MAU MAU
AND KENYA

Blacks in the Diaspora
Darlene Clark Hine, John McCluskey, Jr., and David Barry Gaspar
General Editors

MAU MAU

AND KENYA
An Analysis of a Peasant Revolt

Wunyabari O. Maloba

INDIANA UNIVERSITY PRESS
Bloomington and Indianapolis

JAMES CURREY
Oxford

First paperback edition published 1998 in North America by
Indiana University Press
601 North Morton Street, Bloomington, Indiana 47404

and in the United Kingdom by
James Currey Publishers
73 Botley Road, Oxford OX2 0BS

The paper used in this publication meets the minimum
requirements of American National Standard for Information
Sciences—Permanence of Paper for Printed Library Materials,
ANSI Z39.48-1984.

Manufactured in the United States of America

Library of Congress Cataloging-in-Publication Data

Maloba, Wunyabari O., date
Mau Mau and Kenya : an analysis of a peasant revolt /
Wunyabari O. Maloba.
p.   cm.—(Blacks in the diaspora)
Includes bibliographical references and index.
ISBN 0-253-33664-3 (alk. paper)   ISBN 0-253-21166-2 (pbk. : alk. paper)
1. Kenya—Politics and government—To 1963. 2. Mau Mau—History.
3. Nationalism—Kenya—History—20th century. 4. Peasant uprisings—
Kenya—History—20th century.   I. Title.   II. Series.
DT433.577.M35   1993
967.6204—dc20   92-31421

3 4 5 02 01

British Library Cataloguing in Publication Data

Maloba, Wunyabari O.
Mau Mau and Kenya : an analysis of a peasant revolt
1. Mau Mau 2. Peasant uprisings—Kenya—History—20th century
3. Kenya—Politics and government—To 1963 I. Title
967.6'2'03
ISBN 0-85255-745-0

4   5   6   7   8   09   08   07   06   05   04

For my mother
Mary Amboko
Whose life taught me the meaning and value of perseverance

Contents

PREFACE

This is a study of one of the more remarkable nationalist peasant revolts against British colonialism in Africa. As a nationalist revolutionary movement, Mau Mau has remained remarkably difficult to comprehend. It has sometimes appeared to be an elusive revolution. This study has been undertaken with the aim of not only clarifying but also explaining the varied contradictory components of this revolt.

In writing this book, I have been struck by the complexity of issues that surround what are generally referred to as peasant protests or revolts. A major problem of analysis involves the composition, ideology, and leadership of the revolts. Also, the study of peasant protests—especially in Africa—has been too particularized. Studies exist that deal with specific peasant-based revolutionary movements, but comparative analyses are still scarce. The result is that a study of the general issues giving rise to peasant revolts continues to be haphazard. Indeed, very few of these studies address themselves to the question of what peasants wish to become after the revolt or revolution. Do peasants rebel to perpetuate their class, or do they hope to change their class, their status, in the new revolutionary society? Are peasants expected to remain peasants?

The majority of the peasant-based revolutionary movements that will be discussed in the Introduction were not led by peasants. This distinction between the leadership, petty bourgeoisie in origin, and the peasants, introduces complex questions about social transformation, values, and institutions in the postliberation era. If the leadership is unable or unwilling to commit class "suicide," as suggested by Amilcar Cabral,[1] can the peasants be expected to continue to support it "in the interests of the country"? Yet another problem arises. If the peasants alone are not able to initiate and lead a successful revolutionary war, are they therefore doomed to subsist in repressive and exploitative circumstances in the event that the revolution is "betrayed"? This could happen if the petty bourgeoisie abandons the peasants in the postliberation era, leading to a definite collapse of the revolutionary alliance that had previously been indispensable in the execution of the liberation war and struggle.

These are important questions to ask, for it is obvious that any critical analysis of the liberation movements of Africa must deal with not only their origins but also their varied legacies. There is a legitimate need to revisit these movements. In that spirit, this book aims to look afresh at the Mau Mau movement.

My interest in Mau Mau goes back to my undergraduate school days. It was, however, in graduate school at Stanford University that my advisor, Kennell Jackson, encouraged my efforts to study the ideology of the revolt. As I read and reflected upon past studies of Mau Mau, I came to realize that because of its varied composition, a study of this revolt must also recognize its multiple ideologies. Kennell Jackson's extensive knowledge of Kenyan history, together with his own interest in Mau Mau as a subject of study, was useful to me as I sought to open new ways of looking at this revolt.

In trying to understand the value of theory in history, I benefited from my numerous discussions with Richard Roberts. His general grasp of this phenomenon proved invaluable as I struggled to formulate a theory of peasant revolts and its relationship to Mau Mau. It was, however, Nancy Kollman who drew my attention to peasant revolts in Russian history and encouraged me, while at Stanford, to attempt a comparative analysis of peasant revolts. Terence Emmons discussed with me theories and complexities of revolutions, while Renato Rosaldo generously acted as my guide on matters related to anthropology. His own scholarship shows that there are definite gains for knowledge whenever history and anthropology cooperate.

At the University of Delaware, I would like to thank Jack Ellis, chairman of the History Department, for his interest in my work, support, and encouragement.

I would also like to thank William R. Ochieng of Maseno University College, Kenya, for his friendship and constant encouragement. This book has benefited from his several criticisms, observations, and suggestions.

The fieldwork for the doctoral dissertation,[2] on which this book is based, was undertaken in 1985 and 1986 on a research fellowship offered by the Social Science Research Council (SSRC), New York. Subsequent fieldwork in 1989 was funded by the General University Research Grant of the University of Delaware. I am grateful to both institutions for the fellowships.

To the many librarians and archivists who were of help to me, I would like to assure you that I valued your help immensely, even if I did not always say "thank you." In particular, I would like to thank the librarians and archivists at the Royal Institute of International Affairs (London); Imperial War Museum (London); Public Record Office (London); Rhodes House Library, Oxford University; the Kenya National Archives (Nairobi); and, of course, the librarians at C. H. Green Library, and Hoover Institution of Stanford University, and Morris Library at the University of Delaware.

This list of acknowledgments would be incomplete without mentioning my sincere gratitude to Elinor Stutz and Gail Brittingham for typing, at different stages, the manuscript for this book.

MAU MAU

AND KENYA

INTRODUCTION

The Theory of Peasant Revolts and Mau Mau

The rebellion that has come to pass down in history as Mau Mau was essentially an uprising of the peasants of Kenya (principally from Central Province) against the colonial state, its policies and agents, in 1952. When the revolt broke out, the colonial authorities refused to acknowledge that there was any legitimate reason for such an uprising. The general opinion of the colonial authorities continued to be that Africans were bound to benefit from colonial rule. Colonialism, so it was argued, had brought with it the benefits of education, religion, modern commerce, and government, and it had rendered the invaluable service of drawing Africans into the mainstream of human civilization and away from the pervasive barbarism which had hitherto enveloped the African continent. So long as this line of argument was maintained, it was impossible for the colonial state to see the genuine legitimacy of African discontent or of nationalistic stirrings. Africans were expected to be grateful for all the benefits that accrued to them as subjects of the empire. At the same time, however, at least in the case of Kenya, they were expected to supply labor and pay taxes. The point at issue is that, so long as the colonial state and its agents continued to find an excuse for whatever they did from their belief in the "white man's burden," it was impossible for them to recognize and respect the legitimacy of nationalism on the part of Africans.

Kenya's colonial history is indeed a study in the intransigence of the colonial state. Since the 1920s when the first organized African protest movements emerged, the colonial state maintained an air of indifference, if not hostility, to African demands. The formation of the Kikuyu Central Association (KCA) in the 1920s and the Kenya African Union (KAU) in 1944 did not by any means alter the position of the state, which was that Africans had no complaints at all. What was happening, so the colonial logic dictated, was the fomenting of trouble by a few disgruntled educated Africans who wanted to use their uneducated kinspeople to advance their own selfish political aims. It was not therefore surprising that as the tension rose toward the end of the 1940s, the hostility was principally directed against the political leaders of African nationalism. It was imagined that if the leaders were removed, then the docile masses would revert to their appropriate position of silence. Little did the colonial state understand the widespread discontent on the part of Africans, which was fueled by economic hardships both in the reserves (land reserved for Africans only) and in urban areas. There was a tragic misreading of the depth of African hatred of the colonial state. This misreading would later on cost the British government "£60 million with the commitment of some 50,000 troops and police" and result in "10,000 Africans . . . killed and 90,000 others impounded in concentration camps under sometimes appalling conditions."[1]

Even as late as June 1952, there were many officials in Kenya, including the governor, Sir Philip Mitchell, "who believed the corner had been turned." Indeed, Mitchell, on the eve of his retirement, could speak of seeing "only happy smiling faces wherever he went in the colony." This general dismissal of the revolutionary stirrings in the colony is difficult to explain. It has been suggested that Mitchell was not willing to accept discontent in the colony on the eve of his retirement from what had been to him an illustrious career. Whatever the reason, when the new governor, Sir Evelyn Baring, arrived in September 1952, he found a country seething with discontent, sporadic violence, and heightened racial tension. On 20 October 1952, he declared a state of emergency, and Kenya's history entered a new unpredictable phase, characterized by violence, prejudice, propaganda, and eventually a strategic compromise.

The Mau Mau uprising of 1952 was therefore the outcome of both state violence and African reaction and counterviolence. It was a movement the colonial state had refused to acknowledge until October 1952 and after this date fought with fury and singular determination, aiming to score both military and psychological, if not ideological, victory. This introduction aims to study some of the issues raised by Mau Mau as both a social and political movement.

The study of Mau Mau as a peasant movement inevitably leads to a comparative analysis not only with past movements but also with more recent nationalist peasant revolutions in the Third World. The major focus of such a comparative analysis is not merely to record the similarities and differences between the movements but to extract any valuable theoretical issues and concerns that can be utilized as tools of analysis of peasant revolutions. However, theoretical issues and lessons so deduced cannot be applied indiscriminately to all movements everywhere. Their value lies in extending our comprehension of why peasant rebellions occur, their composition and leadership, and their impact. Even while concentrating on the theoretical issues, we should never forget that every peasant rebellion is the product of its society. It is the product of a particular mix of social, political, and economic forces in a given context. In this regard, no study can produce comprehensive results unless it seeks to understand the social tensions in the society in which the rebellion occurred.

This introduction attempts to demonstrate the extent to which a study of the Mau Mau peasant rebellion in colonial Kenya can benefit from the theoretical debates about peasant rebellions. In placing the Mau Mau movement within the broad framework of the theoretical debates about social movements, this study can make a contribution to the theory of peasant rebellions. Various facets that make up Mau Mau the movement can benefit from current theoretical debates.

Mau Mau was a nationalist, anticolonial, peasant movement which was similar to and different from both European peasant movements and Third World revolutionary movements.

Its composition, like that of European peasant movements, was made up largely of peasants. But it differed even on this score from European peasant movements, which attracted participants from other social classes. The English peasant uprising of 1381, for example, was composed of "peasants, artisans, minor clergy as well as a good proportion of well-to-do people of both country and town."[2] In the great Russian peasant revolts of the seventeenth and eighteenth centuries, Paul Avrich informs us that

> Cossacks of the Steppe fought against the central government; poor cossacks fought against rich cossacks; rising gentry clashed with declining boyar aristocracy; national minorities attacked Russian colonizers; old believers resisted the new faith, serfs rose against landlords, village went against town, periphery against center.[3]

Likewise, in the more recent Third World revolutionary movements, representatives of every social class joined the struggle. In Vietnam, for example, the liberation army was made up of "the best elements among the workers, peasants, and revolutionary students and intellectuals."[4]

It is, however, the overwhelming support given by peasants to these movements that has given them their specific identification. Peasants, both in European movements and Third World revolutionary movements, supplied the manpower.[5] Peasants in these movements were, like in Mau Mau, decidedly in the majority.

The leadership question also sets Mau Mau apart. European peasant movements never were led by peasants. In the French Peasant Rebellion of 1358, the leadership role was taken by townsmen, including even the richer merchants in Paris.[6] In the Russian peasant rebellions, the cossacks, or townsmen, or "outside agitators" provided the leadership.[7] Third World revolutionary movements, although heavily dependent on peasant fighters, have not been led by peasants.[8] They have been led by revolutionary intellectuals such as Amilcar Cabral, Fidel Castro, Ho Chi Minh, Mao Tse-tung, Augustinho Neto, Mondlane, and others. These leaders, together with the revolutionary cadre, organized the development of the revolution. In Mau Mau, there were no revolutionary intellectuals nor cadres. As a result, the revolt lacked the essential unity of focus normally provided by a revolutionary party.

In European movements, peasants rose in rebellion because of harsh and intolerable financial burdens imposed on them by the state. Peasants in France in the fourteenth-century revolt resisted an increase in taxation.[9] In the sixteenth and seventeenth centuries, peasant rebellions erupted frequently in France. By the seventeenth century the relationship between the peasant rebels and some of the country gentry who led the rebellions was easy to see. In seventeenth-century France, as in most European countries at this time, there was a marked expansion of state control. This expansion was felt at the local level through increased demands by the state, on the part of every section of the population. In resisting the new demands, the peasants and their leaders sought to revive the old system in which social duties were well defined and in which the provincial residents enjoyed considerable independence from the central government.[10] In Russia, people on the outskirts of the expanding empire, such as the cossacks, fought to defend their independence. At the same time, other groups rose up to resist increased taxation and military conscription. The expansion of the empire brought with it the evils of enserfment and the loss of traditional "freedom."

These rebellions should therefore be seen not as agitations for a progressive future but as violent defense of old customs, realities, and duties. "In France, generally speaking, none of the rebels had a single new idea. Princes, grandees, parliaments, officials, bourgeoisie—all wished to go back to the good old customs and traditional political constitution somewhat idealized."[11] If their violent actions can be seen as an expression of intolerance, it was intolerance toward the new and a yearning for the "ideal" past. The rebels did not campaign or agitate against the absolute monarchy or indeed the existent unjust social order in which they carried the burden of taxation. The rebels did not demand the abolition of feudalism. "The rebels did not attack the existing stratification of society, or the totality of social structures and institutions. There was, in short, no question of a struggle by one social group against another."[12]

The successful peasant-based revolutionary movements in the Third World are vastly different from European movements in aims. It should be realized that these revolutionary movements were formed with the express aim of creating a new society, a society different from the existing one, whose injustices had produced the revolutionary movement. These movements therefore were not seeking for a purification of the system but for its replacement. Unlike previous European peasant movements, the premium in Third World revolutionary movements was not placed on the "ideal" past, but rather on the "ideal" future.

In the Mau Mau revolt, there was a direct challenge to the existing social order, which was colonial and racist. To this end, it could be argued that Mau Mau agitated for the abolition of the colonial system and not its purification. The revolt strove for an independent future free from colonial control. Yet most of the participants were peasants who wanted their own land to live on and farm and who wanted to enjoy prosperity as their rich neighbors did in the reserves. The ahoi, or landless peasants, were particularly upset that their age-old access to land had been curtailed by the new landed gentry in the reserves. The ahoi would have clearly preferred the old system, in which their access to land had prevented them from being destitute or laborers on someone else's land. To strive for an independent future did not necessarily mean that Mau Mau activists had a common concrete idea as to the shape of this future. As this study will amply demonstrate, this remained one of Mau Mau's major weaknesses.

Realization of goals in revolutionary wars depends on the effectiveness and appropriateness of strategies employed by the leadership and revolutionary masses. Sometimes the failure of a revolutionary struggle is an indication of the inappropriateness of strategy or poor execution of an otherwise correct strategy. European peasant movements were characterized by lack of a coherent organization. The constituent parts of each rebellion tended, on the whole, to remain separate from each other, and no unitary theory of the revolt was formulated. In Bolotnikov's rebellion in Russia (1606–1607) the gentry rebels and peasants marched to Moscow in two separate armies, emphasizing the clash of interests within the rebel movement. There was no extensive organization that aimed to consolidate the separate interest groups into a unified movement. These movements, therefore, remained amorphous and weak and quickly disintegrated when faced with formidable force. Russian rebellions, like other European peasant rebellions, were not conceived to launch a protracted struggle against the state. There was exhibited, in their tactics, an almost naive estimation of the power of the state and the difficulties to be endured before victory could be achieved. In their tactics, we see an almost unwarranted faith in easy and "prompt" victory. Faced with long and painful struggles, most of the constituent groups deserted the movement and its "leaders."

The power of European peasant rebellions was lodged in their destructive fury. It is immense destruction of property and loss of lives that frightened the state and the ruling classes. This urge to destroy was distinctly motivated by an urge to take revenge. As the rebels traversed the land and struck at the nobles and the state officials, they let their hatred and abhorrence be known of all those who were perceived to be responsible for their misery and hardship. This quality of revenge clearly came close to identifying these rebellions as having characteristics of social banditry. Eric Hobsbawm has pointed out that although the state thinks of bandits as criminals, the local population looks at them as heroes, local sons who were courageous enough to challenge the state and its agents.[13] A social bandit is therefore a rebel, defying state laws and relying for his survival on his courage and the goodwill of the rest of the peasant population. To be able to inspire both respect and fear, the social bandit strikes ruthlessly at those individuals considered social enemies. "Even the best of bandits must demonstrate that he can be 'terrible.' "[14]

Third World revolutionary movements that succeeded to overthrow the state and its repressive machinery were intensely organized. China, Cuba, Algeria, Vietnam, Guinea-Bissau, Mozambique, and Angola are examples of peasant-based revolutionary movements organized into revolutionary parties. In these movements the element of spontaneity was vastly reduced, and instead more effort was directed toward organization and education. The element of education is crucial. In European peasant movements, the leaders of the rebellions relied on commonsense recognition of the ills of society by peasants. But the ready recognition of oppression and exploitation that propelled peasants into rebellion was undirected and unorganized.

In successful Third World movements, emphasis was placed on the politicization of the peasants. It was observed that it was not enough for peasants to hate their lords or the system in which they toiled. It was important for them to understand the causes of their ills and the inescapable need to create a new world free of those previous structures and institutions. The support of the revolutionary movements by the peasants was, on the whole, based on their comprehension of this argument and their acceptance of the need to create a new world. But even this point is not without controversy. Che Guevara, basing his deductions on the unique experience and circumstances of the Cuban revolution, introduced the phenomenon of "foco" theory of revolution. By this theory, a revolutionary does not have to wait for all conditions to be ripe before launching a revolution. "Guevara was intent on demonstrating that rather than concentrating on political education and organisation, the first order is to create a military focus for struggle."[15] The courage and heroic triumphs of the guerrillas would suffice to win new converts to the struggle and hence expand the revolutionary movement's base of operation.

Experience from Africa and Latin America has repeatedly called into question the universal validity of this theory. Many revolutionary leaders have, on the contrary, argued persistently that the most crucial battle to be won is the spread of the political message to the peasants. Once the message is accepted, support is assured.[16] The argument here is that guerrilla warfare, even if based on peasant support, is not merely a display of military prowess but rather a complex mixture of politics and war: war advances politics but is forever controlled and directed by politics. "It must probably be emphasized, even at this late point in time," Basil Davidson writes

> that a successful guerilla-type resistance can never stem from military adventure, however motivated, but only from the political exploitation of a general situation which is felt by a mass of people to be hatefully and obviously unjust to them. "Big" words about freedom and independence can achieve nothing, if the "little words" about local oppression are not persuasive.[17]

A study of Mau Mau political and military strategy, covered in chapter 6, demonstrates a general lack of coherent politicization within that movement. Mau Mau guerrillas did not undertake an organized appraisal of the colonial economic system and how this system needed to be changed. There was no theoretical analysis of the political and economic structures of the colonial system. For politicization, the guerrillas depended on the oaths and widespread oath-taking of both the would-be fighters and the passive wing. But oaths alone were insufficient to uphold a people's resolve and determination. When faced with superior military forces, oaths were found to be an inadequate tool of cohesion and politicization. The revolt also relied heavily on the spontaneous fury of the masses. Spontaneity generally provides a good background from which to build a disciplined movement. However, it can never be relied upon to provide the main force behind a revolutionary movement. Any movement that relies solely on spontaneity generally suffers the same consequences as those experienced by European peasant movements: defeat and disintegration. Spontaneous enthusiasm of the masses has the tendency of being a temporary engagement upon which a revolutionary movement cannot depend for long-term sustenance.[18]

Successful Third World revolutionary movements combined courage of the peasant fighters with a progressive ideology under the general direction of a revolutionary party. No successful revolutionary warfare has ever been fought without the unity of focus given by a respected party led by dedicated revolutionary cadre or "political entrepreneurs." The failure of any revolution is not just a military defeat but, more crucially, a political defeat. "Without a political goal, guerilla warfare must fail, as it must if its objectives do not coincide with the aspirations of the people and [when] their sympathy, cooperation and assistance cannot be gained."[19] Because success is not easily attained, the party offers continuity of hope and perseverance and resurrects the struggle after every setback. It is easily observed that after 1954 Mau Mau suffered a series of military (and political) defeats and was never able to "resurrect" the struggle after 1956.

The struggle against foreigners is a powerful tool to use in the mobilization of the masses. It is increasingly apparent that nationalism has not been given due emphasis as a vital factor in the recruitment of peasants for revolutionary war in the Third World. This unfortunate point has been arrived at, no doubt, because it was felt that peasants do not think beyond their villages. European peasant movements were not a struggle against foreigners, although it could be argued that the expanding state may have been perceived as foreign, at least in its requirements. In the Third World, there are a number of theories that prominently emphasize the economic aspects of the struggle at the expense of the political, and especially the nationalist, dimension. One such theory is the one about "moral economy," which emerged out of the Vietnam revolutionary war.

The chief argument of the moral economists is that "social relations in precapitalist settings are invariably 'moral' and that, whenever capitalist institutions are introduced, the fabric of the moral economics is rent—in extreme cases destroyed—by the introduction of the cash nexus."[20] It follows from this assumption that peasant upheavals in such a society are associated with the introduction of capitalist relations of production. These capitalist relations of production lead to a loss of security and communal solidarity, which are presumed to have been prevalent in precapitalist moral economy. The resultant tension leads to rebellions. On the other hand, Samuel Popkin, in a remarkable counterargument, postulates that indeed the precapitalist society is not free of social stratification and therefore has tensions in it. He suggests that more attention should be placed on individuals and the choices that these individuals are willing to make and the risks they take to further their economic welfare. According to Popkin, then, the decision of peasants to join a revolutionary movement is determined largely by individual calculation of gain at the end of the upheaval. By the same logic, Popkin implies that indeed peasants are not hostile to capitalism and that the decision to revolt is individual and not societal. In his own emphatic words, "peasants do not necessarily act to further their group or common interests, . . . they often opt for individual interests over common interests and . . . there is a free rider problem."[21] Popkin further believes that the peasant does not support the revolution for grandiose aims promulgated by the revolutionary cadre but rather because of selfish individual goals whose realization the revolutionary cadre guarantees. Again and again, the emphasis is on economic gain.

Both the moral and political economists miss the crucial element of nationalism and freedom. Nationalism as a motivating factor in these peasant rebellions is given scanty attention, and, as a result, the deductions of moral and political economists are wanting in crucial details. Peasants are presumed to be concerned only about economic welfare with limited horizon and are not concerned with nationalism and national dignity. The historical experience of other countries, and in particular of Vietnam, eloquently contradicts such a simplistic interpretation. The history of Vietnam, insofar as a simple summary can be made, is a history of resistance against foreign intrusion. "Whoever the invader may have been at a particular time, it has been one long, continuous fight for national independence and freedom from oppression."[22] This statement is crucial in our bid to understand the long and heroic struggle of the Vietnamese people against foreign colonial or neocolonial aggression. From the start, the Communist party of North Vietnam (later of the whole country) sought to unite the ideology of Marxism with nationalism, national dignity, and culture. The resultant ideology was both Marxist and nationalist, and the triumph of the Vietnamese people is in no small measure the direct result of this strategic linkage. To underestimate the force of nationalism is to miss the main ingredient of success of peasant-based revolutionary movements of the Third World. Nationalism and national dignity are powerful tools in those societies in which racism and racial prejudice are keenly felt by an indigenous population. Revolutionary movements that succeed are those which link a progressive ideology to cultural heritage and nationalism.

A recent article by Allen Isaacman[23] raises important points about peasant revolts in Africa. In particular, Isaacman has highlighted the importance of considering the value of "everyday struggles" and other nondramatic forms of protest. The thrust of his informative and exhaustive article, commissioned by the Social Science Research Council, is to argue that peasants differed from the urban and rural workers in their relationship with the "colonial state and the appropriating classes." This difference in relationship was the result of what he calls "the relative autonomy of the peasants," which issued from "their ability to mobilize their own labor power through the household and their access to land, which together, gave them command over subsistence."[24] This formulation presumes a level of "partial autonomy" which was not always present in a lot of the so-called settler colonies. Certainly in Kenya, the plight of the ahoi, or squatters, and peasant migrants to the urban areas demonstrates the degree to which the colonial state, through its economic and political policies, was able to seriously undermine precolonial agricultural opportunities and kinship obligations.

On another level, peasant revolts in Isaacman's article are examples of "limited struggle" within the system as opposed to wholesale challenge to it and its legitimacy. If both the colonial state and the peasants were merely interested in "jockeying and negotiating to reshape this partial autonomy," then a question must be raised about the ultimate aim of peasant struggles. Do the activities of peasants, including "subterranean protests," demonstrate that they had basically accepted the colonial political economy and all that they required was "partial autonomy" under colonialism?

A study of successful peasant-based revolutionary struggles in the Third World shows that no revolutionary leader ever assumed that peasants were docile, passive country folks.[25] Indeed the success of these revolutionary struggles depended upon the participation of peasants in large numbers. This participation, secured after politicization, linked the legacy of "subterranean protests" to revolutionary struggle in a focused national effort aimed at dismantling not only economic exploitation but also political oppression and racism.

This study clearly emphasizes the economic dimension of Mau Mau revolt. As chapter 1 demonstrates, colonialism, and with it the introduction of capitalist relations of production in Central Province, caused the destruction of the traditional political economy. The resultant economic hardships, especially of displaced peasants and former tenants and squatters, complicated rural social relations and generated tension both in the rural and urban centers. But these economic problems were never viewed as distinct from political struggles by Mau Mau supporters. To them it was manifestly clear that the colonial state and its multiple demands and requirements were responsible for both the economic and political problems in the country. The colonial state's identification with European settlers was complete. In these circumstances, it would have been impossible to distinguish economic needs from political needs, for neither could be satisfied independent of the other. In Kenya, there was a problem of distinguishing between economic and political causes of the revolt; for after all, political and economic injustice were intricately intertwined.

How has Mau Mau been studied and discussed in the past? The writings about Mau Mau, at the time when it occurred, were essentially undertaken by what can, in retrospect, be termed enemies of the movement. These were essentially local white settlers who painted it as dark and satanic in content and inspiration. J. F. Lipscomb's *We Built a Country* and even L. S. B. Leakey's *Defeating Mau Mau* must be understood as examples of efforts by white settlers and residents of Kenya to explain and denounce the Mau Mau movement as essentially destructive, illogical, barbaric, and, of course, unwarranted. Sir Michael Blundell's *So Rough a Wind* provides another interesting reading characteristic of this period. Apart from being autobiographical, the book is also a record of the author's activities, especially during the state of emergency (when the colonial government declared war on Mau Mau). Blundell was a member of the War Council. In his book, we read of details worked out by the War Council to defeat Mau Mau, but nowhere are the legitimate aspirations of the fighters acknowledged. The aim of the council was to devise means and ways of defeating Mau Mau. The alleged nature of Mau Mau and its irrelevance and nuisance are forever emphasized. This group of books therefore forms the hostile appraisal of Mau Mau. This hostility was not just limited to private people. The colonial state felt compelled to offer explanations of the movement. Two studies were commissioned by the state. The first one, *The Psychology of Mau Mau* by J. C. Carothers in 1955, explained Mau Mau in terms of psychology. Carothers looked at it as mass madness, a case study of a people whose weak tribal cohesion and worldview, if not culture, had been broken down "in the face of a superior and more profitable culture"—the Western European culture. The emphasis in this study was placed on psychology, not on politics or economics.

The *Corfield Report*, written by F. C. Corfield, emphasized the oaths and the Kenyatta factor. The explanation of the troubles, according to Corfield, lay in the atavistic oaths, with Jomo Kenyatta as the chief priest and key administrator of these oaths. According to this report, Kenyatta as the chief architect of Mau Mau, aimed it "against western civilisation and technology and, in particular, against government and Europeans as symbols of progress" (*The Corfield Report*, p. 220). The official reports, like the writings of private white settlers, did little to clarify the origin and spread of Mau Mau, let alone its basic characteristics. There was an overemphasis on what was seen as the dark side of the movement; the oaths and their administration, and, of course, the maiming of cattle and killings in the rural areas. Refusing to acknowledge that they were dealing with a genuine expression of frustrated nationalism, the colonial state and its agents looked at and interpreted the actions of Mau Mau as criminal acts. The propaganda was aimed at creating horror among law-abiding citizens by describing unimaginable crimes attributed to the fighters. It is this propaganda war which the colonial state was quick to claim as its first sizeable victory over Mau Mau. The movement did not have a propaganda organization that could rival the colonial state's bulletins and analyses. Mau Mau could rely only on the goodwill of the people toward whom the colonial state's propaganda was aimed. In the absence of an authoritative counterargument, most people were left with the official explanation; and however much they may have wished to sympathize with the movement, they found it difficult to do so in the face of what they saw as unimaginable atrocities allegedly committed by Mau Mau fighters.

It is this victory by the state in the propaganda war that would, in years to come, haunt Mau Mau and the ideological positions it represented. It became a movement that was shunned by both the conservative and radical left-wing populace. The conservative wing which was comprised mainly of the converted Africans (Christians) and professionals, went along with the evaluation of the missionaries. They saw in Mau Mau the dark forces that had to be confronted and defeated by Christianity. It symbolized a past era, an era from which Africans had been delivered through the opportune intervention of Christianity. It was therefore impossible for these converted Africans to sympathize with, let alone recognize, the legitimate claims of Mau Mau. Grievances should, according to this group, be expressed through the appropriate channels. Violence and especially oath-taking were barbaric, and any movement which utilized these means to achieve its ends was equally barbaric and despicable.

As the colonial state heightened its propaganda war, the legitimate claims of the nationalists were drowned out by the disgust of the conservatives over oaths and the symbols used. Bethwell A. Ogot argues that the tribal elders were reluctant to join in the movement because they felt that the traditional symbols and values had been abused and defiled by the youth. The elders accordingly sought to safeguard "pure" culture from being spoiled by youthful mischief, no matter the legitimacy of their complaints. The colonial state, its agents, and African conservatives adopted a very simplistic explanation of the Mau Mau movement. They looked at it as a "disease," as madness, as deviation from normal behavior.

The overseas left-wing radicals, and even the liberals, were equally uncomfortable with Mau Mau. In their writings they denounced British imperialism but failed to identify with the revolt. The revolt was seen as the inevitable outcome of racism and the brutal tactics of colonialism. These sympathizers, however, never took the next step on the path to complete identification with the Mau Mau movement. It was a movement which was, according to them, unfathomable. Acknowledging that it was an anti-imperialist uprising, the Marxist scholars and sympathizers saw no characteristics of a genuine people's war of the kind their studies and reflections had led them to believe in. Certainly the movement had no Marxist ideology, nor did it have a cadre of revolutionary intellectuals propounding well-knit and stimulating ideological positions. Instead of the standard agents of propaganda and politicization of the masses, it was found, to the dismay of the radical scholars, that Mau Mau fighters employed ancient oaths and even invoked deities in these ceremonies. It was, therefore, a backward-looking movement which did not pass the litmus test of ideological purity and methodological application of Marxism to its environment. Mau Mau rebels had not even heard of Marx! These realities led left-wing intellectuals into an ambivalent posture.

Although Mau Mau was the result of imperialism's oppression and exploitation, it did not symbolize the uprising or revolution of the proletariat. Many of the workers held out, as did the educated class. Many peasants gave passive support; but the bulk of the fighting was shouldered by those displaced in the rural areas, the landless squatters, and the urban unemployed, the marginals of society. It was led and organized by a group of semiliterate men who chose to use traditional symbols to enlist support. We are told that the symbols, especially the oaths, "seemed inexplicable to overseas liberals and thereby may have jeopardised support for Kenyan African nationalism."[26]

It was not just the physical support that was jeopardized, but also the ideological identification of the radicals with the movement. It is therefore possible to argue that Mau Mau is an orphan movement. It had ideological support from neither the Left nor the Right. The movement was executed using means and symbols that offended the conservatives and were inexplicable to the radicals. The net result of these developments is that the movement itself has remained mysterious. In colonial and postcolonial Africa, no movement has been so misunderstood, so much talked about, and remained so stubbornly incomprehensible as Mau Mau. It shall be recalled that when Eric Wolf wrote his pioneering text *Peasant Wars of the Twentieth Century* (1969), he failed to include Mau Mau as a case study. This was an interesting omission considering that probably "there is scarcely a major language group that has not had some writing on the Kenyan rebellion."[27]

The two books that came close to shedding some scholarly light on this controversial movement are *The Myth of Mau Mau* by Carl Rosberg and John Nottingham, and *Mau Mau from Within* by Donald Barnett and Karari Njama. *The Myth of Mau Mau* is unfortunately not restricted to Mau Mau, but is rather an exhaustive study of African resistance and the evolution of African nationalism in Kenya. As a result, Mau Mau is given limited treatment. The book's key point is that Mau Mau was the result of the colonial state's stubbornness and intransigence. The Mau Mau violence, the authors argue, was the direct result of government policies. "As the full weight of Government power was brought to bear on the Kikuyu, the assertive character of their radical politics was transformed into desperate resistance as they sought to preserve their hopes and ideals as people under increasingly severe siege conditions."[28] The book leaves several questions unanswered, principally the nature of the movement itself, the composition and even leadership, let alone its impact. Barnett and Njama's *Mau Mau from Within*, produced almost at the same time as Rosberg and Nottingham's book, seeks to shed light on the movement itself. Barnett definitely looks at Mau Mau as a genuine peasant people's war, although bedeviled with contradictions. However, his aim is limited to "the structure, and organisation of the guerilla forces."

It appears that the problem which has haunted Mau Mau has been that those who sought to study it aimed to interpret it holistically; to offer a single all-encompassing theory of interpretation. This is difficult to arrive at given the contradictions that plagued this movement and its zigzag legacy. What all these studies have been unable to do is to study the revolt as it was. It is important that the various elements comprising the uprising should be studied.

Recent scholarship, while avoiding a comprehensive study of Mau Mau, has nonetheless concentrated on what may be termed micro-issues. In this regard, Luise White's article,[29] appropriately identified as provocative, "argues that gender was at the heart of the Mau Mau struggle."[30] This argument, which partially links colonial political economy and the government-imposed rehabilitation process of Mau Mau detainees, is intent on showing that the colonial state's policies were based on this premise: "Men living together bred revolt; men living with their wives were satisfied."[31] White states again and again that the basic thrust of colonial policy was to avoid congregation of single men, especially in urban areas. Such single men "would be drawn to political action" and destabilize the colonial structures. In her analysis of the nature of the conflict between Africans and the colonial state, she concludes without qualification that "it was the nature of gender, and the proper division of labor by sex that followed gender relations, that was the contested terrain of colonial control."[32] This conclusion clearly oversimplifies the nature of colonial control and varied African responses to it. On the central question of her article about single and married men and political agitation, Luise White fails to inform us whose worldview this is. Is this a Western or an African worldview? If it is Western it may be instructive to be given evidence of this policy in action in Western countries. Did Western men who lived with their wives in urban areas avoid political agitation and even confrontation?

White's deductions become more troubling when she deals with Mau Mau gender relations in the forest and the outcome of the rehabilitation process. Although it is true that questions related to marriage, sexual relations, and division of labor were discussed in the forest meetings, it would be inaccurate to conclude that these were the principal or only topics discussed. Statements issued about marriage do not by themselves signify that the revolt was more concerned about this aspect of life than about land and freedom, as White's article implies.[33]

In her rather brief remarks on the nature of the revolt itself, White concludes that "the struggles within Mau Mau were about housework."[34] Is this really true? Without a doubt, there were struggles about housework and other gender-related questions. This is true of any revolutionary movement. It would however be inaccurate to conclude that all the struggles in Mau Mau can be reduced to the single issue of housework. Luise White's thesis raises new and interesting questions, but it is over-drawn in its conclusions.

Rehabilitation was a more complex and pervasive phenomenon whose mission went beyond detention camps. Indeed we need constantly to remember that even the "passive wing" underwent its own version of rehabilitation. Those men who were detained remained a small fraction of the Kikuyu society. Not all of them were "boys" or single men. Upon release, some did not have families or farms to return to and would not have been able to marry and settle down as a "reward earned by hard work" in detention camps and prisons. Even in the urban areas, the economic hardships that had made life for couples impossible to sustain before the emergency still prevailed afterwards, as *The Carpenter Report* revealed in its findings.

About the nature of labor performed by men in detention camps, which White identifies as "women's work," it may be important to recall here that this was not and is not unique to Kenya. Prisons in Kenya before and after the emergency routinely employed men (prisoners, detainees, etc.) to perform "women's work"; and so do many prison systems elsewhere.[35] Besides, the rehabilitation program in Kenya was based on the Malayan example. Did rehabilitation in Malaya produce the same or similar gender-related results as in Kenya? If not, it may be worthwhile to determine the reasons.

John Lonsdale's article briefly touches on the gender question.[36] The thrust of his article, however, is on the intellectual construction of Mau Mau. Specifically, Lonsdale demonstrates the mental response of the varied white groups in Kenya to Mau Mau. These responses were in large part determined by what Mau Mau was believed to be all about: oaths and atavism. This determination, as chapter 5 shows, was the result of a deliberately well-orchestrated propaganda offensive. In this regard, Lonsdale is correct in drawing our attention to the effectiveness of the propaganda. However, by concentrating largely on the intellectual construction of Mau Mau within the white community, Lonsdale is unable to highlight the various "Mau Maus of the mind" within the African society. The struggles within Kenyan nationalism are discussed in a rather sketchy way, and this in turn makes the rise of Mau Mau somewhat inexplicable. Although Lonsdale argues that "Kikuyu were engaged in a struggle about class, not in class struggle,"[37] there is ample evidence to suggest that indeed class struggle was underway in Central Province by 1952.

A detailed consideration of the colonial political economy shows that land scarcity, population explosion, unemployment, and increasing class distinctions made it difficult for the younger Kikuyu generation to attain wealth, status, and therefore honor. Chapter 1 deals with this question of shrinking land and opportunities and how economics of desperation led to radical politics. Yet even here, these struggles cannot be satisfactorily looked upon as a narrow Kikuyu phenomenon. For if the Mau Mau revolt is viewed as "a parochial war, obsessed with parochial honour,"[38] then the movement sheds its nationalist credentials. It becomes a mere tribal war.

A perpetual and crucial question in the remaking of post-emergency Kenya is the role played by Christian churches in the rehabilitation process. Lonsdale concludes that "neither fundamentalists nor liberals exercised the influence which has been attributed to Christian rehabilitation as a whole."[39] Available evidence, as shown in chapter 7, points to the central role played by Christian churches in rehabilitation. As early as 1953, the government reported that Christian teaching formed the basis of the curriculum in the rehabilitation process.[40] Confessions, the government believed, left the detainees "rudderless," and Christianity provided "a new sense of direction."[41] The churches themselves, apart from receiving some money from the government for evangelical purposes at this time, believed strongly that "a strong current of demonic energy" ran "through the whole history of the crisis."[42] The church believed that its challenge was to help in forging a new society "founded on the sanctions of Christian revelation."[43] Postemergency Kenya, although largely "a political creation," was in many respects possible because the rehabilitation process, based on conservative Christian ideology, had been much more effective than Lonsdale discusses in his article. This "political creation" was further helped by the military defeat of Mau Mau. As subsequent events showed, this defeat "left the politicians who are more amenable to a peaceful handover, and also for making life more comfortable for themselves."[44]

The importance of these and similar articles to the study and comprehension of Mau Mau should not be overexaggerated. They raise new and interesting questions, pointing out the subtle and complex nuances that continue to characterize this revolt. But they are focused on an aspect of Mau Mau and not on the whole story. Also, none of these articles is able to explain satisfactorily why the revolt broke out when it did. With regard to White's thesis, it is not possible for problems of gender and division of labor to have been restricted to Kikuyu urban residents. If these were urban problems, how did the non-Kikuyu population respond to them? How, for example, did the Abaluyia and Luo urban residents (and even rural residents) respond to these new social forces, which White argues "were galvanizing the rest of the continent"? Since the Abaluyia and Luo were on the whole not detained, were gender relations and division of labor within them markedly different from the Kikuyu before and after the emergency?

On a more conceptual level, recent scholarship, by deemphasizing nationalism and racism, runs the risk of inadvertently reinforcing the colonial model, whose main thrust was to deny the force and centrality of African nationalism. There is the danger of overemphasizing the various economic factors (and even social factors) without linking them to a people's struggle for freedom, justice, and dignity. This struggle for freedom and dignity does not seem to have made a convenient and impassable distinction between economic and political factors or to have looked at nationalism with cold suspicion, especially in the 1950s.

The preceding analysis emphasizes several crucial points. In the first instance, the Mau Mau movement cannot be fully understood unless we identify its composition. Who joined Mau Mau and why? The other revolutionary movements, so far analyzed, had peasants as the bulk of their members. The same could be said of Mau Mau, but if left at that, it would not clarify this key question of membership. In his article "The Social Composition of the Mau Mau Movement in the White Highlands,"[45] Frank Furedi greatly emphasizes the squatter movement and the action of the squatters to resist being turned into a rural proletariat away from their previous position as "independent producers." The search for unity to withstand the settlers' onslaught led to the need for oathing as a bond of unity and solidarity. Oathing spread throughout the highlands and into Kikuyu reserves, where landlessness had become a problem. According to Furedi,

> The squatter movement, which came to constitute an important wing of the Mau Mau revolt, emerged out of lengthy agrarian struggle between Kikuyu squatters and European settlers. . . . Thus, the rank and file of the movement was the Kikuyu squatter, who had long experienced an erosion of his wealth and status, and was at the point of proletarianisation.[46]

The support of Mau Mau, according to this view, grew out of economic welfare and not out of any ideas about nationalism. This would seem to put Mau Mau on the same footing as European peasant movements, in which peasants struggled against oppressive landlords. Although Furedi highlights the importance of economic, and specifically land, grievance, he underplays the role of nationalism. Surely to these squatters, white settlers were not just ordinary landlords, but foreign white landlords who had gained land and power as a result of conquest.

The political aspect of this struggle must pay attention not only to the social status of the participants but also to their acquaintance with national politics. The decision to participate in the revolt must be seen against the background of education, economic hardships, landlessness, age, and general disgust with the prevalent colonial racism and exploitation, not to mention oppression and political insensitivity to African demands. As these categories clearly indicate, a study of Mau Mau must recognize its multiple ideologies, in themselves the result of its varied composition.

What makes Mau Mau unique is not this question of multiple ideologies. Every revolutionary movement starts off with a myriad of aims, often conflicting because of its varied membership. The success of any revolution is in many ways measured by its having managed to reconcile these contradictory aims so as to allow the emergence of a unifying aim to which all other aims are subordinate. This can only be realized through the activities and direction of a single revolutionary party. It is this party that Mau Mau did not have. The rise of Mau Mau is connected, however weakly, to the Kenya African Union. It grew as the militant wing of a section within KAU that had, by 1950, opted for more militant nationalism. The evidence from Bildad Kaggia's autobiography suggests that when the emergency was declared in October 1952, the Mau Mau central committee had not finalized its preparations for an armed uprising.[47] Everything seems to have been in the preparatory stage, with emphasis placed on building intricate lines of communication and a chain of command originating from Nairobi slums and extending to far-flung rural areas of central Kenya. What is not clear, however, is whether the movement was, at this time or in the foreseeable future, prepared for a protracted struggle or for shocking but isolated attacks which would force the colonial administration to negotiate on terms favorable to Africans. And indeed in 1952, what were these terms that would be taken to be favorable to Africans? How had the Mau Mau central committee and its adherents arrived at these terms?

The absence of a unifying party continued to haunt the fortunes of Mau Mau in the forests. Once the emergency had been declared, the various military leaders in the Aberdaress and on Mount Kenya found themselves faced with problems of administration, coordination, and struggle for which they were singularly ill-equipped to handle as a result of limited formal education and revolutionary experience. It was a case of these leaders assuming both military and political leadership on a trial-and-error basis at a time when forthright and more imaginative leadership was required. "It was militarily organised by men, such as Dedan Kimathi, who clearly understood the material cause-and-effect of modern warfare, and showed when it came to the point, a remarkable ingenuity of method,"[48] but this ingenuity had a limited political dimension.

Since the publication of Waruhiu Itote's *Mau Mau General* (1967), a number of other fighters have written about their experiences in the forest. We now have Ngugi Kabiro's *Man in the Middle* (1973); Mohammed Mathu's *The Urban Guerilla* (1971); and G. G. Gikoyo's *We Fought for Freedom* (1979). What comes out clearly in these accounts are descriptions of individual heroism on the part of the writers. Emphasis is on the hardships endured and the great courage of these writers, who endured it all to face an enemy so well equipped materially but bankrupt in justification of the war. The torrential rains, the dangerous trekking through the dark and inhospitable forest, all these are emphasized. These are stories of great courage, singular determination, and perseverance. In content, the books are weak on analysis of the movement itself. They all include general references to the possible reasons for participation in the rebellion. But they lack analysis of the causes of the rebellion and why the authors personally and collectively joined in the uprisings. Moreover, these books are silent on the question of the impact of the movement then and in subsequent times. Ogot raises important questions when he asks, "But what was the Mau Mau ideology—if we exclude the demands for our stolen land and for independence which the Kikuyu Central Association (KCA) and Kenya African Union (KAU), among others, had made? And did Mau Mau really aim at the reorganization of Kenyan society? What happened to their efforts in that direction?"[49]

It would appear that even when the movement had the military initiative in the struggle up to 1954, the emphasis was on military effort with little energy expended on politicization of the masses and the thought of creating a new Kenya. This movement had no intellectual revolutionary cadre and was plagued with internal rivalry and increasing isolation from the masses, whose support was crucial. In the successful peasant-based revolutionary movements of the Third World, it has been seen that their leadership was not of peasant origin. Mau Mau may be one of the first few nationalist movements whose leadership and membership was essentially composed of peasants. Faced with a formidable enemy, they counted on the traditional, supposedly unquestionable loyalty of their kinsmen, hoping that kinship loyalty could be easily translated to political loyalty.[50] Experience shows that this political transition was never achieved. To create and uphold loyalty, the fighters relied on secrecy and traditional symbols—oaths, which later became misused. Terror against loyalists was supposed to win support for the guerrillas. But as the military balance shifted, the loyalists disobeyed Mau Mau with impunity, confident of the protection supplied by the colonial state. Loss of military offensive was quickly translated into loss of political support.

It is evident then, that Mau Mau cannot be understood if approached with a one-theory interpretation. There are several facets within it that do not fit neatly into any one theory. The purpose of previous and current theoretical debates should be to help us gain a deeper insight into the movement, always aware that it is riddled with contradictions. It is these contradictions that must be highlighted.

This study maintains that it is of immense historical value to find out how the revolt's various components united and disagreed over aims and objectives and how this lack of an all-uniting and revolutionary ideology influenced the shape and destiny of Mau Mau. Under the umbrella of Mau Mau, there existed ethnic nationalism, the squatters' problem, unemployment and lack of housing in urban areas, and landlessness in the rural areas of Central Province. All these issues frustrated the politics of nationalism. The racial problem, essentially the African reaction against white racism and discrimination in Kenya, also became a factor in the general grievances that gave rise to the revolt. It is therefore important to distill from this complex mixture and interrelationships the aims and objectives of these various groups and how the aims contradicted each other at one level and reinforced each other at another level.

It is easily observed that, after 1954, there was a significant erosion of local support for Mau Mau within the Kikuyu reserve. The general tendency had been to blame Mau Mau's military tactics, which are said to have alienated the movement from its base of support. In part, this is true, but it does not explain everything. This loss of support was a combination of Mau Mau's military tactics, its weak political organization and base, government counterinsurgency, and more crucially, the social and economic changes instituted by the government within the larger society. Emphasis on this linkage seeks to place the Mau Mau peasant revolt within the context of any social movement. Mau Mau and its fortunes must be analyzed against the background of the larger society. "The course of development of a movement," Robert H. Lauer has written, "cannot be adequately understood apart from the social context, in particular, apart from the changes which are occurring in the context." He adds that, "events may effect changes in the climate of public opinion and strip a movement of its appeal and even of its legitimacy."[51] Lauer concludes by saying that "whether we are dealing with genesis, growth, ideology, program, recruitment of members, selection of strategies, or decline—all are a function of changes that occur in the social context."[52]

What then makes this book different from other past projects on Mau Mau? In the first place, it seeks to produce a systematic and comprehensive analysis of Mau Mau from its inception to the military and ideological battles within the movement, and lastly, the rehabilitation period followed by decolonization and its legacy. It therefore covers a broader time frame and addresses more issues about the revolt than many of the previous studies. Four recent publications give admirable analysis of parts of this peasant revolt, without offering a comprehensive analysis. David Throup's *Economic and Social Origins of Mau Mau* (1988) is essentially an analysis of official economic policies and the failure of these policies to redress the economic grievances of the Kikuyu. This failure, of course, led to the revolt. Throup's study, while detailed, does not deal with Mau Mau in action nor with its consequences on the decolonization process and beyond. Tabitha Kanogo's *Squatters and the Roots of Mau Mau* (1987) was one of the first books to give a detailed account of the squatters' problem and its linkage to Mau Mau. Concise and well researched, the book nonetheless is limited to squatters. It does not deal in detail with the agrarian crisis in Central Province nor the urban economic crisis in Nairobi. Like Throup, Kanogo does not deal with Mau Mau military and political strategy nor with rehabilitation and the legacy of the revolt.

Mau Mau (1989) by Robert Edgerton is a well-written, fast-flowing summary of the revolt. Unlike other studies, Edgerton attempts to bring the story up to 1988. However he avoids dealing with several issues. There is no analysis of the oaths, the propaganda, government counterinsurgency, nor the legacy of the revolt. His discussion of rehabilitation fails to link this program to the nature and character of nationalism that emerged after 1960. A more ambitious study is Frank Furedi's *The Mau Mau War in Perspective* (1989). Furedi lays a lot of emphasis on the squatter problem and looks at squatters as main actors in his drama.[53] Clearly the interrelationship between squatters and Mau Mau cannot be denied. It would however be inaccurate to look at squatters as having played the leading role in "the drama" throughout the course of the revolt. Besides, it would be problematic to explain the concentration of armed struggle and military activity in Central Province, and not in the Rift Valley, throughout the emergency years. Furedi's study is suspicious of the value of comparative analysis and looks at Mau Mau as "essentially an ad hoc response to changing conditions."[54] Furedi avoids dealing with Mau Mau the movement—the organization, the military and political strategy, and then the rehabilitation. For if it is true, as he argues, that by the time of decolonization, radicalism and mass resistance to conservative politics were on the way to being defeated, then we must look for the ideological preparations for this outcome in the rehabilitation process.

On another level, this book aims to revitalize the study of African nationalism. It aims to enhance our comprehension of the interrelationship between an essentially populist movement and the conventional mass-based political parties. How do they interrelate in a colonial context?

The book itself is divided into three sections. Part 1 is devoted to the background to the revolt. It describes and analyzes the economic, social, and political reasons that led to the revolt. The immediate events leading to the 1952 revolt are covered separately in chapter 3. Part 2 deals with the "military phase" and covers not only British counterinsurgency strategies but also the propaganda offensive against Mau Mau which proved so effective. Mau Mau's own military and political strategy is covered in chapter 6 and demonstrates its complex composition and contradictions. Part 3 deals with the rehabilitation of Mau Mau detainees. As will be seen, this was an extremely important undertaking by the British and may have affected Kenyan society more profoundly than is readily realized or even acknowledged. This section also deals with the question of decolonization, especially Mau Mau's role in the politics of decolonization. Lastly, there is the complex and sensitive question of the legacy of the revolt. What factors have influenced the shaping of the varied legacies of Mau Mau?

This study has paid special attention to published texts, newspapers, films, news magazines, tape recordings, and archival documents. The expiration of the thirty-year restriction on documents at the Public Record Office in London for 1952 documents enabled me to gain access to a wealth of documents hitherto unutilized. I also benefited from consulting the archives and libraries at Rhodes House Library, Oxford University; Royal Institute of International Affairs, London; Imperial War Museum, London; University of London Libraries; and Kenya National Archives, Nairobi. I had originally intended to make an extensive use of oral sources on two questions: oaths and legacy. Unfortunately during my field trip in 1986 (and even in 1989), there was a remarkable national renewal of public discussion in Kenya on Mau Mau which became heavily politicized.[55] Consequently, many of those individuals I contacted were either very wary about talking to me or gave standard answers that corresponded to the discussions in newspapers and those uttered at public rallies. As for the oaths, I found almost no individual willing to talk about the details.[56] On these two questions, I have therefore relied on archival documents and secondary sources to reconstruct what I think is a balanced and fair analysis.

The history of Mau Mau is inevitably a complex and controversial story. Yet this should not deter us from studying it. We should study it to understand and appreciate the causes and impact of its successes and contradictions.

PART ONE

Background to the Revolt

ONE

THE ECONOMICS OF DESPERATION

Before the establishment of colonial rule, the Kikuyu people of central Kenya were involved in a significant southward expansion which had established them in Kiambu and which was still in progress. It was a slow but steady expansion, which in the past had led them to occupy Nyeri and later Kiambu. As they expanded, they came to formulate significant customs and kinship obligations that regulated the occupation, ownership, and utilization of land. "The *Mbari* was the most important social grouping in Kikuyu society, as it combined land owning with the regulation of marriage. The *Mbari* was a lineage group of all Kikuyu who traced their descent through the male line from a known ancestor."[1] A mbari ordinarily occupied specific lands, reputedly owned by its founder. Such lands were known as *githaka*. To be sure, not all githaka lands were in one large plot. It was quite possible for githaka lands to be scattered over a wide area.

As population grew, it was normal in the early days for some mbari members to go out on their own to break new ground, thereby founding a new mbari, with of course a new leader, the *muramati*. The muramati technically owned the githaka lands initially, but this individual ownership soon gave way to mbari ownership as the population grew and more and more kinsmen were accommodated on the land. What however didn't change was the unrestricted access to githaka lands by male members of the mbari for cultivation and pastoral purposes. ". . . all land belonged to the mbari and . . . any member of the mbari had the right to utilise any part of it so long as no one else had made prior claim to it and, more important, provided the head of the *mbari*, the *muramati*, was informed."[2]

The Kikuyu country had a distinct group of landless people prior to colonization. What, however, distinguishes landlessness in precolonial times from that of the latter part of colonial rule is that in precolonial times landlessness did not spell economic disaster. There were tested mechanisms and client relationships in place that cleverly ensured that the landless were not destitute. These landless people entered into a tenant relationship between themselves and a mbari, usually through its muramati. The most prominent categories of tenants were the *muthami*, the *ahoi*, and the *muthoni*.

A muthami was a resident tenant. He negotiated with the muramati for permission to occupy a specific piece of land belonging to the muramati's mbari. He moved his whole family and became a local resident on "his" new land. He was expected to provide, "at every harvest the first full *kiondoo* (string bag) of each crop . . . as a tribute to the landlord, and failure to provide this would result in eviction."[3] It was, however, rare for the muthami to be evicted unless there were serious accusations leveled against him, for example, witchcraft. After his acceptance as a tenant, the muthami had "reasonable security of tenure." L. S. B. Leakey contends that most tenants sought to increase the security of their land tenure by entering into a marriage union with the landlord's family and changing their status from muthami to muthoni (in-law).[4]

During the colonial period, the most talked about tenant relationship was that of the ahoi (the tenant-at-will). The ahoi were landless tenants who ordinarily did not reside on the land allocated to them. The muhoi was expected to provide a portion of his crop to his landlord at each harvest and be of general military and economic use to the landlord as need arose. In the early days of clan warfare and more especially warfare between the Maasai and the Kikuyu, these tenants were particularly useful as soldiers and defenders of githaka lands from enemy intruders. These tenants did not pay rent for the land they occupied. Their presence constituted a functional relationship between them and the mbari and its muramati. Land remained the property of the mbari, which was watched over by the muramati.

These customary and traditional obligations could be fulfilled only in traditional circumstances in which customs were uniformly obeyed and honored and, perhaps more crucially, in which there was enough land for the reproduction of these obligations. These circumstances changed dramatically with the coming of colonialism. Colonialism effectively stopped the southward expansion of the Kikuyu and therefore offered no possibility for the occupation of new githaka by an enterprising member of the Kikuyu society. It was in Kikuyu country that the first land alienation for the white settlers' benefit occurred, especially in Kiambu.

The history of settler occupation of Kenya from 1900 is indissolubly linked to the railway—then called the Uganda railway. The railway was built using British government funds and represented the most expensive official expenditure in the newly acquired territory. This expenditure in itself demonstrated the British government's commitment to securing a firm foothold, not only in Uganda but also in British East Africa, a territory that, after 1920, became known as Kenya.

Once the railway had been constructed, it had to be put to profitable use. Because Kenya and Uganda lacked minerals, the railway could be profitable only if it stimulated agricultural production in the interior.

In the early years of Kenya as a protectorate, several schemes were encouraged by the Foreign Office in London to stimulate agricultural production in the territory. On the one hand, the Foreign Office considered making Kenya "America of the Hindus" by encouraging Indian colonization. Others in the office favored Jewish colonization of the territory.[5] In the end European colonization of Kenya's highlands was settled upon as the most viable alternative.

The white settlers' occupation of Kenya was achieved largely through the efforts of the newly appointed High Commissioner, Sir Charles Eliot, and a few newly arrived settlers who congregated around Nairobi. It was Eliot's view that the new territory would have to be developed by Europeans as "a white man's country." He proceeded to bar Indians from occupying the highlands, allowing only a few to occupy the low-lying areas.

In these early years no proposal was as bothersome, irritating, and emotional to the already resident settlers in the territory as the possibility of the country becoming a Jewish colony. These Jews were "refugees from eastern Europe, fleeing from Pogroms in Russia and Rumania. They were sponsored by the Zionist organization and encouraged to apply for land in East Africa by Joseph Chamberlain, the Secretary of State for Colonies."[6] In this encouragement the British government was lending recognition to the fact that Jews had invested heavily in the empire, especially in the "Rand Mines." However, the conditions of settlement laid out by the Zionist organization were clearly unacceptable to the British government.[7] The Zionist Congress eventually voted to reject the offer of settling Jews on the Uasin Gishu Plateau in Kenya. But this rejection came after considerable emotional antisemitic outbursts on the part of the resident white settlers. They resisted the possibility of Jewish settlement with intense emotional fervor. They argued that only Christians, and not Jews, were ideally suited to bring the benefits of Western civilization to Africans.

At no time in these discussions was any thought seriously entertained of using indigenous Africans as the agents of commercial agricultural production in Kenya. It was postulated that Africans were so primitive, so disorganized, that it would be centuries before they would be able to assume the gigantic task of commercial farming.[8] Sir Charles Eliot thought that although

> the African is greedy and covetous enough, . . . he is too indolent in his ways, and too disconnected in his ideas, to make any attempt to better himself, or to undertake any labour which does not produce a speedy visible result. His mind is far nearer the animal world than is that of the European or Asiatic, and exhibits something of the animal's placidity and want of desire to rise beyond the stage he has reached.[9]

In the mind of Eliot and subsequent governors of Kenya, the development of the territory could not be left in the hands of such a race that inhabited a "section of the world which has hitherto been a prey to barbarism."

Eliot initially turned to South Africa, and it was from there until 1912, that a majority of settlers in Kenya came. This initial South African majority had several implications for Kenya. M. P. K. Sorrenson asserts that "the European settlement in Kenya highlands was in a very real sense (though not legally) a South African colony."[10] These settlers saw their position as being similar to that of earlier settlers in other British dominions, like Canada, New Zealand, Australia, and of course South Africa. They were in Kenya to found a "white man's country" modeled specifically on South Africa. The political and economic implication of these sentiments was that Africans would be treated as laborers, providing labor which would in turn give settlers the prosperity needed to lead a comfortable, secure life. The Africans would in the circumstances have to be controlled and disciplined. In years ahead, up to 1923 and beyond, the settlers agitated for self-rule in one form or another, and especially for severe legislation in dealing with Africans, or "kaffirs."

The most important step taken by the colonial state to demonstrate its commitment to European settlement in Kenya was the alienation of African land. In 1896, "the Land Acquisition Act allowed the administration to acquire land compulsorily for the railway."[11] This was followed by the Land Ordinance of 1902. This ordinance enabled settlers to acquire land, allocated by the commissioner, on a ninety-nine year lease. In ordinances like these and others that followed, the colonial state allocated to itself the responsibility of giving out land to white settlers and other alien economic establishments in the territory. The theory and practice was that all Africans were tenants at the imperial government's will, and therefore had no land rights that could not be abrogated by imperial decree. Besides, it was felt that Africans' occupation of land and their claim to it were detrimental, for they did not contribute to what the colonial state regarded as economic development. What all these ordinances meant to the economic future of Africans in Kenya is that their access to land, their principal means of production and livelihood, was severely limited, especially in central Kenya. This, together with the labor needs of settler capitalism mediated through the colonial state, drastically reduced and eventually destroyed the economic independence of the African population.

The 1915 Land Ordinance is most significant. Apart from increasing the powers of the governor, it also increased the lease years from 99 to 999 years. The governor could now ". . . grant lease or otherwise alienate, in His Majesty's behalf, any Crown Lands for any purpose and on any terms as he may think fit."[12] This ordinance also established the native reserves and empowered the governor to reduce the reserve lands as he deemed fit. This ordinance in effect established the creeping boundary of the Highlands and created great insecurity on the part of Africans over their land tenure in their reserves. The boundary for the "White Highlands" was not established until 1939, "because the colonial government accepted the settler argument that land found suitable for permanent European settlement should be added to the highlands, whenever it became available."[13]

The strategy of perpetual reduction of reserve lands was advocated by the settlers as an effective tool to "induce" laborers from the reserves to seek a livelihood on European farms. The taxation policy of the colonial state also aimed at "encouraging" the flow of labor from rural areas to European farms. In this way, therefore, the taxation policy of the administration, although aimed at raising state revenue, also sought to furnish the labor needs of settler capitalism.

Many of the settlers were in reality men of limited economic means and as a result were forced to rely on government aid, especially over the recruitment and retention of labor. African labor was not flowing to European farms voluntarily, but as a result of direct or indirect coercion. In other words, settler capitalism failed to be the engine of economic growth in the colony and continually relied on the colonial state for survival. Settlers did not and were not able to sustain an independent economic growth unaided by the state.

During the depression of the 1930s, settler capitalism was saved from extinction by the state. "The price of land collapsed, leaving behind a level of debt which weakened the future of white settlement in Kenya. As a result, Government instituted a number of interim measures to save the settlers from extinction."[14] This unswerving commitment to settler capitalism by the colonial state in Kenya produced insurmountable economic and political problems in the African reserves, especially in Central Province. The chief economic problem was scarcity of land.

Land scarcity in Kikuyuland during colonialism has generally aroused controversy in both colonial and postcolonial Kenya. During the struggle for political freedom, the nationalists tended to explain landlessness as being the result of land alienation by the colonial state for settlers. The implication of this line of argument was that the settlers had taken most land from the Kikuyu and that if this land were returned to them there would be no problem of land scarcity. Available evidence suggests that land shortage in Kikuyuland was multifaceted and therefore cannot be attributed solely to land alienation for the settlers. The percentage of the Kikuyu who actually lost land to the settlers was about four percent,[15] and the total acreage of the land lost was certainly smaller than that suffered by other Kenyan tribes, for example, the Maasai. What made loss of land in Kikuyuland dramatic was population pressure and lack of room for further expansion. The frontier of expansion had been sealed off with the advent of colonialism and the consequent proclamation of reserves. In Kikuyuland itself, there occurred significant population increase in the first two decades of this century. Population pressure worsened the changing traditional roles and rights toward land ownership and utilization.

The advent of colonialism introduced new classes of people in the society who could not be accounted for in the traditional hierarchy of power, but who came to wield an increasing amount of power and authority in society. Perhaps the principal new centers of power were the chiefs appointed by the colonial administration. The institution of chiefdom was lacking in Kikuyu society, and so when the British sought for local agents of colonialism they chose people who had no traditional claim to power. In Kiambu, for example, the leading colonial chief was Kinyanjui, "a man of no traditional standing, a hunter without property."[16] The background of the early and subsequent chiefs did not stop them from wielding a lot of power and accumulating considerable property. These men owed their offices to British colonial administration and not to the traditional institutions. They were government appointees and served without being unduly worried about their popularity with their subjects. The most significant acquisition of these chiefs was land. They acquired this land as individuals, and it became their personal property and not that of their mbari or any traditional association.

The rise of chiefs and the corruption that inevitably accompanied the execution of their duties accelerated the process of loss of respect for, and later abandonment of, customary obligations, especially over individual rights to mbari land. The introduction of formal, Western-style education, usually through missionaries, by 1920 had started to produce a number of Africans with access to money and influence by virtue of their literacy and the salaried employment they were able to obtain. They worked as teachers, government servants, and church servants. These, together with chiefs, tribal elders, and other government employees, started the process of individual land aggrandizement in Kikuyuland, which paid little heed to traditional rights and obligations. Individualism had set in, and it was to tear down the thread of unity that had hitherto existed in Kikuyuland. The land that these people accumulated was acquired through corruption and intimidation, and also through a lengthy litigation process in which they were assured of victory, for only they had the resources to appeal traditional judgments and to bribe tribunal elders.

As land ownership became increasingly individualized, the ahoi found that friendship alone was not enough to assure them of their traditional rights to cultivation. The ahoi found to their painful dismay that the options facing them were either to remain in Kikuyuland and become servants of the new landlords or to migrate to the Rift Valley out of economic necessity. Moreover, there was official pressure for them to migrate and supply labor on the farms.

The ahoi had been tolerated as tenants in the past when land was relatively abundant and when family members of the landlord were effectively catered to. It became increasingly difficult to honor these obligations in fast-changing circumstances in which shortage of land was also accompanied by the introduction of a cash economy requiring agricultural commodity production for profit. These changes in traditional obligations led to rural tension in Kikuyuland.

There was tension between the ahoi and the new landed gentry who curtailed their access to land and actively started to turn them into laborers. There was also tension between those families that had lost what they claimed were their ancestral lands and the new landed gentry who had acquired such lands through corrupt means, including lengthy litigation processes. The major source of rural tension was, of course, the actual loss of land to white settlers. But even here we should remember that some members of Kikuyu society had actually sold mbari land to settlers without the consent of their mbari. Disclosures of such dealings inevitably created bitter enmity between those who lost their land and those who had "feathered their own nests by selling their own *Mbari* or even other people's land without their knowledge or consent." [17]

The journey to the Rift Valley to work on European farms as squatters was undertaken not solely by the ahoi, but also by those who owned small pieces of land in the reserve at this time. For a while at least, the migration to the Rift Valley was demonstrably a worthwhile option to take in the face of dwindling opportunities in Kikuyuland. There was the prospect of "owning" large pieces of land for cultivation and grazing and therefore of prospering on the new lands. It was the option that came closest to founding a new mbari and especially gaining new githaka. As will be shown later in this chapter, this proved to be a situation of false security for the squatters. They had no security of tenure over the new lands allocated to them by the settlers. They were tolerated when it was profitable and necessary to their new masters and ignominiously evicted when they were deemed unnecessary. It is the bitterness of these squatters who saw no future back home in Kikuyuland that gave a significant impetus to the growth of the Mau Mau movement. It was estimated by the Carter Land Commission that by 1934, 110,000 Kikuyu were living outside the reserve. [18] By 1948, "there were 294,146 or 28.65% of their total population living outside the reserve." [19] In these circumstances the colonial government undertook, from 1937 on, to implement its most unfortunate and tragic decision: to repatriate "undesirable" squatters to the reserves. It was perhaps its most mistaken decision since the proclamation of the 1915 Land Ordinance.

This decision embittered a large number of desperate people, who saw no future ahead for them nor for their children. Many had been forced out of the reserve for lack of land and had accepted work and land on settler farms in Rift Valley where they had hoped to create a new life for themselves. The decision to repatriate them was therefore a fatal blow arousing feelings of hatred toward the settlers and the government. The decision to repatriate some of the squatters was part of the 1937 Resident Labourers Ordinance, which severely restricted the land available to squatters for cultivation and grazing. This reduction in land was in part because the settlers' era of prosperity had started and more land was needed for cultivation, and also because more land was needed to settle white ex-servicemen after the Second World War.

During the Second World War, Kenya had to make its contributions to the imperial war effort. There was a significant rise in the demand for agricultural and tropical goods to be used by the far-flung imperial army and for domestic consumption in Britain. Relying on established precedent, the colonial state turned to settlers to provide most of the food and cash crops needed on the world market. It was an official decision. What however underscored the favorable treatment of the settlers by the government were the terms to induce and sustain production of the necessary crops on settlers' farms.

> As part of a drive for increased production, Increased Production of Crops Ordinance was passed. This legislation provided in the case of non-native production, for guaranteed prices to farmers for such crops, for advances against the minimum guaranteed returns, and, in approved cases, for payment of free grants for the breaking of new land.[20]

The board that supervised this wartime production was the Agricultural Provision and Settlement Board whose chairman was Major Cavendish-Bentick, a prominent settler farmer. These favorable terms naturally led to settler prosperity—perhaps the greatest prosperity in the settler enterprise in Kenya. It was prosperity that was artificial, for it relied on extraordinarily favorable economic and labor terms guaranteed by the state. It would therefore be inaccurate to attribute this prosperity to settler ingenuity and workmanship. Settlers prospered by farming under no risks whatsoever.

The availability of funds and the guarantee of profit induced settlers to break new lands which had lain fallow in the past. They had the funds to mechanize their farms and thereby reduce significantly their reliance on massive manual labor. Mechanization of settler agriculture, together with the expansion of the acreage under cultivation which had started in the late 1930s and greatly increased after 1942, occurred at a time when scarcity of land had become a destabilizing factor in central Kenya. The subsequent reduction of squatter labor by the settlers put more strain on the reserve in Central Province, which was called upon to shoulder not only its excess population but also the excess labor thrown out of the White Highlands. The "excess" squatter labor was the casualty of settler prosperity. Settler capitalism reached its hour of economic triumph during the Second World War, but this was to be short-lived, for past official policies on its behalf had produced insurmountable economic and political problems in the African reserves, especially in Central Province.

The reentry of ex-squatters into the reserve was resisted by the local residents. Kinship ties were not enough to assure these repatriates of a warm welcome. Even those who had owned small pieces of land prior to their migration to the Rift Valley found that their land had been distributed to other members of the mbari or had been acquired by a variety of means by the new landed gentry. This loss created yet another source of bitter rural tension between the landed gentry and the expanding class of ahoi.

Land scarcity in Kikuyuland inevitably led to over-utilization of land, which in the end aggravated the agricultural and economic problems of central Kenya after 1939. This deterioration in land fertility had been noticed as early as 1933 by the Carter Land Commission. But it is also worth noting that the colonial government, in spite of this fact, had encouraged an expansion of agricultural commodity production, especially during the depression and Second World War. "During the Depression, and even more so during the war, however, Africans were encouraged to maximise production, regardless of the effects of soil fertility, to bolster the finances of the Colonial State and to supply the troops."[21] Occurring alongside population explosion, this official encouragement to overcultivate led to two tragic consequences in Kikuyuland. In the first place, an increase in population meant that there was more demand for food, which led to extensive cultivation even of areas previously reserved for grazing or generally held to be unsuitable for cultivation. This led to extensive soil erosion, reducing even further the amount of land available for cultivation. Secondly, the introduction of a cash economy produced severe social differentiation between the landed gentry who seized the opportunity to make profits from their large land holdings and those who were slowly edged out of land into the class of the ahoi. This rural economic strife, the result of land scarcity, gave rise to a definite struggle between the landed gentry and the ahoi, and consequently a sort of rural class struggle, however modified, was in place in Kikuyuland by 1948.[22]

The general agrarian problems facing Central Province were surprisingly well known to the colonial government. The colonial government had some information about overpopulation, congestion of the land, soil erosion, and falling living standards in Kikuyuland from 1934 up to the outbreak of the emergency in 1952. What is however sadly apparent is that the colonial government was not at all convinced that these problems required a radical and urgent solution to the question of land ownership and utilization. The solutions were thought of on a long-term basis, being seen as the natural outcome of improved agricultural techniques in the rural areas.

A government-commissioned report entitled "Post War Five Year Development Plan, Central Province" clearly acknowledged that overpopulation existed in Central Province. It stated, "The basic problem for solution, when considering plans to develop the native areas and raise the native standard of living and education, in its broadest sense, is one of excess population." It went further and explained, "The position is that occupation of tribal lands has now become static, migrations have ceased, and in the case of small movements in Kikuyu, these have actually been checked."[23] According to this report, population in central Kenya was "far outstripping the capacity of the land." In a well-known document on the agrarian problem, the governor, Sir Philip Mitchell, arrived at similar conclusions. He believed the problem in Kikuyuland was largely due to unchecked population increase. His explanation was that the Kikuyu were the "most prolific of Kenya tribes and had bred so freely as to be seriously congested in their own areas."[24] In his handing over the report in 1950, the district commissioner for Nyeri, P. S. Osborne, noted that "the fundamental problem of the district is overpopulation." He gave specific statistics and observed that, "in addition to the 180 odd thousand persons found to be residing in the district on the day of the 1948 census, there are more than 35,000 males with Nyeri identity certificates out of work of whom only a small proportion is detribalised. This formidable total has to find the only land it owns in the 300 square miles of the district."[25] What solutions were offered by the colonial government to these problems?

The response of the state to the agrarian problems in Central Province was governed by two policy considerations. In the first place, it was held as an irrefutable fact that all African land complaints and grievances had been adequately settled by the Carter Land Commission, whose findings were published in 1934. The colonial government held the report as the final arbiter on the land question.[26] The commission thus gave the settlers the formal assurance that there would be no further alteration of the boundaries of the White Highlands.

The second policy consideration was that the settlers and their occupation of the Highlands had to be protected at all costs. The solutions to the African agrarian problems had therefore to be found in the African reserves. The problem was not one of lack of land, but of increasing the carrying capacity of the land. Africans had to be guided into improving their farming techniques, stopping the spread of soil erosion, and abandoning "primitive farming methods," especially shifting cultivation. In his recommendation toward solving the congestion problem in Kikuyuland, S. H. Fazan stated that "the remedy would appear to lie in the direction of improving their skill rather than reducing their relative numbers either by emigration or by addition of their land."[27] The government felt that it was not going to provide more land for African settlement, although a few settlements were vaguely contemplated along the Tana River and on the coast. There was also the proposal of officially encouraging migration to Tanganyika.[28]

What the state and the settlers failed to realize is that land scarcity and the need for more food to feed an expanded population had inevitably led to overutilization of available land, ruining some of it in the process. Soil erosion and loss of fertility were the most visible results of serious agrarian problems. It should never be forgotten that all through the colonial period there was very little technical and capital investment by the state in African agriculture. The department of agriculture was principally concerned with settler farming. Although the department of agriculture knew of the broad contours of the problem, it had no intimate knowledge of the agrarian problems in Central Province. It had general information about congestion on the land, and of soil erosion, but no accurate statistics or reliable information about soils. It knew less about disparities in land ownership. It is no wonder then that the solutions which the state offered were both unrealistic and general. They proved to be worthless up to 1952.

The "Post War Five Year Development Plan" recommended that in Central Province, "natives therein must be impressed with the fact that they should not consider the growing of food crops for themselves as a primary and customary need, but must concentrate on other crops from the proceeds of which they can purchase staple foods."[29] This was a government-commissioned report urging vigorous and widespread cash-crop farming without as much as hinting as to how this could be accomplished without provision for adequate transport and commercial and communication infrastructure. There was also the sad fact that the landless peasants who were the cause of intense rural tension at this time had no access to land and would therefore not have the money to buy food from other areas.

The other solution generally toyed with was to imagine that excess rural population would be absorbed in industrial employment in urban areas. This again was unrealistic. In the first place the industrial development in Kenya at this time was minimal, even with the boost from wartime production. Secondly, those who were eager to move out of the rural areas were poorly educated, mostly illiterate peasants who would not have been easily absorbed as factory workers. Besides, the colonial government had no comprehensive plan to absorb Africans in urban areas as workers and permanent urban residents.

Most of these unrealistic solutions were put forward for official consideration during the governorship of Sir Philip Mitchell. It is worthwhile, therefore, to discuss briefly the views of this governor toward Africans and their development. Mitchell came to Kenya as governor in 1944, after a long service in East Africa.[30] It was a service which had earned him some distinction in the Colonial Office in London as an expert on Africa, especially on African agrarian problems. Mitchell achieved his status an expert largely on account of his commentaries and lengthy dispatches to the Colonial Office.[31]

Perhaps Mitchell's most famous document on African agrarian problems is *The Agrarian Problem in Kenya*. In this document Mitchell strove to offer the origin, development, and solution of the agrarian problem. The document, however, reflected Mitchell's views on Africans and their problems. He simplified the history of colonialism and felt that Kenya had been colonized as an act of humanitarianism by Britain to stop the slave trade![32] He was convinced that there had been no African precolonial development. But he had difficulty explaining this. "For reasons which remain a mystery today and do not derive from the slave trade," Mitchell said, "the People's of East and Central Africa were found in the 1890's to be in an extra ordinary condition of backwardness and ignorance." He proceeded to offer illustrations of this inexplicable backwardness.

> They had no wheeled transport and (apart from the camels and donkeys of the pastoral nomads) no animal transport either; they had no roads or towns; no tools except small hand hoes, axes, wooden digging sticks and the like; no manufactures, and no industrial products except the simplest domestic handiwork, no commerce as we understand it and no currency . . . they had never heard of working for wages.[33]

The list is long. To such a people, therefore, it was expected that the white man should carry on his civilizing mission and introduce them to modernity and contact with human civilization. Africans, Mitchell reminded his audience, "are a people who, however much natural ability and however admirable attributes they may possess, are without a history, culture or religion of their own, and in that they are, as far as I know, unique in the modern world."[34]

Mitchell felt convinced that it was in the interests of the empire, and especially of the Africans, for the colonial state to support the settlers who would then bring prosperity to the colony. There was no question in his mind that settlers were indispensable in the dual enterprise of civilizing Africans and developing the economy of the colony. Almost by way of a final verdict on the Africans, Mitchell stated, "I must repeat that they are a people who in 1890 were in a more primitive condition than anything of which there is any record in Pre-Roman Britain."[35] Mitchell was clearly prejudiced against Africans, their values, or even their role in the development of the colony except, of course, as obedient servants.

Mitchell believed that opening up more land for African occupation was distinctly injurious to the economy of the colony because it would inevitably lead to more land being ruined by African primitive farming methods.[36] And so in 1944 Kenya received a governor who was singularly unsuited to tackle its pressing economic problems and political frustrations that naturally were the result of the economics of desperation. He identified himself closely with settlers at a time when these settlers were belligerent, insensitive, and arrogant. He failed to appreciate the desperate nature of displaced and expelled squatters, landless ahoi, and perhaps worse, he refused even to contemplate the wisdom of providing more land to African peasants. Mitchell, graphically portrayed by D. W. Throup as "a blunt, unattractive, fat, little man without any social graces,"[37] easily succumbed to settlers' pressure and was personally hostile and contemptuous of African peasant agriculture.

Apart from these land problems, Kikuyu society was, at this time, starting to experience a severe clash of generations between the old and the young, notably between the old and the young men. A general disintegration of traditional cultural obligations had led to a clash between the old people, who insisted on upholding these traditions, and the youth, who felt it impossible or undesirable to fulfill these obligations in a fast-changing society. The traditional elders had lost to the chiefs the power to deliver binding verdicts on matters of local duties and obligations. As government appointees and supported by an array of administrative and paramilitary forces, chiefs had power to implement decisions and to confer favors on their supporters. As chiefs became centers of power, the prestige of the traditional elders was slowly but surely diminished. It was now possible to disregard their views and decisions with impunity, without the fear of being automatically ostracized. These contending centers of power naturally caused tremendous damage to the unity of the Kikuyu people.

By 1951, the combination of all these forces had produced a distinctly restive and increasingly defiant mood among the economically depressed population in Central Province. Crimes of violence increased tremendously from 1948, as poor, landless peasants, and frustrated young people attacked the landed gentry and other rural agents of colonial administration. By 1949 the district commissioner of Kiambu was already warning of an "alarming increase in crime, particularly in Chura Division, with crimes of violence figuring large." He thought that "most of the crime was directly or indirectly attributable to excessive drinking."[38] But he failed to mention that "excessive drinking" was in itself the result of intense rural social tension, which was directly or indirectly linked to land scarcity that had made economic survival an insurmountable problem for a sizable section of the population. Drunkenness became a common feature in Central Province in the last four years before the declaration of the state of emergency in 1952. In his "handing-over report" the district commissioner for Nyeri in 1948 noted that "crime, drunkenness, juvenile delinquency and general indiscipline are all common features of the present unhappy social state of the Kikuyu people."[39] Diminished economic opportunities in the rural areas of Central Province led to a drift of displaced persons to the urban areas. Urban areas were the last option for survival for many of these young people, the ahoi, and repatriated squatters from settler farms in the Rift Valley.

Urban areas rose in Kenya after 1900 principally as government administrative centers. They provided living quarters and entertainment centers for the immigrant administrative communities. The colonial white civil servants lived in these centers, together with members of the Asian community, who had become traders and technicians after being barred from farming in the White Highlands. Urban centers arose in colonial Kenya, therefore, to serve the interests of a limited section of the population—aliens. The housing and general welfare facilities of most of these cities were planned to cater to the interests of those immigrant communities. The institution of racism in the colony made it imperative for the development plans of urban centers in Kenya to proceed along racial lines. Residential estates were strictly along color lines, with whites occupying the best parts of the towns. Commercial centers that catered to whites were generally well planned and so were their residential estates. Government workers recruited from overseas and even locally were generally provided with superior, comfortable accommodation and servants. The Asians lived in separate areas, usually more crowded than those occupied by whites. In the initial years, it was generally held that urban areas were not for Africans.

The administration did not envisage that Africans would become permanent residents of the urban areas. The place for Africans was the rural areas (the native reserves), where they were expected to live according to their customs under the guidance of chiefs and district commissioners who represented the colonial state. Yet the economic and administrative needs of the colonial state continually conspired against this naive view of the realities in African reserves. In the first place, the white and Asian urban residents relied on African manual labor for survival. Africans were needed to work as domestic servants, refuse collectors, general manual laborers, clerks, artisans, and railway workers. These laborers had to reside in urban centers away from their original rural homes. Secondly, land alienation and the subsequent development of agricultural commodity production in the rural areas, especially in Central Province, had produced a class of people who could no longer rely on land for their livelihood. The prospect of urban employment had inevitably led to migration of the economically dispossessed persons to urban areas. And so, in spite of colonial beliefs, migration to urban centers continued all through the colonial period. What is interesting here is that in the initial stages up to 1939 the colonial state refused to acknowledge the possibility of Africans residing in urban areas on a permanent basis. As a result of this mistaken belief, municipal authorities in Kenya, which tended on the whole to be dominated by Europeans, never developed or created any social welfare facilities to cater to African residents.

African urban residents were from the start a forgotten people. Neither the government nor the municipal authorities officially acknowledged their presence, although they relied on these forgotten people for survival and existence.

Problems of urban existence for Africans were particularly serious in Nairobi, which was close to the Kikuyu reserve. It was therefore understandable that the majority of Nairobi's African residents were mainly Kikuyu. Their numbers grew steadily so that "by 1948 there were 28,886 Kikuyu living within the municipality of Nairobi, 45% of the total African population in the city"[40] Which categories of the African population migrated to Nairobi from Central Province? The principal category of migrants comprised the landless peasants, the ahoi, who had lost land and cultivation rights in the rural areas. They were generally a desperate people with a bleak future. In addition, migrants came who had small pieces of land in the reserves, land that was unable to support a man and his expanding family. There were young migrants who had clashed with the older generation or whose economic fortunes had been seriously diminished in the reserves. These young people hoped to get employment and accumulate enough cash to pay bride price or to buy land back home. There were also women migrants composed of "divorced, widowed, or barren women for whom Nairobi was an escape from the derision of their community."[41] Clearly these were not industrial workers or even the industrial urbanized proletariat. They were recently arrived rural people who strove to make a living in a harsh, fast-moving, color-bar ridden town.

The limited nature of industrial development in Kenya, in general, meant that these migrants remained either unemployed or were absorbed in low-paying manual work. Even for those lucky to secure manual work, life was not easy or tolerable. Their wages were punitively low. The colonial state and private employers paid very low wages to their African workers, basing their actions on the belief that high wages for Africans were unnecessary and injurious to the economy. Low wages were seen as justifiable because it was held that African workers did not solely depend on them for survival. The general premise of this tragic policy was that all African urban residents had land in the rural areas that was cultivated by their kinsmen or wives and thus effectively supplemented their urban wages. Likewise, permanent, planned family housing was unnecessary since "home" for Africans was in rural areas and not towns.

As land scarcity became more serious in Central Province after 1946, Nairobi was flooded by migrants from Kikuyuland and also from the Rift Valley, squatters who had either been expelled or edged out of settler farms. To this pool of urban residents was added the recently demobilized African ex-servicemen who had seen action in the Second World War. Unlike their white counterparts in the British imperial army, there were no official plans to settle them on any prime agricultural land or even to offer them key technical or capital aid in their commercial enterprises. The result was that many of them were frustrated and embittered, feeling betrayed by a government and a system which had only recently valued their courageous contributions to the war effort. The limited crafts training offered by the colonial government was deemed as an inappropriate and ineffective alternative to resettlement and capital aid. Many of these ex-soldiers drifted to the urban areas or market centers, where they hoped to set up general retail shops. Many of these shops never became profitable enterprises. And so these ex-servicemen became part of the angry, embittered, urban unemployed. How did these African urban residents survive in Nairobi up to 1952?

The absence of any housing schemes for government employees before 1930 led to a mushrooming of what came to be known as "African locations"; these were essentially slums housing wide-ranging categories of African workers and the habitually unemployed. Pumwani became, perhaps, the most famous of such slums. Others developed at Dagoretti, Ngata Rongai, and Quarry.[42] But even for those Africans housed in newly established government units after 1930, there was inevitable congestion and overcrowding in their small houses as more people flocked to Nairobi and sought refuge with their kinsmen. The slums housing the majority of the African population were not planned nor did they have adequate sanitary facilities. They were overcrowded and hazardous to decent existence. As early as 1947, the colonial government had acknowledged lack of housing for African urban residents.[43] The Royal Commission Report (1953-1955) acknowledged that overcrowding was a serious problem in Nairobi. "Evidence was given that in Nairobi, 3,000 men, women and children were occupying accommodation in one estate designed to house 1,200 people."[44] But as usual, no serious massive housing schemes were contemplated.

Unplanned and rarely supervised by the municipal law-and-order authorities, African locations were plagued by poverty and discontent. The wages received by those lucky enough to be employed were, as already remarked, very low. They were calculated to meet the minimal requirements of an individual male African urban resident without his family. *The Carpenter Report* on African wages published in 1954,[45] after the declaration of the emergency, pointed out the realities of African wages and housing which had not really changed much from those of 1952 or even earlier. The committee felt that "African wages and living costs lead us to the conclusion that approximately one half of the urban workers in private industry and approximately one quarter of those in the Public Services, are in receipt of wages insufficient to provide for the basic needs of health, decency, and working efficiency."[46] As grim as this may sound, these calculations were all the same based on estimates and not hard statistics. The colonial authorities kept no reliable statistics on Africans and their problems except, perhaps, where they entered into an employment contract with members of the immigrant communities. The Carpenter committee frankly admitted that we know all too little about population and housing in our urban centres. No accurate up-to-date information is available as to the numbers of African men, women and children living in these centres, whether they live there on a permanent or temporary basis or how and where they are housed.[47]

After the Second World War, inflation became a big problem in Kenya, but especially for the lowly paid urban residents. It was an aggravating problem not simply because of the increased hardships for the employed African worker, but also because any such worker found it impossible to provide for his kinsmen who had come to Nairobi and sought refuge with him. Tolerance and kinship ties were put to a severe test. Inflation and its effects on African workers were generally known to the colonial authorities. In its annual report for 1947 the colonial state noted that "it is apparent that the cost of living has arisen considerably during the year and a new index, recently prepared by the Director of Statistics, based on consumer goods for Africans, reflects very nearly a hundred percent increase in a wide range of commodities."[48] Most of these commodities were food, drink, tobacco, clothing, and housing. The cost-of-living index in Nairobi, where most of the economically depressed people from Rift Valley and Central Province had congregated, made life practically a nightmare for most of the African residents. As Table 1.1 indicates, the cost-of-living index in Nairobi had steadily increased from 1947 to 1951; and every increase made survival in the town more and more difficult.

Although it could be argued that all racial groups were affected by post–Second World War inflation, there can be no doubt that the brunt of its effects were borne by Africans whose prewar and postwar wages were very low in real and comparative terms. As the *Carpenter Report* later observed, "For a large section of the

Table 1.1
Nairobi Cost-of-Living Index (excluding rent)
[August 1939 = 100]

| Month/Year | Major Groups | | Average Weighted Index Nine Groups |
	Food, Drink, Tobacco	Clothing	
June 30, 1947	163	232	167
December 31, 1947	175	240	175
June 30, 1948	185	257	183
December 31, 1948	185	253	183
June 30, 1949	187	252	184
December 31, 1949	191	248	187
June 30, 1950	209	249	198
December 31, 1950	211	265	203
June 30, 1951	216	269	213
December 31, 1951	229	283	225

Source: East African Statistical Department (Nairobi: Government Printer, 1953), p. 13.

Table 1.2
Distribution of Employees by Earning Groups, 1947 and 1951
(percentage)

| £s per annum* (total emoluments) | European Males | | | |
| | Private Industry | | Public Services | |
	1947	1951	1947	1951
up to £599	46.0	31.6	36.8	11.8
£600–£1,199	44.0	50.6	57.4	71.8
£1,200–£1,799	6.9	12.0	5.1	13.7
£1,800–£2,399	2.0	3.2	0.5	2.1
£2,400–£2,999	0.5	1.2	0.1	0.4
£3,000 and over	0.6	1.4	0.1	0.2
Total	100.0	·100.0	100.0	100.0

| £s per annum* (total emoluments) | Asians and Other Non-African Males | | | |
| | Private Industry | | Public Services | |
	1947	1951	1947	1951
up to £179	27.8	17.8	16.7	5.4
£180–£359	58.7	47.6	65.3	54.2
£360–£539	10.7	25.8	16.8	28.6
£540–£719	1.7	5.6	1.1	10.1
£720 and over	1.1	3.2	0.1	1.7
Total	100.0	100.0	100.0	100.0

| Shillings per month | African Males (excluding agriculture) | | | |
	1947	1951	1947	1951
0–40	70.0	30.7	79.6	21.7
41–60	19.2	37.0	13.0	38.1
61–100	8.3	20.7	5.5	25.1
100 and over	2.5	11.6	1.9	15.1
Total	100.0	100.0	100.0	100.0

*£1 = Shs. 20
 Source: East African Statistical Department: Estimates of Geographical Income and Net Product, 1947–1951 (Nairobi: Government Printer, 1953), p. 12.

urban labour forces, wages were inadequate in relation to the work performed for the wages."[49] Table 1.2, showing the distribution of earnings between the different races in Kenya in 1947 and 1951, illustrates both the Africans' depressed wages and their economic plight during this difficult period.

As the figures in the table demonstrate, Africans earned the lowest wages of all racial groups, with the highest-paid African earning less than half of the annual total emoluments received by the lowest-paid Asian worker. The highest-paid African male worker earned about one-tenth of the wages received by the lowest-paid male European worker. The position of the lowest-paid African worker was considerably worse. By 1948 wage rates for agricultural workers (squatters) mainly on settler farms showed that resident laborers earned between Shs. 1/60 and Shs. 3/60 per week plus housing, plus the value of farm holding (permission to cultivate a certain acreage of crops and to graze a certain number of stock).[50] These were inadequate wages, especially given the fact that the settlers by then had started to reduce the number of squatters they needed and thus had fewer laborers to pay. Since 1937 the settlers also had reduced considerably the amount of land available to squatters for cultivation and grazing. The *Carpenter Report* was critical of the supposed positive attributes of the squatter system. "A system which compels a worker to rely, for the satisfaction of many of his essential needs, upon income derived, not from his own direct employment, but from the use of his employer's land," the report noted, "must in the long run be detrimental to the best interest of both the worker himself and his employer."[51]

In Nairobi, the weekly wage by 1948 was officially Shs. 9/25 for nonskilled labor, a category principally made up of manual laborers. With high levels of urban unemployment during the postwar years, it is difficult to imagine that unscrupulous employers, eager to exploit these desperate workers, bothered to stick to the official wage rate, which was in itself inadequate in the inflation-plagued years after the war. The official weekly wage rate for the rest of the African workers is shown in Table 1.3.

The general lack of provision for housing for African workers, especially in Nairobi, became a major point of discontent and later on provided an emotive issue around which political and trade union activists rallied African workers' support against the colonial state and its policies. The most important outlet for African anger against the colonial state was trade unionism.

Table 1.3
Weekly Wage Rates for Skilled and Semi-Skilled Labor

(1) Domestic Servants: (Cooks and Houseboys)
—Rural: from Shs. 7/50 to Shs. 25 with food and housing.
—Urban: from Shs. 10 to Shs. 30 with food and housing.
(2) Clerks:
—from Shs. 11/50 to Shs. 69 usually without food and housing.
(3) Drivers:
—from Shs. 14 to Shs. 35 without food and housing.
(4) Artisans:
—from Shs. 16 to Shs. 45 without food and housing.

Source: *Kenya: Colonial Annual Report, 1948* (HMSO, 1950), p. 16.

In postwar years, the growth and development of trade unionism in urban areas was linked to the career of Chege Kibachia, whose rise to national prominence lay with his organization of a dockers' strike at Mombasa. Widespread discontent in urban areas led Kibachia to form the African Workers' Federation as an all-African militant trade union seeking immediate solutions to the plight of thousands of African workers. He had hoped to form a nationwide trade union movement, and to this end he traveled to Nairobi, Nakuru, Gilgil, Nanyuki, Uplands, and elsewhere, "spreading the word." Usually local strikes, however ineffective, were reported after his visits. There was, therefore, the possibility of arousing the urban workers into militant agitators for economic reforms. The colonial state was clearly not willing to let this happen. Kibachia's attempt to organize a general strike in Nairobi in 1947 failed "possibly because it lacked the support of the African politicians."[52] He was arrested and deported, and soon the rudimentary organizational structure of his trade union disintegrated.

The collapse of Kibachia's federation was followed in 1949 by the formation of yet another trade union organization—the East African Trade Union Congress (EATUC), founded by Fred Kubai, a Kikuyu activist and Makhan Singh, an Asian who was "a self-avowed communist." This trade union consciously combined the economic and political struggle of the workers. Politics and especially nationalist agitation for reforms became an integral part of the union's agenda. The resultant confrontation between the colonial state and the union was therefore inevitable. In 1950, the EATUC called for a general strike after its leaders had been arrested. It was an emotional strike supported by a significant section of African residents in Nairobi. The colonial state responded not by granting reforms or pledging any promises, but by a heavy show of force most probably aimed at intimidating the strikers and their sympathizers.

In May 1950, the EATUC was banned, leaving the workers with no central trade union organization through which to channel their legitimate economic grievances. The perpetual clampdown on all trade union organizations led many activists at this time to believe that the colonial state was not able or willing to listen to nonmilitant and nonviolent agitation. The road to peaceful negotiation and resolution of problems was effectively closed by the insensitive and negative response of the colonial state to legitimate complaints. This rigid and arrogant posture by the state led to the formation of underground and multifaceted militant organizations that embraced the political and economic struggles of African urban residents.

Perhaps the most tragic and yet expected aspect of urban existence for the unemployed people in Nairobi at this time was the evolution of an alternative subculture in which crime was dominant. Shut off from the mainstream urban culture, the unemployed and the poor resorted to crime and violence to survive in an increasingly hostile environment. This violence was initially confined within the African locations, where gangs preyed on their victims normally at night. There were those drawn to this criminal existence out of sheer desperation and those who probably hoped to reap profit by robbing and intimidating defenseless victims. African locations degenerated into violent neighborhoods in which individual safety was usually not guaranteed.

Criminal groups organized themselves along mbari, or clan, lines. This was the urban application of rural kinship ties. The majority of the African population in Nairobi was Kikuyu, many of whom had migrated there out of sheer economic desperation. Unemployed and without accommodation, many of these newly arrived migrants resorted to crime for survival. It is noticeable that there was no transtribal class solidarity among the African workers or lumpen proletariat in Nairobi at this time. Rural kinship loyalties remained strong, even if they were now being turned to criminal activity. Residence in an urban environment alone does not turn a peasant into an urban proletariat conscious of his class interests. Many of these residents in Nairobi would have preferred land and life on their githaka to misery-ridden urban existence. Besides, lack of employment denied them an opportunity for effective urban socialization. They lived on the periphery of urban society, poor, unemployed, insecure, and desperate. Naturally the forms of loyalties they recalled were rural and ethnic.

The incidence of crime reported to the police increased considerably in Nairobi after 1947. This increase may have been due to two factors. In the first place, ordinances were passed which led to the arrest of Africans for petty crimes, vagrancy, and activities engaged in for survival, for example, prostitution and beer brewing. The Vagrancy Bill (or Amendment) of 1949 and the Voluntarily Unemployed Persons Ordinance of 1950 were used to banish from Nairobi all those Africans who were unemployed. Of course this was never achieved. Those ordinances increased police powers to arrest and charge Africans with vagrancy, thus condemning them to repatriation to the reserve. Secondly, this increase in crime was due to spiraling inflation and mass migration to Nairobi in spite of official hostility. Desperation led to crime. Most of the crime, however, occurred in African locations in which the colonial forces of law and order were sparsely represented. "During the second half of 1947, it became increasingly apparent that the rule of law had collapsed in Pumwani and Shauri Moyo."[53] In fact, it would be accurate to state that the police had no effective presence in African locations from 1947 to 1953. In the intervening years, gangs effectively controlled these locations. It would have been suicidal for anyone to report the presence and activities of these gangs to the police, whose everyday presence was almost nonexistent.

Police statistics indicate a steady increase in crime from 1948 to 1951. In a report to the Member for Law and Order, the police commissioner summarized the crime statistics for 1948 and 1949 in Nairobi (see Table 1.4).

These figures indicate only crimes committed against property. They do not deal with crimes committed against individuals or physical violence against individuals. The figures also do not deal with intimidation, harassment, or general insecurity, which is difficult to quantify. Given the sporadic presence of police in African locations, it is fair to state that these reported crimes do not tell the whole story. Many more crimes went unreported or undetected, thereby increasing general insecurity in the city. The same is true of adjoining rural areas in Central Province. Although the police continued to report a general increase in crime, it should still be appreciated that these areas were not effectively controlled by police and that many areas lay outside police supervision. It is quite possible that crimes in those

Table 1.4
Crime-Nairobi

1. *Burglary*

	Jan.	Feb.	March	April	May	June	July	Aug.	Sept.
1948	44	26	39	21	47	40	40	42	23
1949	15	21	36	41	43	41	64	76	65

Comparison Totals:
Number of Cases 1948=322
Number of Cases 1949=402

2. *Housebreaking by Night (external kitchens, etc.)*

	Jan.	Feb.	March	April	May	June	July	Aug.	Sept.
1948	20	11	8	7	15	12	26	5	2
1949	9	18	11	17	23	21	26	17	26

Comparison Totals:
Number of Cases 1948=106
Number of Cases 1949=168

3. *Warehouse, Shop Breaking, etc., by Night*

	Jan.	Feb.	March	April	May	June	July	Aug.	Sept.
1948	10	22	20	11	10	14	6	9	5
1949	16	23	21	18	5	11	12	10	13

Comparison Totals:
Number of Cases 1948=107
Number of Cases 1949=129

4. *Housebreaking by Day (dwellings, external & internal kitchens)*

	Jan.	Feb.	March	April	May	June	July	Aug.	Sept.
1948	22	31	50	33	20	20	12	15	13
1949	9	5	14	16	19	13	27	33	20

Comparison Totals:
Number of Cases 1948=216
Number of Cases 1949=156

10. *Thefts from Vehicles (other than cycles)*

	Jan.	Feb.	March	April	May	June	July	Aug.	Sept.
1948	40	31	27	22	33	35	34	19	26
1949	25	39	39	46	41	41	41	60	24

Comparison Totals:
Number of Cases 1948=267
Number of Cases 1949=356

Table 1.4 (*continued*)

11. *Theft by Polefishing*

	Jan.	Feb.	March	April	May	June	July	Aug.	Sept.
1948	13	10	19	12	17	9	2	4	1
1949	5	9	12	18	26	26	25	18	28

Comparison Totals:
Number of Cases 1948=87
Number of Cases 1949=167

15. *Total Offenses against Property*

	Jan.	Feb.	March	April	May	June	July	Aug.	Sept.
1948	418	416	477	405	414	424	368	235	280
1949	317	340	359	360	403	400	446	468	430

Comparison Totals:
Number of Cases 1948=3,437
Number of Cases 1949=3,523

Source: Defence, Deposit 13, Piece 123, Kenya National Archives.

areas went unreported. Besides, it should never be forgotten that police were not trusted by the majority of the African population, who saw them as brutal representatives of the colonial state and its unpopular policies.

The response of the municipal and government authorities was to repatriate "undesirable natives" to the reserves. This act in itself demonstrated not only the insensitivity of the state to Africans' problems but also its lack of imagination in policy formulation. Those people who were repatriated under the 1949 and 1950 ordinances found their way back to Nairobi, thereby creating an endless flow of people back and forth from urban to rural areas. This later proved extremely useful in the expansion of oath-taking as an instrument of politicization in 1952 and beyond. Police arrests and searches were interpreted as constituting harassment. For a people with little or no economic security, police harassment was resented and later vehemently resisted. Colonial authorities forgot that crime cannot be solved merely by exporting desperate people from one location to another. In instances in which economic misery abounds, increased police supervision merely creates further reasons for popular resentment against the state. In a colonial context, economic misery becomes all too easily and readily associated with alien rule, and in the struggle to improve their living conditions many of the workers and peasants listen with understandable sympathy to those activists who link economic progress to political freedom.

The racial component of the Africans' economic struggle in Nairobi must not be forgotten. Discrimination in jobs, entertainment facilities, residential areas, and general racial hostility by the immigrant races against Africans fanned local hatred against the state. To be sure, it is not every African who would have wanted to go to European hotels, schools, hospitals, and cinemas. The point at issue is that these prohibitions against Africans were racist and derogatory and consequently aroused bitter resentment against colonial institutions. These prohibitions underlined racial and economic distinctions between the rulers and the ruled, between prosperity and misery. To defend these racial distinctions was to defend the colonial economic and political system, which was oppressive, racist, exploitative, and insensitive.

TWO

FRUSTRATIONS OF NATIONALISM

In the development of African nationalism in Kenya, no factor was as important to Africans as the attainment of literacy. The organization of African protests to colonial policies shifted from the warriors to literate Africans. They understood the ways of white people; they spoke their language, and they were expected by other Africans to know how to protest colonial policies without arousing brutal physical response. In effect, literate Africans became the new "warriors." The missionaries' original aims in providing education for Africans were mainly to produce literate evangelists and minor functionaries for the colonial state and the settlers—not to train nationalists. Yet one of the remarkable and unintended outcomes of missionary education was the production of African nationalists.

African nationalism after the First World War did not involve the struggle for self-determination. It referred instead to a general awareness of the oppression and mistreatment of Africans by the new colonial regime. Nationalism began as resentment toward specific colonial policies and did not in these early years include a determination to overthrow the colonial state. After the First World War in which so many Africans died as porters, the colonial state instituted stringent labor laws aimed at recruiting labor from the reserves for European farmers. There were famine, disease, taxation, and of course the loathsome *kipande,* an identity card "placed in a small, solid metal container, which usually hung from the neck of the owner on a piece of string."[1] This kipande system was to remain in place until 1947.

An emotional issue around which many African protests revolved was land. Land became a problem in Kenya because both the settlers and Africans competed intensely for its possession and utilization. It came to represent power, integrity, and security both to Africans and to the settlers. Land alienation on behalf of settlers and the subsequent labor needs from the state and the settlers greatly alarmed the Africans. Complete subjugation by colonialism clearly demanded more than the surrender of political independence. It entailed provision of labor, payment of taxes, and surrender of land on an almost endless basis. The most critical demand by many Africans at this time was for provision of individual title deeds to land to forestall further alienation. It was a request which the colonial government refused to grant, believing as it did that all Africans were "tenants at the will of the Crown" and could have their land alienated any time it was deemed necessary.

It was these grievances which gave rise to the formation of protest movements, organized and led by literate Africans. These movements formed a significant development beyond the initial primary resistance. Their focus was on the problems unleashed in their societies as a result of the consolidation of power by the colonial state. These movements initially were formed, as one would expect, in those areas where the colonial cash economy had been actively incorporated and which also had had a significant exposure to missionaries and mission schools. These were Central Province (especially among the Kikuyu) and Nyanza Province (among the Luo and Abaluyia). The Kikuyu Association (KA), formed in 1919, was the first movement to articulate Africans' grievances and present them to local colonial administrators for redress. It was based in southern Kiambu and was led by a new breed of chiefs—those who had acquired some missionary education and were therefore literate. Its moving spirit was Chief Koinange, assisted by Mathew Njoroge, Josiah Njonjo, and Waruhiu Kungu. It sought to draw the attention of the colonial government to Kikuyu land grievances that arose from land alienation for white settlers. In the initial stages the association merely wanted compensation for "lost lands" but later wanted the return of the "stolen lands." It also voiced concern over taxation, labor recruitment, and limited opportunities for education for Africans. Its leadership of chiefs and headmen was strongly guided by missionaries. Most of these chiefs were products of missionary education and were devout defenders of the new Christian faith. They were moderate men appealing to the colonial state for redress and quite conscious of their power in the rural areas. The colonial government, although not acceding to the demands of the association, felt that it was more representative of African opinions than any other organization. Chiefs under the influence of missionaries represented "responsible leadership."

Harry Thuku's East African Association (EAA), while Nairobi-based, looked at itself as a more radical alternative to the cautious and conservative KA. It protested government threats to cut urban wages by a third because of the depression and poor economic performance in the post–World War I period. African urban residents, initially few, were free from chiefly powers and better educated. They looked at themselves as the elite, as the people who were best suited to articulate the grievances of their fellow Africans. To them, chiefs were oppressive collaborators with the colonialists and therefore unrepresentative. Chiefs, of course, looked at themselves as the true leaders of the people, who knew their people on account of living among them.

Thuku dispatched a telegram to London to appeal directly to the Colonial Office.[2] It was a decision that later propelled him into a brief, though exceedingly memorable, political career, culminating in his detention in March 1922. Before his detention Thuku and the EAA constituted the most vocal opposition against colonial policies in Kenya. His organization had been deliberately named the EAA to appeal to a wider constituency than the Kikuyu. Its leadership and membership and even key grievances remained, however, largely Kikuyu, and therefore his problems lay with the struggle for power in Kikuyuland between his organization and the KA. A triumph by Thuku would have greatly undermined the authority of the chiefs. And so the colonial state chose in its own interest to back the chiefs and the conservative rural society against Thuku and his populist politics. The chiefs and missionaries, whose teaching he had criticized, conspired against him and had him arrested and detained.

In a bid to secure his release, crowds of enraged Africans gathered in Nairobi outside the police station in which he was being held. The tension in the crowd and the fear and panic of the police officers resulted in the worst urban massacre in Kenya at that time. In its inquest the government found that the shootings were justified.[3] This massacre has generally come to be seen as the first shedding of blood for freedom in Kenya. The career of Harry Thuku reached its peak on the day of his arrest. He may not have advocated national independence; but in organizing Africans to agitate for their rights even within the stifling confines of colonialism, he brought into being both the need and the method of struggle that subsequent organizations emulated with varying degrees of effectiveness. Thuku's career also demonstrated that an effective protest could not be launched without cooperation between urban activists and rural peasant support. Yet in his detention, another power was demonstrated: the power of chiefs and their readiness to go against any-one who challenged their rural supremacy. Thuku, by sending the telegram directly to London, showed that it was possible to be heard in London without going through the "proper channels."

Missionary influence in African political organization was again seen clearly in Nyanza Province through the activities of Rev. W. E. Owen and his skillful conversion of Young Kavirondo Association into Kavirondo Tax Payers Welfare Association, which steered the original organization away from being a protest movement into being a welfare organization.[4]

The organizations arising in Central Province and in Nyanza were small-scale movements that addressed local grievances about colonial policies. This is not to diminish their eventual value to the cause of nationalism. But all the same it would be inaccurate to look at them as representatives of territorial nationalism. They relied on local support because they articulated locally familiar and keenly felt problems whose resolution was supposed to be local. Although Thuku tried to forge alliances with separate internal groups and alerted several international agencies to the plight of Africans in Kenya,[5] there does not appear to have been any successful attempt to build a national protest movement at this time.

The proscription of the EAA in 1922 after Thuku's detention dealt a significant blow to the cause of African nationalism. Many of his followers and the peasants in the countryside saw firsthand the reassertion of brutal imperial power and felt their own powerlessness against such a formidable enemy. It was to be many years again before the peasants in central Kenya and Nyanza Province came to be enthusiastically involved in political agitation. The grievances were still there, but what was lacking was inspired leadership that promised and delivered concrete results. It was against this background that former colleagues and associates of Harry Thuku formed the Kikuyu Central Association (KCA) in 1924 in Kahuhia, Murang'a, in Central Province. The KCA arose thereafter as a direct successor of the EAA.

Unlike the EAA, the KCA did not pretend to represent a constituency other than the Kikuyu. It agitated against land alienation, lack of educational opportunities, and especially the power of chiefs in the Kikuyu reserve. Its immediate concern was to contribute money for Thuku's welfare in detention,[6] while still calling for his release. Although it represented a more uncompromising attitude to colonial policies than the KA, it did not however have a coherent program of action. It responded to events and lacked a general long-term plan. Its significance, like that of Harry Thuku's was in its psychological effect on the Kikuyu population. Its members represented those who had refused to abandon the struggle against colonial injustices even if this struggle produced no immediate spectacular results. "The KCA was far from a unified or disciplined political party. It was a loosely structured grouping, mainly of the younger mission men, who in varying degrees were suspicious of European overrule."[7] It faced perennial problems with regard to expansion of its activities and membership outside Murang'a.

Even after introducing the oath of loyalty in 1925, the KCA still faced the wall of political apathy in Kikuyuland and government suspicion and obstruction. Thus the KCA and its influence in Kikuyuland should not be exaggerated. "At the peak of its popularity, it claimed over 10,000 members, but the number of people who remained active, attending meetings and paying dues, was much smaller, certainly no more than 300 at the most in the three Kikuyu Districts."[8]

Its influence rose noticeably during the female circumcision controversy in Kikuyuland between 1929 and 1930. It became the chief advocate of Kikuyu cultural traditions and the necessity of female circumcision. This appealed to a large section of people and won it a lot of temporary supporters. In championing the circumcision issue, the KCA appeared responsible and respectable to both the young and old in Kikuyu society who were worried about the loss of their cultural heritage at the hands of Christianity as taught by white missionaries. The KCA therefore won tribal respectability by appealing to old tribal customs. But this popularity lasted as long as circumcision was an issue of controversy. With the formation of independent schools and churches, enthusiastic support for the KCA slowly diminished.

The female circumcision controversy constituted cultural nationalism on the part of the Kikuyu. It must be remembered that not all Kikuyu Christians participated in this controversy. There were many who chose to remain faithful to the orthodox missionary interpretation of Christianity and therefore stood against the KCA-led struggle against missionaries and the subsequent establishment of independent churches and schools. This rift in the interpretation of Christianity was to have a crucial bearing on the development of nationalism. Those who stood with the missionaries included the chiefs, the better-educated elite, the majority of African evangelists and teachers, and members of African tribunals. Thus, supporters tended to be older, richer, and better educated. The KCA supporters tended to be younger, poorer, and not well educated. Although this rift has generally been looked upon as a religious controversy, it also had a social dimension. It brought out the essential individual differences that had arisen in Kikuyu society since colonialism. There were now differences in power, opportunity wealth, influence, and perhaps more crucial was the fact that the powerful and the rich also tended to be orthodox Christians.

In the rest of the country political organizations had not yet advanced beyond the level reached by the KCA. In western Kenya, the Abaluyia of Kakamega district formed the North Kavirondo Central Association (NKCA) in 1932 to rally opposition against what they perceived as a threat to their land at this time. This had been triggered by the discovery of gold in Kakamega in 1931 and the resultant minor gold rush, which the inhabitants of Kakamega felt would deprive them of their land. The NKCA was never able to command a mass following in Kakamega or among the rest of the Abaluyia people.[9] Being an issue-centered organization, it lost its initial appeal with the passage of time but specifically when there failed to occur a wholesale land alienation for gold prospecting and mining.

Another issue-centered organization was formed by the Akamba just before the Second World War. The Ukamba Members Association (UMA) was formed in 1938 to protest an impending destocking decree. By this decree, the government intended the cattle from Kambaland to supply a meat factory opened in 1938 at the Athi River. The Kamba resisted, formed the UMA, and marched onto Nairobi to protest. Later the decree was abandoned, and the UMA soon disintegrated.

The last movement of significance formed in the interwar period was the Taita Hills Association (THA). It was formed by the Taita in 1939 to protest lack of land for expansion of their population. The immediate cause however was the government's plan to alienate land below the hills for a "European Sisal Plantation." This association, like the UMA and the NKCA, received some strategic help from the KCA in terms of organizational techniques. This help from the KCA to the rest of these organizations was not overwhelming as has been supposed in the past, nor was it the key factor in their formation.

These organizations, like the KCA itself, were local protest movements formed in response to local grievances. They did not claim a national constituency or even a mass following in the areas in which they were established. The linkage between the KCA and these other organizations was therefore not crucial to their formation and existence. No attempt was made to form a national movement representing all of them and their grievances. The KCA, the THA, and the UMA were proscribed in 1940, while the NKCA dissolved itself "at a meeting with the D.C. at Kakamega . . . voluntarily for the course of the war. In fact the D.C. continued to use them (leaders) to help with the recruiting campaign and other war time measures."[10]

The development of African nationalism up to 1939 was a series of protests against colonial policies. Many of those who protested and formed protest organizations were aware of the physical power of the state. Their objectives remained, therefore, modest requests for reform within the colonial system. The educated elite and the chiefs believed that with due "responsible pressure" the colonial state could grant reforms.

The development of African nationalism was complicated further by the establishment of the African reserves in 1915. Each reserve occupied, as far as possible, a separate ethnic group. This had the effect of emphasizing "the distinctiveness of each tribal grouping'' and limiting any chances of interethnic solidarity. Separateness led to suspicion and ill-feeling, some deliberately fostered by the British in their strategy of divide and rule. Problems affecting each community tended to be viewed in local terms, with almost no consideration given to their national dimension. This was officially sanctioned parochialism, and it was to be many years before territorial nationalism emerged in Kenya. The government did not recognize the utility and need for African nationalist parties. After the establishment of Local Native Councils (LNC) in 1925, the government looked at them as the only appropriate channels for the expression of African complaints. In its view African parties were therefore redundant. It persistently obstructed the establishment and expansion of such parties, looking at them as agents of disruption. It is significant to note that no major shift of official policy, especially over land in the Highlands, was adopted as a result of African petitions.

The lack of unity and of strong leadership of African nationalism was not helped much by the release of Harry Thuku from detention in 1930. In his absence several songs of praise and stories were deliberately circulated about him to raise the political consciousness of the Kikuyu and also money for the KCA. He was the hero of African nationalism in the 1920s. However when he returned, people noticed that he was different in temperament and in commitment to the politics of agitation. "Thuku was noticeably different when he returned. . . . He had become stuffy, the old fire had gone, replaced by something very close to arrogance."[11] He continued to look at himself as the pioneer nationalist, the natural leader, and he resented opposition from his colleagues. He also refused to be accountable to the KCA's executive committee after he had been elected its president in 1932, especially in regard to the association's finances.[12] He became a disagreeable personality with close ties to the government.

Although this change in Thuku's behavior was a shock to his colleagues, a study of his activities during detention as given in his slim and sketchy autobiography clearly shows that by the time he left detention he was in a different frame of mind. During his detention he became a fairly successful farmer, raised horses, and fraternized with the District Commissioner, or D.C., and other local white administrators in Marsabit.[13] He had not suffered extensively in detention, nor is there any evidence that he was bitter or harshly treated. He had been "converted" in effect and became a staunch supporter of the government before and during the Mau Mau revolt. By 1933, however, points of dispute between Thuku and the KCA led to a split in the association, and in 1935 Thuku formed the Kikuyu Provincial Association (KPA), an exceedingly conservative and progovernment organization. In its rules and regulations, the KPA required that "every member of this organization . . . be pledged to be loyal to His Majesty the King of Great Britain and the established government and will be bound to do nothing which is not constitutional according to British traditions or do anything which is calculated to disturb the peace, good order and government."[14] It was a requirement which was bound to upset many of his former colleagues. But Thuku "did not care."[15]

The formation of the KPA with different emphasis and aims from the KCA effectively subverted Thuku's earlier goals and strategies during the EAA era. In actual fact, Thuku subverted Thuku! This led to immense confusion, not only in Kikuyuland but throughout the country. There were those who remembered Thuku from the EAA era and who now found it difficult to reconcile his past with the stand he had assumed by the formation of the KPA. Yet his name was the best known in the country, and so the KCA and other African nationalists found that they had to struggle to come out of Thuku's shadow and show the people that their former hero was now in the service of the government. It was a very difficult exercise.

By 1940, the voice of African nationalism was weak, timid, and not united. Yet the economic problems in the urban and rural areas were becoming intolerable, giving rise to the necessity of adopting more forthright methods to resolve them. Perhaps more crucial was the fact that many people who were dispossessed and landless or unemployed had started to lose faith rapidly in the ability and willingness of the colonial state to grant reforms in response to petitions. In perpetually dismissing all petitions with scorn, the government undermined the process of peaceful change.

The formation of the Kenya African Study Union (KASU) in 1944, later known as the Kenya African Union (KAU), marked the first attempt to organize an African political party with territorial ambitions—the first attempt at territorial nationalism. It was formed by the mainly Nairobi-based African elite, many of whom were employees of the government. Other than fostering their unity and offering "a club" in which to meet and be acquainted, the KAU also specifically afforded an opportunity to continue the politics of moderate petitions to the government, a strategy which had yielded almost no results since 1919.

From its inception, the party was faced with immense problems. There was the problem of ethnic nationalism, or tribalism, fostered in large part by the colonial government. Then there was the constant failure of the politics of petition, which had left the majority of the African population uninterested in politics. Politics were dangerous, for they exposed one to the wrath of the chief and the D.C. and ruined one's chances to advance in life. The KAU therefore had to compete against ethnic nationalism, political apathy, even hostility, and official obstruction. The rift in Kikuyuland caused by the clash between the Kikuyu Association and the East African Association, the circumcision controversy, and now the KCA and the KPA all complicated the political map in Central Province. Unity was difficult to achieve in the face of such deeply felt emotional issues.

The KAU was also correctly seen as a party of the educated, and as a result very few ordinary peasants showed any marked enthusiasm to be associated with it.

The KAU's claim to prominence was that it was the only national African political party at this time. Many Africans looked at it as their legitimate political outlet. These expectations were heightened in 1947 when Jomo Kenyatta assumed the party's presidency from Gichuru.

Kenyatta had been away for fifteen years in Europe, mainly in England. His political career had started with his joining the KCA in 1924, but more crucially with his appointment as its Secretary-General in 1928. Although he had not participated in the formation of the KCA, he was later approached to join as an official, largely on account of his command of English which was higher than that of its other officials.[16] When the KCA decided to send a delegate to London to plead its case before the British government, Kenyatta was again chosen largely on account of his education.[17]

In his second journey to London, which was to last fifteen years, he continued to be a representative of the KCA. His prominence in African politics from 1928 to 1946 lay largely in the fact that he was the first African emissary to go to London. He was thus not part of the several controversies that arose in Kikuyuland from 1929 until 1945. He was aloof, with his reputation no doubt enhanced by his absence. He had visited not only Britain at a time when it was uncommon for an African to do so but also other European countries. He stayed in Europe for a long time and even married a white woman, while professing to be a true Kikuyu patriot. He had been the "eyes and ears" of the Kikuyu in London and had not abandoned them, and had in fact reaffirmed his cultural pride in *Facing Mount Kenya* (1938), a book about Kikuyu cultural traditions written as part of his studies for a Diploma in Anthropology at the London School of Economics.[18]

In 1946 when he returned to Kenya he was a towering figure in African politics. "As a politician during the post-war period Kenyatta never really had any competition: the Kikuyu were solidly for him, and at that time none of the other tribes had thrown anyone of comparable stature."[19] But he had been away for fifteen years and had been influenced by the British political traditions and culture much more than he knew or wished to acknowledge. The British, according to Guy Arnold, "are perhaps the subtlest of brainwashers."[20] He had acquired immense political and personal experience abroad, helped the Pan-African Congress in Manchester in 1945, and "absorbed a great deal of the British approach to politics: pragmatism, only dealing with problems when they become crises, tolerance so long as the other side is talking, and the sense, despite everything that might be wrong, of living in a fundamentally settled society."[21]

Kenyatta came back with political sophistication but not with burning radicalism. Having been away for so long, it was quite possible for him not to comprehend immediately the urgency of the economic and social problems that faced the Africans in Kenya in general and in Central Province in particular. He was determined to build a disciplined, mass political party with long-term interests of forging national unity at a time when his old comrades in the KCA looked at him principally as a Kikuyu warrior. He felt that many of the problems facing the Kikuyu would be solved through meaningful cooperation between the colonial state and his people and also through individual initiative and hard work. Such sentiments were out of tune with the times. Many ahoi and the unemployed peasants in urban areas wanted land and work and were not keen to listen to speeches or to be admonished about their laziness and insincerity in business. The colonial state also saw no need to cooperate. It granted no reforms. But Kenyatta's reputation continued to be his key asset. It was not surprising, therefore, that when he assumed the presidency of the KAU in 1947, there was a new interest in the party by the ordinary masses who still looked at him as the "Burning Spear."

His initial thrust of activity was naturally in Kikuyuland. He addressed large enthusiastic crowds. This mass enthusiasm was not about the KAU but about Kenyatta. Many of those who came to the meetings came to see him, the man the KCA had "lionized in party songs." It was curiosity that principally drove many of the rural masses to the meetings. But still Kenyatta seized the opportunity to spread the KAU messages across the province. They were not always flattering messages. "He spoke of African failings and insisted that Africans should raise their own standards; he attacked the African practice of litigation over land; the embezzlement of funds by officials, low moral standards and dishonesty by African traders."[22]

Even with Kenyatta as president, the history of the KAU from 1946 to 1950 was one of failure. It failed to register any victory and also failed to expand its influence beyond Nairobi and Central Province. "It stirred up expectations it could not fulfill and made promises it could not keep."[23] The failure of the KAU during this time was the result as much of its weak organization and political apathy as of the hostile intransigence of the colonial state.

What was the political relationship between the colonial state and the white settlers? Since the founding of the colony, the general policy of the colonial state had been considerably determined by the settlers, through their organizations locally and through petitions directly to London. The Colonists Association formed in 1902 was largely responsible for the "preservation of Kenya" as a "white man's country." Its organized pressure managed to exclude Jews and Indians as competitors for land in Kenya. The Convention of Associations formed in 1910 became the unofficial white Parliament, and many of its resolutions ultimately became official policy. The white Parliament agitated for severe labor laws to ensure the flow of African labor to European farms. Fearful of Asian demographic superiority, European settlers continually petitioned for immigration laws that would severely restrict Indian immigration to the colony.

Their aim since the days of Sir Charles Eliot was to ultimately attain self-government. They were confident that the British government and the local administration shared these sentiments and therefore would facilitate their work by disciplining and controlling Africans and Asians. They never tired of pointing out that they had been invited to the colony and were therefore an integral part of the British administration's mission of spreading Western civilization among Africans. To be sure, there were disagreements within the administration over the demands of settlers, but these were private, the exception, and communicated under confidential cover. Other than Charles Hobley and John Ainsworth, who were worried over excessive settler demands for forced African labor,[24] there were also other examples: "F. W. Isaac defended the rights of the Kamba to Mua Hills; H. R. Tate, H. H. Horne and C. S. Reddie, the rights of the Kikuyu to Kiambu and Fort Hall Land."[25] Nonetheless, these administrators had been socialized through their education and training to see the supremacy of British "traditional values." What this meant in practice was an unquestioning implementation of colonial directives.

Whatever disagreements there may have been between officials, they were not over fundamentals or over the purpose and destiny of British imperialism.

The high degree of agreement over fundamentals made it possible for the system to sustain a considerable degree of conflict over detail; it ensured that the contradictions which existed between the interests of the various sections of the ruling class would take on non-antagonistic forms and be resolvable by peaceful means.[26]

Besides, these officials were highly dependent on their superiors for recommendations for promotion. This reduced any chances of open "rebellion" on the part of the administrators. By 1930, settlers' representatives dominated key development committees in the colony. They were also represented in the Legislative Council and the Executive Council. The implication of these developments was that it was not possible for colonial administrators to act with impunity against the interests of the settlers.

An issue over which both the settlers and the colonial administrators agreed was what was termed the "primitivity of the native races." Because Africans were held to be primitive, they had to be disciplined, organized, and guided. They were faceless masses with uniform characteristics. This gave rise to the notion of "African characteristics," and practically every European whatever the level of his or her education and knowledge became an authority on Africans.

The settler and the administrator alike in Kenya, influenced by prevailing writings, opinions, economic necessity, and racial prejudice, came to evolve a stereotypical picture of the "real" African. He was primitive, lazy, morally depraved, smelly, illogical, given to cheating, ignorant, and immature. After all, Lord Lugard had concluded that Africans "were child-like races of the world."[27]

When the 1923 *Devonshire White Paper* was issued declaring that Kenya was primarily "an African territory" and that the British government would not delegate or share the colony's administration, it was clear that it would be impossible for the settlers to attain the dominion status. Yet it should be remembered that this White Paper declaring the paramountcy doctrine was essentially a statement of purpose. It was not a program of action. It was up to the local administration to formulate policies that would advance African interests. This was not done. The 1923 White Paper had forbade taking "drastic action or reversal of measures already introduced" to foster European interests in Kenya. Subsequent government policies from 1923 to 1952 do not reveal any conscious efforts to formulate policies in the colony that would have ensured the paramountcy of African interests; rather they eloquently demonstrate the abundance of policies and legislation that effectively postponed indefinitely the paramountcy of African interests.

Against this background, it is easy to understand the hostility of the colonial state toward African political parties, and especially toward the KAU in the postwar era. The view of the state and especially of the outlying provincial administrators was that the ordinary African masses were meek, law-abiding citizens, even if lazy, who were likely to be aroused into uncontrollable fury against the Crown by African politicians. It became the special duty of these white administrators to harass, intimidate, and bully African nationalists, both in rural and urban areas. Their persons and messages were ridiculed and contradicted. These administrators conveniently refused to acknowledge the presence of overwhelming economic and social frustrations in the country that had given rise to restiveness and the need for Africans to organize into political parties. Any problems mentioned by the KAU officials or other African nationalists were conveniently seen as products of the mischievous imagination of African politicians, now targeted as troublemakers. This cynical indifference assumed tragic proportions over the emotional question of racism and the color bar in Kenya.

Although racism had been part and parcel of the colonial enterprise in Kenya, it was not an official policy; rather it was implemented through a series of administrative decrees, discriminatory tradition, and convenient interpretations of the law.

> Officially, segregation by race was not a part of British colonial policy, yet such distinctions operated both residentially and in public facilities. In both cases, the legitimation was one of health and sanitation, for it was felt that only by isolating the European community could desirable standards be maintained."[28]

Official or not, racism and the color bar were cornerstones of official agenda in colonial Kenya. The thing that reminded Africans every day that they were colonized was their harsh discriminatory treatment under whites. They were mistreated, shouted at, beaten, sneered at, ridiculed, derogatorily described, and reminded often that they were inferior to whites in their own country. It is difficult to describe adequately the feeling and emotion of being treated as an inferior person when you know you are not. The weight and suppressed anger felt by Africans at being treated as inferior persons was one issue over which there was general agreement: such treatment was wrong, hurtful, and had to be removed. It is difficult for those who have not been discriminated against to understand the gravity of the situation, the gravity of walking and knocking against a pervasive wall of prejudice every day.

Because racism precluded any possibility of meaningful contact between whites and Africans, most of the racist pronouncements were based largely on imagination, lies, and self-serving prejudices. Even after Western education had become commonplace in Kenya, there existed very limited contact between Africans and whites. The claim by whites that they "knew Africans" and their problems was therefore ill-founded. In a remarkable study on the question of human relations and racism in colonial Kenya, Richard Frost reminds us of the dangers that followed from official policies based on limited knowledge or, in some cases, on utter ignorance of the realities in African lives. "Misunderstandings arising from lack of correct information were accepted as truth and, because they were believed, had adverse effects on race relations."[29] Frost further states that Europeans, in spite of their claim that "we know the African," came into contact with few Africans except farm labourers, domestic servants and office-boys."[30] The Europeans therefore could be said to have "known" only the least formally educated Africans, the laborers, over whom they had absolute power and who of necessity behaved in a meek, subservient manner, never engaging as equals in discussions with their white employers.

Were Africans justified in looking at all whites as racists? In the context of colonial Kenya, whites appeared to Africans as a united band of foreigners determined to dominate and oppress the indigenous populations. Apart from cultural harmony if not uniformity among whites, Africans also saw them as part of the same ruling machine. They fraternized with each other, frequented similar clubs, and always stood together against Africans and their demands. There were no cases of open rebellion from any group of whites on behalf of Africans and their demands. If private individual whites harbored no racist feelings, it was difficult to discern this from the general behavior of whites as a group. Racial prejudice was particularly hurtful to educated Africans. By 1944 many of them felt frustrated and humiliated by the white establishment.

In March 1944, Europeans in Kenya formed a new party, the Electors' Union, with the express aim of forging and sustaining white unity in the face of what was seen as turbulent years ahead in the postwar era. The thrust of this new party was to safeguard old privileges against any attempts by the local administration or London to institute reforms that could cause irreparable damage to the luxurious lifestyle whites now saw, after almost fifty years, as their right. To underscore their determination, the Electors' Union published in 1949 the memorable *Kenya Plan*,[31] an authoritative statement that clearly spelled out the Europeans' determination to continue in their dominance of the country's economic and political affairs. Like the *Outline of Policy* of 1946, the *Kenya Plan* emphatically restated that leadership of the country was to remain in white hands and these leaders, while assuming an increased role in the governance of the country, would determine the rate at which Africans would be included in the government. The possibility of Africans in government was seen by settlers as too remote to warrant any immediate attention.

The Electors' Union wished to consolidate and expand on the economic success Europeans had achieved under the wartime production schemes. They realized they needed more power to safeguard their economic privileges, and so by 1944, the major thrust of white agitation in Kenya was to attain more control over the local government by drastically limiting the supervisory role exercised by London. This was the united front of white nationalism in Kenya; adamant, racist, powerful but increasingly insecure. Their past history in Kenya had completely spoiled them, leading them to be unrealistic and uncontrollable. Like overindulged children, they were used to having their way by throwing tantrums before the authorities. White nationalism in Kenya, however, forgot one basic reality: namely that whites were numerically too few and could not continue to dominate millions of Africans without yielding to some local demands or broadening the scope of local cooperation. Past triumphs had mistakenly led them to believe they could dispense with local cooperation and still continue to dominate. Arrogant exercise of power, indifference to African economic troubles and petitions, and perpetual racist pronouncements clearly demonstrated that they were not interested in compromise or reasonable appeals. By adopting an uncompromising position, white nationalism clearly singled itself out for violent confrontation with angry, bitter, and numerically superior African nationalism.

Confronted with such a powerful adversary, Kenya's African nationalists in the KAU under Kenyatta felt they had to walk a tight rope between African anger and demands and European power and intransigence. Kenyatta steered the KAU clear of any immediate direct confrontation with the colonial state. He realized that ''as a British colony, the formal rights of freedom of speech, association and public assembly were recognised in Kenya and the Administration could proscribe KAU only at the risk of public outcry in Britain and the possibility of active intervention of the Labour government."[32] Kenyatta wanted the KAU to remain an above-the-board moderate political party committed to constitutional nationalism. To this end he dissociated the KAU from confrontational politics in order to avoid being banned. Constitutionalism entailed gradualism, and as Joseph Murumbi states, "For some time there was a feeling in KAU of gradualism."[33] And so although delegates to the KAU meeting of 1 June 1947, at which Kenyatta was elected president, mentioned political independence as their ultimate object, it was a goal that was perceived to be quite far off in time; none of the delegates at this meeting expected to be able to see this independence.

The major concerns of the KAU up to 1952 continued to be the age-old grievances of past associations: return of "stolen lands"; land for the landless, which the KAU thought would be available from the unused land in the highlands; and

> increased representation for Africans on the Legislative Council, the Nairobi City Council and other local bodies and boards, at first to give Africans equal elective representation with Europeans, ultimately to give them control; restrictions on European and Asian immigration; . . . the absolution of barriers preventing African promotion in the civil service; and the ending of discrimination in hotels, theatres, and social clubs.[34]

In 1951, Kenyatta, at a public rally at which he denounced Mau Mau and dissociated the KAU from subversion, reiterated the party's main demands. He said, "We want equal pay for equal work, we want good hospitals and good roads in the Reserves. We want education for our children, the same as that which is provided for the children of other races."[35] This gradual approach to African nationalism was doomed to failure because of the intolerable economic conditions of the African masses as detailed in chapter 1. The KAU's constituency was impatient and restive and demanded immediate solutions. This was especially true in Central Province, land of the Kikuyu, where landlessness had given rise to both rural violence and increased migration to the urban areas, especially to Nairobi.

It was in Nairobi that most of the landless ahoi and evictees from European settler farms and Olenguruone (a Rift Valley settlement) congregated. They were joined by the youth—young men and women who were mostly unemployed. In the postwar era, ex-soldiers (ex-Askaris) formed another important layer of disgruntled people in the city. The ex-soldiers were never able to form a national organization to advance their interests and articulate their grievances against the government. In about the only detailed study yet on the role of ex-soldiers in the development of nationalism in Kenya, O. J. E. Shiroya found that "ex-Askaris did not succeed in forming a politically powerful organisation. This was mainly due to the government's rigid control of the ex-Askaris' activities." As for their contribution, Shiroya discovered that "their major contribution to Kenya's nationalism; the spreading of the newly acquired ideas, was by individual ex-Askaris."[36] Their contributions were as individuals and not as representatives of any ex-Askaris organization.

In Nairobi, some of these ex-Askaris, embittered by government treatment, formed the "Anake 40 Group," or the Age Forty Group. They were not the only members of this overwhelmingly Kikuyu organization. "Its first members were unemployed, petty traders, thieves, prostitutes and other members of the Lumpen proletariat of Nairobi."[37] Although Frank Furedi looks at this Age Forty Group as having formed "the most successful populist initiative in Kenya's history to this day,"[38] it is not clear that this group in fact constituted a well regulated and disciplined party. The nature of its membership shows that uppermost in its drive was economic survival in an increasingly hostile environment. It capitalized on widespread economic misery and general discontent of the largely Kikuyu urban population in Nairobi at this time. This was the age of amorphous radicalism in the urban areas, especially in Nairobi.

"Anake 40" continued to be a loosely organized, almost informal, movement not initiated by the trade unions or the KAU but later linked to them. It came to be closely associated with violence, intimidation, and gang warfare which terrorized the nonKikuyu residents, especially the Luo and Abaluyia. "It carried out armed robberies and obtained a regular flow of funds from Asian and African merchants through an arrangement similar to a protection racket."[39] Political consciousness or disciplined nationalism was certainly not a top priority of this group. It also did not control all the underworld criminal activity in the city, even in the African locations of Pumwani and Shauri Moyo, where other independent thieves, prostitutes, thugs, and hawkers continued to operate.

This crime wave and violence were of course the results of unemployment and lack of housing and also because the colonial police, although not trusted by Africans, were not effectively represented in these African neighborhoods, leaving them in the hands of gangs and thugs. It is crucial to note that this widespread violence, but more especially this widespread amorphous radicalism, was not within the political structure of the KAU. Many of these radicals were young, unknown outside their immediate neighborhoods, unemployed, and politically inexperienced. Impatient and largely uneducated they did not trust the efficacy of constitutional nationalism, whose record was one of failure in the face of settler hostility and the government's intransigence. Besides, the educated elite who were the leaders of the KAU were not part of them; the KAU leaders belonged to a well-groomed and educated class, and whatever frustrations they experienced in their bid to rise in status, they were more secure economically and even socially than these young, desperate, and largely illiterate youth of the Nairobi slums.

The political energies of Nairobi African residents were again aroused in 1949 with the formation of the East African Trade Union Congress by Makhan Singh and Fred Kubai. This union would be banned in 1950. The significance of this phase of trade unionism is that it led to a revitalization of the KAU in Nairobi, the center of widespread urban discontent. This onslaught on the KAU's complacency was led by two young trade union activists, Bildad Kaggia and Fred Kubai. Both of these men were closer in temperament and radicalism to the youth in the Nairobi slums than to the established African elite in the KAU, the churches, and the administration.

Kaggia came from an extremely humble background, the son of a landless man. He states, "My father was a poor man. He lived all his life outside his own district. . . . My father had no land which he could call his own."[40] After primary school and employment as a clerk, Kaggia enlisted in the army during the Second World War and served (performing largely noncombat duty) in the Middle East and Britain. In his autobiography in which he portrays himself as a natural radical and revolutionary comparable only to Kubai and Makhan Singh, Kaggia is critical of educated Africans. He clearly saw them as the stumbling block on the road to freedom because of their caution and gradualism. His aim and that of fellow young radicals was therefore "the elimination of educated Africans from KAU leadership."[41] It was as if, through him, the urban radical youth and the masses were intent on overthrowing the educated leadership so that they could lead themselves. Kubai, Kaggia's key associate, was a product of interethnic marriage. He was the son of a Kikuyu father and a Giriama mother and described as "educated privately." He was not well educated and was inclined to radicalism unhampered by niceties of political sophistication and caution, qualities which had almost paralyzed the KAU.

On 10 June 1951 Fred Kubai, Bildad Kaggia, and other radicals associated with the trade union movement were elected to offices in the Nairobi branch of the KAU after a protracted struggle with the party's national leadership. The KAU's national leadership was alarmed at the increasing radicalism in Nairobi slums and the violence in Central Province and refused to associate the party with violence. In the general strike of May 1950, Kenyatta opposed it as "inconsistent with the main strategy of KAU."[42] The capture of the Nairobi KAU office by this radical group and later of a large section of the national KAU leadership in 1951[43] demonstrated that political initiative was slowly passing from the elite and cautious leadership of the KAU into the hands of radicals: young, politically inexperienced rebels with a formidable connection to the discontented urban masses whose importance could not be neglected. Kaggia, Kubai, and their associates aimed at capturing the KAU leadership and thereby being able to reformulate the party's program of action to include the radicalism that had been characteristic of the trade unions.

Although there was widespread general discontent on the part of the Kikuyu people at this time, it was still obvious that there existed no unity among them. Discontent had given rise to amorphous radicalism, especially in Nairobi, but this was not easily translated into political consciousness and unity behind recognized political leadership. There were various sectional interests, old grudges, clan rivalry, the power of Christianity and chiefs, individual agenda for development and survival, and a general deterioration of the traditional authority of the elders. Against this background,

> on February 20, 1950 an important meeting of influential KAU and trade union leaders from many parts of Central Kenya was held at ex-Senior Chief Koinange's home at Kiambu just outside Nairobi. These leaders recognised to a greater extent

than ever before the immense potential for an oath as an instrument for achieving unity and concerted action.[44]

The oath that was planned at Kiambu in 1950 was to be a massive enterprise administered to as many Kikuyu as possible. Solomon Memia, one of the key Mau Mau leaders, states that the major objective of the oath was to inject courage into those who were initiated.[45] This meeting at Kiambu gave rise to *Parliament* as the key body behind the oath-taking campaign in Kiambu. *Parliament*, based at Banana Hill in Kiambu, was dominated by the old KCA leadership and ex-Senior Chief Koinange. It spread its influence throughout Kiambu and the Rift Valley, especially among the squatters. The squatters, alarmed by reductions in their land by white settlers and threatened by evictions which were already being carried out, immediately joined in the oath-taking campaign.[46] The major concern of the squatters continued to be land; they talked of the return of stolen lands, which for them meant land which had been taken away from them by the settlers as part of the 1937 Resident Labourers Ordinance. In the eyes of the squatters, the White Highlands were now part of the Kikuyu frontier, and they treated their loss of land with the same seriousness and anger as that evinced by the landless and dispossessed ahoi in the Kikuyu reserve.

Parliament wanted the oathing campaign to proceed slowly and with caution and to convince even the educated elite to join the underground movement in order that complete Kikuyu unity would be achieved. When this militant unity had become reality the Kikuyu-dominated KAU leadership would with strength and confidence confront the colonial administration, seeking reforms and answers to prevailing problems, especially regarding land. As originally envisaged at Banana Hill, *Parliament* in instituting the oathing campaign did not see the resultant unity as a natural stepping stone to an armed uprising. Armed rebellion was not entertained by *Parliament* nor did it ever abandon the politics of petition. However as the oathing campaign increased and expanded, there developed different interpretations within the Kikuyu leadership over the ultimate use of the oath.

The Nairobi radicals who had participated in the *Parliament* proceedings became convinced by 1951 that oathing had to be expanded even further and that armed uprising against the government might become inevitable. Neither of these positions was immediately met with consensus in the *Parliament*. The increasing rift between *Parliament* and Nairobi militants can be attributed to variation in age and political sophistication. *Parliament* was under established and recognized Kikuyu leadership, while Nairobi radicals were young, largely unknown till then and with no general prestige of established power or authority in Kikuyuland. Besides, *Parliament* looked at the oathing campaign as merely a strategy to achieve unity to make constitutional nationalism more likely to succeed, while by 1951 the Nairobi radicals had completely discounted the likelihood of success for constitutional nationalism. The radicals also represented young, impatient people willing and ready to enter into armed resistance. So as the oath of unity campaign swept through Kikuyuland and beyond, there were already points of disunity and disagreement among its chief sponsors and advocates.

In the oath of unity the initiates, as Kaggia tells us of himself, "vowed unity, a readiness to do anything for the advancement of the movement, never to sell land and the brotherhood of all the members."[47] In a secret memorandum prepared by the police for the Member for Law and Order, the state intelligence community thought that this oath of unity contained the following conditions: "Not to disclose the workings of Mau Mau to government or to any European; not to inform against a fellow member of the organisation; not to sell land to any European; not to assist any European; to chase the Europeans from Kenya."[48] The central feature of the oath however was its quest for unity and the recovery of land for the Kikuyu. To be effective it employed symbols whose significance was easily comprehended by the initiates. These were Kikuyu symbols, and the Kikuyu attachment to their mythical founders of Gikuyu and Mumbi was especially emphasized. It was also the practice at these ceremonies to swear to carry out orders and to learn of the aims of the KAU. What needs to be understood is that the oathing ceremonies and the Kikuyu-centered version of Kenyan history sketched out during the ceremony were conducted orally. Dealing with a largely illiterate society, the oath administrators, many of whom were simple illiterate men, relied on symbolism and ethnic nationalism and loyalty to achieve and sustain ethnic unity of the Kikuyu.

In a bid to impose some discipline and give direction to the widespread oathing activity in Nairobi slums, a central committee was established by the Nairobi radicals. Many members of the committee were also officeholders of the Nairobi branch of the KAU.[49] Kaggia and Kubai, together with Mutonyi and Isaac Gathanju, were members of this super-secret committee, which now aimed to control the city oathing activities from its headquarters in Kiburi House, in Nairobi.[50] Soon afterwards, however, the central committee (*Muhimu*) decided to open the administration of the oath to almost every Kikuyu without much scrutiny. By the end of 1951 and early 1952, the aim of Muhimu was to enroll as many people as possible in the movement, and this now involved mass oath administrations of the Kikuyu, especially in Nairobi. The committee also expanded its activities to include the northern districts of Nyeri and Muranga. "It was decided to accelerate oath administration—our people were dispatched to Murang'a, Embu, Nyeri and later Meru."[51] This was a period of tension, anger, frustration, and rapid activity mixed with excitement.

By 1951 the introduction of the Kikuyu oath of unity had given rise to serious complications in the nationalist movement. As the administration of the oath expanded rapidly throughout Central Province and in Nairobi, the KAU meetings became more emotional and were well attended by people who appeared defiant to the colonial authorities. But this was in Central Province. In the rest of the country the KAU remained inactive and largely moribund. The KAU as the sole representative of African nationalism in Kenya had two faces by this time. There was the open face, legal and constitutional; and another face that was private, hidden, defiant, and conspiratorial under the control of *Parliament* and the Muhimu. The hidden face of the KAU, which was the most active at this time, was essentially an expression of militant Kikuyu nationalism, forged by years of economic deprivation and colonial intransigence and given its militancy by the ethnic oath of unity.

Having lost faith in "polite politics," the Kikuyu engaged from 1950, but especially from 1951, in militant agitation for the goals long advocated by the KAU. Yet in doing so, the Kikuyu effectively alienated themselves from other ethnic groups that still subscribed to constitutional nationalism.

The unity that the oath was destined to deliver was Kikuyu unity, and there does not appear to have been any thought given to the implications of this exclusive, ethnic nationalism on territorial nationalism. Militant Kikuyu nationalism with its long-term goal of ethnic unity effectively excluded other ethnic groups and postponed even further the possibility of attaining national unity in African nationalism in Kenya.

As violence raged in urban areas, especially in Nairobi, there occurred confrontations between the Kikuyu and African groups who were not part of the organized gangs that terrorized neighborhoods in African locations. It became difficult to distinguish between criminal violence and political violence instigated by Muhimu, for indeed Muhimu came to rely on street gangs not only to administer the oath but also to enforce discipline, compliance, and acquisition of funds and, later, of weapons.

> Between 1947 and 1954 the presence of the Administration and the police was extremely weak in the locations, which were abandoned to the control of the political militants and their allies among the Kikuyu dominated street gangs, which terrorised Luo and Abaluyia inhabitants of the city. This freedom from government interference enabled the radicals to establish a secure headquarters in Nairobi from which they controlled the introduction of the Mau Mau oaths into the Kikuyu Reserves and the White Highlands, and concerted political action against the colonial state and the moderate African politicians.[52]

A significant problem arose regarding the overall discipline and control of African nationalism at this time, especially in Central Province. The oathing campaign was secretive, irregular, with intricate networks of activities and personalities. It was not under the control of the KAU national executive committee, many of whose members remained largely ignorant of the burning ground underneath the surface. *Parliament* occasionally worked through the KAU branch offices in Central Province, but at no time did these branch offices control the conspiratorial and secretive activities of the oathing campaign. In Nairobi, the branch office had reconstituted itself into Muhimu, but even this committee was not open to all branch officebearers. Kaggia states that "after KAU's usual committee meetings in the evenings, the other members of KAU started their meetings."[53] Even then, no KAU official was an official of Muhimu.

For all practical purposes, Muhimu and *Parliament* were separate entities, although they were both engaged in the administration of the oath of unity to all Kikuyu members. Though each of them had a working relationship with individual members of the KAU, at no time did the KAU national executive committee know about the details of their existence and operation. The KAU executive committee did not therefore define their agenda nor were they accountable to it for their conduct and activities. Yet neither *Parliament* nor Muhimu attempted to form a new political party or parties to replace the KAU. They both needed the overall umbrella of respectability and legitimacy that the KAU leadership, especially Kenyatta, immediately accorded to African nationalism. Fred Kubai describes why Kenyatta was important to Muhimu. "Kenyatta was very important to us. People in all tribes knew him and respected him. We found it very difficult to convince old people they should support us. We wanted Kenyatta to join us so that he could get the old people on our side."[54]

By 1951 problems of control and accountability had arisen in both Muhimu and *Parliament*, but perhaps more crucial were problems of overall control of African nationalism in Kenya at this time. The oath of unity had created formidable obstacles to unity and discipline. These problems became more profound in 1952, the year of ultimate confrontation between the colonial state and African nationalism.

THREE

1952

YEAR OF COLLISION

The year 1952 was in many respects a dangerously fluid one for African national-ism in Kenya. The main activities were of course centered on the decision by the central committee (*Muhimu*) to expand the oath-taking campaign to as many people as possible and in the process to use force if necessary to enlist compliance. The rationale given by Kaggia for this expansion of the campaign was that "the move-ment could not succeed unless it was a mass organisation."[1] The central committee at this time believed that politics is nothing but demography and that the would-be victor must always aim for a quantitative advantage. Although laudable as a general premise, it interfered immensely in the orderly administration of the oath, which had been proceeding at a steady pace since 1950. As the numbers rapidly increased, it became impossible for the Muhimu to determine the pace of activity within Nairobi let alone in the outlying districts of Murang'a and Nyeri. The oath admin-istrators dispatched from Nairobi to various parts of these districts in turn created new oath administrators who in their everyday duties did not necessarily, if ever, respond to the directives from the central committee.

A multiplicity of oath administrators and fund collectors made the administration of the movement extremely difficult, especially since most of its personnel and ad-herents were illiterate and so most business had to be conducted orally. At this point then, most of the business operated largely on the principle of trust, and regrettably there was a disproportionate trust placed on the immediate efficacy of the oath in creating and sustaining commitment to the cause. Admittedly, the taking of the oath of unity was generally accompanied by a sketchy outline of the generally known grievances about land scarcity and sometimes of the aims of the KAU or the KCA,[2] but such a brief exercise in politicalization could not sustain spirited loyalty to the movement. Besides, there is no evidence that there was any standard message de-livered at these oath-taking ceremonies. The oath administrators therefore acted as semi-independent ideologues, even though they were under the general umbrella of the KAU, Muhimu, or *Parliament*.

Spurred on by the impatience and enthusiasm of the radical youth in Nairobi, Muhimu and its subordinate organs mistakenly came to look at enthusiasm as being synonymous with commitment to the struggle. Enthusiasm in these emotional times and in this fluid year of 1952, led to an overconcentration on a largely uncontrolled expansion of the oath-taking campaign, while largely dispensing with the niceties of elaborate organization, establishment of effective command structure, control, and above all accountability. As it turned out, this loose organizational structure had by 1952 become susceptible to infiltration by government spies and chiefs.

In Nairobi, the central committee relied immensely on the courage and knowledge of criminals, prostitutes, and thieves to spread the oath and to collect funds and later weapons. Kaggia states that "after the ex-army people we started to recruit criminals. Most of our people, except for those who had been in the army, were afraid to touch guns. Criminals were prepared to do so."[3] Kubai affirms this point, stating emphatically that "we had a team of thieves. We organised them. We asked them to steal guns. They stole money as well from the Asians."[4] Although acting on behalf of Muhimu, and therefore by extension and association also of the KAU in general, these criminals and prostitutes did not suddenly give up their previous life-styles and start acting as knowledgeable, committed nationalists. The loose nature of the organizational structure and accountability made it possible for some of the procured funds and weapons to be diverted toward nonnationalist endeavors. It should also be remembered that there was a financial reward for procuring weapons, and this reward may have been a more appealing motive for criminals than the as-yet-to-be-defined armed struggle. Waruhiu Itote tells us that

as an incentive, rewards were offered: Shs. 200 for a .303, Shs. 100 for a pistol, Shs. 10 for a grenade, and other amounts depending on the size of the weapon. A Bren gun, for example, fetched Shs. 500 and a Sten gun Shs. 250 while ammunition was worth 25 cents a bullet. In actual fact, few people received any rewards—Nevertheless, the incentive was necessary to make our younger people aware of the vital need for weapons.[5]

It would be wrong to conclude that all thieves, prostitutes, and other criminals acted in their own selfish interests. No doubt there were some whose actions were inspired by nationalism. Yet it should be recognized that the extensive inclusion of these people to act as the elite unit of Muhimu significantly complicated the administrative structure of the movement. Nor can we underestimate the inherent difficulty of convincing the general public, however positively disposed it may have been, that these people were now suddenly politically conscious and respectable nationalists. Some of the resistance to the oath-taking campaign must be accounted for by the general prejudice, however founded or unfounded, against this category of Muhimu activists.

The spread of the oath of unity in Central Province and in Nairobi relied on political cells for both the control of initiates and solidarity with other cells of the movement. As it happens, these cells were on the village level, especially in the rural areas of Central Province where members were often relatives or close associates and where it was possible to identify those who had joined the movement and those who resisted it by refusing to take the oath. The movement utilized pre-existing social structures for political mobilization. Pressure from neighbors, fear of being ostracized, intimidation, all played their part in ensuring that as many villagers as possible swore to support militant nationalism. It should be remembered that the oath of unity was not a warrior oath and did not commit the initiate to guerrilla warfare. It is vital to note that by September 1952 "between 75 per cent and 90 per cent of the Kikuyu population had taken the Oath of Unity."[6]

By 1952 there had started to evolve a recognizable pattern of administration and control, stretching from the sublocation level to the division, the district, the province, and then to the central committee in Nairobi. The intention was to create a control structure that would have allowed for the center to be informed of village problems and progress and for the villages to be informed of general policy and directives from the center.[7] Each of these levels of hierarchy apparently had different duties.[8] In Nairobi, members of the movement were organized along the same lines as in the rural areas, culminating in a provincial committee which was represented on the central committee. Liaison between the provincial committee in Nairobi and district committees in Central Province was maintained through roving ambassadors who shuttled between Nairobi and the rural areas to maintain contact and deliver instructions from the central committee. These district committees would be expected in turn to pass the information and instructions to the village level. This command structure relied essentially on the integrity of the office-bearers and the commitment of the members. Its effective operation relied on a controlled environment in which information was not leaked to the authorities and in which the members obeyed instructions without resentment or controversy. As a result there was an overemphasis on secrecy to protect the movement from exposure and betrayal.

At the same time there was a noticeable lack of internal debates about strategy and progress, a lack which limited the movement's options and vitality. The need to enforce discipline inevitably deteriorated into high-handed brutality against suspected deviationists, resisters, and rumored spies. Another significant drawback of the movement was the carelessness with which new members were recruited. It was assumed that the taking of the oath of unity alone was sufficient to ensure loyalty and devotion. Admittedly there were paramilitary functionaries who patrolled neighborhoods and disciplined betrayers or resisters, but this alone, as subsequent events aptly demonstrated, was not sufficient to ensure loyalty and commitment to the movement. Lack of proper scrutiny of new members became a special problem in 1952. Mass oath-taking ceremonies brought into the movement an assortment of committed nationalists, opportunists, resisters intimidated by threats of violence, and spies. Kaggia reveals that even the central committee itself was not safe from government spies. A member of the central committee was found guilty of spying and sentenced to death in a mobile Mau Mau court: "The court session took place in a taxi, and the judges consisted of the chairman of the committee, myself, and two others. The court decided that the man knew too much. He was condemned to death. The sentence was carried out immediately."[9] In an extraordinary development, J. M. Mungai, who apparently had been a key figure among the taxi drivers who transported the movement's leadership to oath-taking ceremonies, confessed that he had after all been a spy for the notorious CID officer, Ian Henderson.[10] In his confession in detention he alleged that

> from 1944, I was helping Mr. I. Henderson of CID with information concerning burglaries, etc. I gave information to him concerning Makhan Singh, Fred Kubai, KAU leaders, which led to the arrest of and deportation of Markhan Singh—I got this information through the Transport and Allied Workers Union which had appointed me to represent them in the EATUC.

He further stated that after being invited together with Fred Kubai to take the oath by Mbiyu Koinange at Kiambaa, he passed this information to

> Mr. Henderson of the Special Branch, who gave me Shs. 100 in order to meet Mau Mau oath fee. Mr. Henderson wanted me to take Mau Mau oath in order to be able to get information from Mau Mau leaders, and African political leaders.[11]

The loose nature of the administrative, control, and recruitment structure enabled spies to infiltrate the movement almost at every level.

The effects of such infiltrations had become apparent by 1952 when "there were over 400 persons in prison for having taken or administered Mau Mau oaths and several hundred others were awaiting trial."[12] This development necessitated the rather frequent resort to capital punishment meted out to individual offenders as a deterrence to would-be spies. But the movement grew and expanded in both Nairobi and outlying areas, and the Muhimu found that it was not effectively able to administer and control it. This was especially serious, for this breakdown of effective control occurred at a time of unprecedented expansion in the oath-taking campaign when careful administration was extremely essential to regulate and moderate an otherwise runaway public fury.

The Muhimu's obsession with secrecy had led it to introduce an executive body immediately beneath it called "The Group of 30" through which it communicated to the district committees and eventually to individual members in Nairobi slums and rural villages. Unfortunately, "the district leaders had no direct dealings with the Central Committee and did not even know who the leaders were."[13] The relentless pressure from the government interfered considerably with this flow of information from the center to the periphery, leading to premature "de facto devolution of decision making power to lower level councils and individual leader-organisers."[14] What must be remembered is that the administrative structure of the movement had been in existence for about a year before this breakdown and the resultant devolution of authority. These lower-level leaders were therefore not experienced leaders nor tested strategists. The resultant duties and tasks were without doubt overwhelming.

The inevitable consequence of this devolution of power by the Muhimu to local committees was that there was no effective coordination between various committees with regard to formulation of strategy and no cooperation over recruitment and employment of physical and human resources. Occurring at a time of intense mobilization and harassment from the government, the movement was without an overall plan for revolutionary violence and lacked a firm and central leadership. The unprecedented expansion of the oath-taking campaign in 1952 caused the disintegration of central control and direction. It was only natural that in such circumstances there should emerge local strongmen: district or location-based leaders exercising a more direct and effective control over their neighborhoods than the remote, secluded leadership in Nairobi. Alongside this we must remember that Kiambu district had always maintained an independent position regarding the administration of oaths. In Kiambu, *Parliament* exercised a moderating influence, and the oath-of-unity campaign proceeded in a relatively orderly fashion with limited regard paid to active preparation for armed rebellion.

Although the militants in the Rift Valley and in Nakuru and neighboring townships were in touch with Muhimu and *Parliament*, these central bodies did not exercise direct control over the activities of local committees. The inspiration for the work undertaken by these committees may have come from Kiambaa and Nairobi, but the nature of the organization, rate of expansion of the oath-taking campaign, and calibre of leadership were all determined at the local level. As Tamarkin has ably shown in a study of Mau Mau in Nakuru,[15] the change from mild militancy to radical militancy and the initial preparations for armed resistance were all connected to an apparent rebellion within a rebellious underground movement. The youth in Nakuru town, many of whom had been expelled recently as squatters from the surrounding white farms, had joined the local KCA and gradually changed their role from mere guards at oath-taking ceremonies to a separate body loosely connected to the local KCA branch.[16] These young men eventually introduced the militant form of administering oaths to unwilling people by force. "The elders," Tamarkin notes, "appreciating their inability to control the course of events and fearful of arousing the militants' rage, chose to abstain from action. The KCA committee was withering away, its leaders intimidated by the militants."[17]

In Nakuru the administration of the oath by force and the obsessive preoccupation with secrecy and absolute loyalty occupied the major part of the militants' energies and strategic planning. It is not clear that they knew what to do with the resultant militant unity. "With no specific operational plans, unity seems to have become the end rather than the means."[18] This strict enforcement of discipline and loyalty to the movement became even more severe toward the beginning of July 1952 after the introduction of the *Batuni* oath, or "platoon oath," which was the warrior oath. In these turbulent times, this oath was initially administered selectively to young men of fighting age who were expected eventually to take up arms and fight against the British colonial government.

The Batuni oath demanded high standards of courage. It demanded a complete commitment to militant action and violence, as opposed to mere demonstration of solidarity with the movement.[19] "It committed those who had taken it to action and violence and to a higher degree of loyalty and discipline."[20] After July 1952, the movement was getting closer and closer to a military confrontation with the colonial state. During this period, stretching up to October 1952, a lot of ammunition was acquired, and the first groups of fighters were dispatched to Aberdare Mountains and to Mount Kenya. Waruhiu Itote, "General China," left for Mount Kenya at the instruction of the Nyeri (Nairobi) Committee on 18 August 1952.[21] He took his Batuni oath enroute to the forest.

The introduction of the Batuni oath did not signal or imply a readiness on the part of the radicals to declare war on the state and its allies. This oath, as Donald L. Barnett correctly observes, "was intended almost certainly as the initial step in long-range military preparations."[22] The movement still faced administrative problems pertaining to coordination of its various facets. Besides, the Batuni oath had not been administered to a sufficient number of would-be warriors. Military training had not yet progressed beyond instructing a few young people in the art of handling firearms. It would be fair to state that no overall military strategy for the movement had been arrived at by October 1952. These were rocky times in which the leadership, almost at every level, was variously preoccupied with procuring and storing arms, eliminating spies and informers, enforcing discipline, expanding the oath of unity and now the Batuni oath, and avoiding arrest by the government. Indeed the Muhimu had started to dispatch fighters to the mountains, but this was still a secondary preoccupation of the movement's leadership by October 1952.

The cache of arms procured by the movement was also not sufficient for an armed rebellion. John Spencer has concluded that "there simply were not enough weapons for any sustained fight to be made against the British."[23] When Waruhiu Itote was dispatched to Mount Kenya to establish a major guerrilla base, his "most treasured possession" was "a pistol and twenty bullets."[24] He later assembled his recruits and discovered that none of them "had been in the army, and thus they knew nothing of the secondary organisations which supported the actual fighting men."[25] As tension rose in 1952, there was a noticeable increase in violence—assassinations and murders occurring in both the urban and rural areas. This violence convinced the colonial government, at the instigation of settlers, chiefs, and missionaries, to declare a state of emergency in October 1952. Before this, however, several huts were burned down and several people were killed and their bodies thrown into rivers or trenches. What had happened to lead to this violence? Basically it was the preoccupation by the adherents of the movement to secure total loyalty from the Kikuyu population. At the height of the tensions in 1952, it was the chiefs, police informers, orthodox Christians, and government employees who resisted taking the oath of unity. If resistance was allowed, so the militants argued, then there would be a breakdown of the efforts to bring unity to Central Province. Thus chiefs, subchiefs, or their messengers were special targets of this sporadic but formidable violence.

In its *Catalogue of Assaults on Government Servants in 1952*, the state concluded that "the attacks have in the main been directed against Chiefs and Headmen but the more junior government servants such as instructors, teachers . . . and loyal Africans in general have also suffered."[26] These acts of violence were not planned nor were they part of a well-orchestrated campaign of revolutionary violence preceding a declaration of war. They were rather the work of local initiative by various local committees who felt that a particular chief or headman had to be struck down. These events, Spencer notes, "occurred . . . outside the direction of any central movement-wide controlling body.''[27] On a symbolic level, these acts of violence against chiefs, headmen, and ''loyal Africans'' represented a definite challenge to the prestige and authority of the colonial government and no doubt served to enhance the prestige and power of the militants in their locality.

Against this background of heightened tension and violence, Kenyatta went on a speaking tour throughout Central Province and some parts of Rift Valley to emphatically dissociate the KAU from Mau Mau.[28] These were government-sanctioned gatherings, and Kenyatta was under pressure and instructions from the government to denounce Mau Mau and violence. ''Kenyatta,'' Kaggia has remarked, ''was asked to denounce Mau Mau in these meetings.''[29] He addressed large rallies at Kiambu in April 1952, at Naivasha in June, at Nyeri in July, and at Kiambu again in August. The message delivered at each of these meetings was standard:

> that freedom must be achieved by peaceful means, and that once they had gained their independence, Africans would safeguard other races living in Kenya . . . that KAU stood for all-round improvements in Africans' living and working conditions and the party expected its followers to work hard and abandon laziness, theft and crime.[30]

The largest of these meetings was at Nyeri on 26 July 1952, which was attended by about fifty thousand people, ''an unprecedented size for those days.'' Apart from emphatically denouncing Mau Mau, Kenyatta also seemed to link Mau Mau to theft and lawlessness stating, ''I do not want people to accuse us falsely . . . that we steal and that we are Mau Mau. . . . Beer harms us and those who drink it do us harm and they may be so-called Mau Mau.''[31]

Certainly his strongest denunciation of Mau Mau was at the Kiambu meeting called by the Kikuyu elders under the general direction of Senior Chief Waruhiu. At this meeting, attended by almost thirty thousand people and most members of the Kikuyu establishment elite, Kenyatta told his enthusiastic audience that ''Mau Mau had spoiled the country'' and that it should ''perish forever.'' He urged his audience to ''search for Mau Mau and kill it.'' There can be little doubt that such powerful messages from the country's best-known African politician caused confusion for many in his audience, many of whom had already taken the oath of unity and even the Batuni oath. Whereas in their huts and at oath-taking ceremonies they were instructed to hate all white people and claim their land by force if necessary, Kenyatta continually urged restraint and racial tolerance. At the Kiambu meeting, he told his audience, ''We do not want to oust the Europeans from this country. But what we demand is to be treated like the white races.''[32] The Muhimu recognized immediately that such messages from Kenyatta would harm incalculably their strategy of radical militancy. They therefore instructed him to stop the messages and not to address the meetings scheduled to take place in Murang'a, Nyeri, Embu, and Meru. They extracted compliance from Kenyatta through sheer intimidation. ''If Kenyatta had continued to denounce Mau Mau,'' Fred Kubai notes, ''we would have denounced him. He would have lost his life. It was too dangerous and he knew it.''[33]

There was, however, confusion in the labyrinth of Kikuyu militant nationalism during this turbulent period. Kenyatta, the towering political figure with a legendary past, as president of the KAU continued to press for constitutional nationalism. The KAU was not however the only political organization active in Kikuyuland at this time. There was the KCA, especially in Kiambu where it had a strong hold over *Parliament* and its activities. Many in Central Province still wanted the government ban on its existence lifted. When Fenner Brockway visited Kenya in 1950, his hosts at Kiambaa, who included Kenyatta, asked him to "request Government House to lift the ban on the Kikuyu Central Association."[34] Although intimidated by the radical youth in Nakuru into relative inactivity, the KCA commanded considerable passive support in the Rift Valley. What needs to be emphasized is that the KCA regarded Kenyatta as its chief spokesman. Feeding the confusion were the militancy and violence associated with Muhimu and *Parliament*, which enabled members of these groups to enlist compliance from the general public through intimidation or assault. Resisters to this strategy of coersion gave rise to disunity and the need for even more violence to help secure the elusive goal of unity. In addition, Harry Thuku continued to enjoy minimal support through his ultra-conservative Kikuyu Provincial Association. Finally, the chiefs, headmen, and orthodox Christians had their own share of local support, however minimal it may have been. For the average politically conscious Kikuyu, there was good reason for confusion. Too many centers of power and influence demanded loyalty and devotion.

The confusion was further exacerbated by the fact that radical militancy through the movement was not yet a separate formal political organization independent from the KAU or the KCA. Its leaders at the national level were remote and not well known, especially in the rural areas where the bulk of the population resided. Even for those who had taken the oath of unity, there was still bound to be confusion. Some had taken it in the name of the KCA, others in the name of the KAU, while others had simply taken an oath. In the political songs that now spread widely in Central Province, Kenyatta's name was freely used; yet in his meetings he feverishly denounced Mau Mau, which had grown out of the oath-taking campaign.

Could Kenyatta control the militants and halt the spread of violence? The answer must be that he could not. He did not control the militants and their radicalism, but more crucially he did not control the spread of the radical oath-taking campaign, either in Nakuru, Nairobi, or in the districts of Central Province. Only the radicals could possibly halt the militancy and violence. But even here it needs to be remarked that by October 1952, Muhimu had devolved power to various local committees spread all over Nairobi, Nyeri, and Murang'a. Many of these committees had no direct dealings with the central committee, but rather relied on local initiative. It would have been impossible even for Muhimu to halt the spread of violence by sheer command. And indeed they had no intention of halting the spread of militancy and radicalism. The quest for land, employment, freedom, education, and housing had made the spread of militancy, and thus violence, possible.

Although violence and intimidation had greatly aided the spread of the oath by silencing overt resistance, nonetheless small pockets of resistance to the movement and its tactics were starting to emerge in Central Province by August 1952. To be sure, such pockets of resistance in these emotionally charged times were few. They were formed initially by orthodox Christians heavily supported by white missionaries. In subsequent years, after the declaration of the emergency, this group proved to be a stubborn and resilient opponent to Mau Mau. At a meeting held at Kiambu and later reported in the London *Times*,[35] African Christians arrived at what they called a "Joint Action." This meeting attended by Kikuyu orthodox Christians "was remarkable because it is one of the few occasions when Protestant and Roman Catholic Missions have acted together in this way."[36] In its six-point resolution, this meeting's participants pledged themselves to oppose Mau Mau because as Christians they felt it was anti-Christ and also "because it is against the Government which maintains law and order of the country and thus our safety and happiness."[37] Participants also demanded the exclusion of Mau Mau adherents from churches and their children from schools "lest they infect others." Perhaps more ominous was the pledge by these Christians to fight Mau Mau. "If the government does not succeed in stamping out the organisation," these Christians resolved, "we are prepared to fight the Mau Mau adherents, even if it is with Pangas [knives]."[38] How much did the government know about Mau Mau and how did it propose to respond to the challenge posed by the growth of militant nationalism? In its annual reports of 1948 and 1949, the colonial government avoided mention of any major political stirrings in the colony among Africans. In 1948 the bulk of the *African Affairs Department Annual Report* concentrated on *Dini ya Msambwa*, a religious sect in western Kenya whose self-proclaimed prophet was referred to by the report as "a certified lunatic"[39] The 1949 report talked of African areas having experienced "progress and development aimed at enabling the ordinary African to live his life more fully."[40] The picture painted by the administration was surprisingly one of endless tranquility and progress, when in fact there was immense economic and social tension in both the Kikuyu reserve and in Nairobi. In 1950, brief mention was made of Mau Mau by name in the annual report.[41] It was however looked upon as yet "another subversive and anti-Government organisation."

Official notice had been drawn to Mau Mau as a result of the now famous Naivasha court trial of Mau Mau adherents accused of forcibly administering an oath to one Kinuthia, son of Njehia.[42] The accused nineteen farm laborers were charged with being members of "Mau Mau Association formed for the purpose of chasing Europeans from the colony of Kenya." All the same the government had no specific knowledge at this time about the movement's aims, membership, office-bearers, or areas of operation. This was a general ban against a society that had not yet had a formal existence. As tension increased in 1951, the government increasingly came to attribute every form of violence to Mau Mau and further to link Mau Mau to the KAU. The provincial commissioner (P.C.) of Central Province noted in 1951 that "a responsible and sincere political body of educated Africans could be of great value in this province," but he felt that "Kenya African Union is not such a one."[43] After dismissing it as a largely Kikuyu body "afflicted internally by Kikuyu intrigues and petty jealousies," the P.C. concluded that all of the KAU's aims and objectives were destructive.[44]

This dismissive attitude on the part of the colonial government proved to be a serious handicap in its response to the crisis. It led the government to treat warnings about African discontent and militancy as alarmist. A particular handicap for the government was the governor, Sir Philip Mitchell. In his last two years of colonial service, Mitchell disengaged himself from the details of the colony's administration.[45] He continued to be heartened by his self-proclaimed expertise on the ways of Africans, professing an unrivaled knowledge of the African continent and its people. It was therefore characteristic of him to dismiss any report about troubles in the colony as merely alarmist and generally a misreading of the reality. Particularly serious for the eventual turn of events was Mitchell's belief that Mau Mau was just another *dini* (religious sect), like the many he had seen in different parts of East Africa. As to why Kikuyu people were engaged in oaths and murder, Mitchell attributed this to their being "a forest and mountain dwelling people" who are therefore "particularly given to black and foul mysteries, to ritual murder, to ordeals by oath and poison and cults of terror, in which murder is the central feature."[46] His explanations, always given with definitive authority however mistaken they may have been, were basically quasi-psychological and quasi-anthropological.

He studiously avoided drawing any linkage between the colonial state and its policies and the prevailing tension in Central Province. As if to affirm his point that there was no trouble in the colony, Mitchell refused to look at intelligence reports from the field early in 1952. "In about March 1952," a colonial district commissioner later recalled, "the administration was informed in a letter from the Private Secretary to His Excellency the Governor that the latter no longer required his copy of the monthly secret intelligence reports from the District Commissioners to be sent to him."[47] The result was that the field administrators who believed they had evidence of subversion failed to convince the Government House or the Secretariat, and many months passed without a concise evaluation or appraisal by the government of the overall security problems facing the colony.

Even before Mau Mau troubles, the intelligence and security system was generally poorly managed. At the district level,

> the D.C. relied on DOs, his chiefs, perhaps the tribal police sergeant, or his own interpreter and the police informer . . . to all this the Kenya Police contributed very little, and indeed on the intelligence side, there was little coordination between the Administration and the Police.[48]

This may be an exaggerated picture by a D.C. who felt betrayed by the central government; nonetheless the crucial point is that the government had no effective system of collecting, assembling, analyzing, and interpreting overall intelligence information in the colony before October 1952. Under these circumstances various branches of the Administration received separate pieces of information and responded to them differently. It could be said that the government suffered from false confidence at this time. Accustomed to securing obedience from Africans by a variety of methods not least of which was physical coercion, the administration felt that its position was safe and intact even at a time when its chiefs and their allies were starting to be isolated and eliminated by Mau Mau activists. It underestimated the force of the economic and social problems which had given rise to the oath of unity and subsequent militancy and violence. Mitchell dismissed warnings about impending trouble, and on the eve of his retirement he saw only what he wanted to see: namely a happy, prosperous colony with a few minor problems instigated by self-appointed African leaders, "usually Kikuyu with a pronounced dislike of honest work."[49] Indeed when he went on a fishing trip (safari) in Central Province in March 1952, accompanied by his wife and Sir Andrew Cohen (Governor of Uganda) he saw only "smiling faces and happy cheerful people delighted to see one and to pass the time of day."[50]

Mitchell retired in June 1952. Meanwhile the spread of militancy and violence continued to lead field administrators and white settlers to be greatly alarmed. Settlers had over the years relied on the government for protection, and so now they petitioned for executive protection. In their usual confrontational manner, the settlers asked the government to declare a state of emergency and to lock up all African nationalists whom they believed were behind the unrest. The Legislative Council debated the security issue on 10 July 1952, after a motion was made by Michael Blundell, a settler leader who wanted the "Government to take the measures necessary to improve the situation." The government still felt that there was no emergency situation in the colony and refrained from petitioning to London for authority to declare an emergency.

In spite of the deteriorating situation, the government, headed by Mr. Potter as acting governor, felt the situation could be contained by introducing stringent legislation giving the police extensive powers of arrest and prosecution. Also, the colonial administrators did not want to assume the professional risk of forwarding such tragic news about the unrest to London. Up to June, this same administration under Mitchell had filed reports to London about the progress and tranquility of Kenya, and now to suddenly petition for emergency powers would surely have sounded incredible. "For the central Government to approach the Colonial office with a request to declare a state of emergency would have been an admission both of its failure to govern effectively and of the inaccuracy of the reports of the peace and prosperity of the colony sent as late as June to the Colonial Office."[51] So the administration stalled in the hope that the situation would improve. But the situation did not improve, leading the administration to resort to some rather unconventional means of containing militancy and halting violence.

On 2 May 1952, the colonial government engaged Kikuyu and Akamba witch doctors and medicine men for the purpose of conducting cleansing ceremonies "by which those who had taken the Mau Mau oaths could be released from the vows they had given to the society."[52] This exercise was seen by the government as a major effort in solving the unrest in Central Province. These cleansing ceremonies were coordinated by the district commissioners through the chiefs whose duty it was to enlist the most effective witch doctors and medicine men for government employment. This was in keeping with Mitchell's diagnosis of the problem, which looked at Mau Mau as essentially a psychological or religious problem. And so the district commissioners toured their districts and addressed several public rallies (*barazas*), dissuading people from joining or supporting Mau Mau.

In the past probably such tactics would have worked. Now, however, economic desperation reinforced by oath-taking had given rise to a level of militancy which could no longer be suppressed or intimidated by the Crown. Imperial rule had been demystified. But still the government did not give up. Funds were provided to pay the medicine men for their services and for the buying of goats, which formed an important part in the execution of these ceremonies. The colonial government had gone native! And so "for the next few months goats were ceremonially battered to death all over Kikuyu reserve by a travelling circus of the government-sponsored medical men, who were jocularly known among Europeans as 'Her Majesty's witch doctors.' "[53] By the end of July it was evident that neither increased police powers nor cleansing ceremonies had been able to stem the tide of militancy and violence. Acts of violence still continued to be reported, and settlers started to make their customary threat of rebellion or taking law into their own hands.[54] Consequently on 17 August 1952, the Colonial Office in London was officially informed for the first time by the government in Nairobi of "a serious deterioration of law and order in the colony"[55] and that it may be necessary to enact even more drastic legislation to deal with the situation. Still the colonial government did not ask for permission to declare an emergency.

There was a very strong feeling in the higher circles of government that even if the Kikuyu were taking oaths, they would not seek a military confrontation with the authorities. The government therefore maintained regal indifference to the widespread worry, frustration, and panic, "taking some comfort from the fact that . . . Kikuyu were an unwarlike tribe and could be crushed in a matter of a few weeks if they really started violence in earnest."[56] This wrong deduction proved very costly once the emergency had been declared. Meanwhile, however, the government decided to display its military might to the Africans in Nairobi slums with the obvious intention of intimidating the militants. "Men of Kenya Regiment drove through the African quarter of Nairobi . . . with bayonets fixed and rifles and Bren guns at the ready. It was a show of the flag demonstration to warn the anti-white underground organisation called Mau Mau."[57]

There can be little doubt that the government's handling of the unrest was further complicated by the absence of a governor since the retirement of Mitchell in June 1952. Though appointed in April 1952, the new governor, Sir Evelyn Baring, did not arrive in Nairobi until 29 September, when he found that, contrary to the positive appraisal of the situation by Mitchell, the colony had serious problems of law and order. The reports from the Chief Native Commissioner referred to widespread influence of Mau Mau in Kiambu, Nyeri, and Murang'a districts and of course Nairobi and that the "show of the flag" or drastic legislation had been unable to contain the situation.

Almost immediately upon being sworn in, Baring went on a short familiarization tour of Central Province, during which he conferred with chiefs, provincial white administrators, missionaries, African clergy, and of course white settlers. All of these groups were uniform in their condemnation of Mau Mau and African nationalists. They singled out Jomo Kenyatta and the KAU as being largely behind the violence and the formation of Mau Mau. Baring's views were therefore heavily influenced by these encounters. His consultants attributed to Kenyatta the responsibility for masterminding Mau Mau and its violence, although they had no proof. However, the theory made a lot of sense to them. Kenyatta, as the most prominent

African politician in the colony, and widely respected by the Kikuyu, was expected, according to these enemies of African nationalism, to know or to be involved in the organization of Mau Mau. The colonial government and the settlers had been wary of his activities ever since 1946 when he returned to Kenya from Britain. "Kenyatta's visits to Russia and his communist contacts, his marriage to an English woman, these damned him in their eyes, whatever he might have said or done."[58] The government had circulated a warning about him upon his return to Kenya, which confirmed the white settlers' prejudice that he was indeed a dangerous demagogue. Every form of violence after 1950 came to be squarely attributed to Mau Mau and therefore to Kenyatta. The government and the settlers felt that there was nothing wrong in the colony except for the disruptive influence of Kenyatta, a communist, who now dominated and directed the activities of Mau Mau through the KAU! It was without doubt one of the more mistaken analyses of the situation and principally self-serving to whites. It absolved them of any responsibility for the unrest or indeed for African frustrations in general.

The chiefs wanted Kenyatta and the KAU officials arrested. Nationalism and militancy threatened their positions of power in Kenya and especially their uncontested supremacy in the rural areas. Kenyatta, as a symbol of nationalism, had to be removed in order that they might be able to reclaim their quickly diminishing authority. Equally the missionaries, settlers, and white administrators all wanted to enjoy the unrealistic claim that they had been doing a good job before their work was interrupted by the KAU and African nationalists. At this period, none of these groups was willing or even able to see that their activities may have contributed to the prevailing unrest.

On returning to Nairobi, Baring came to the conclusion that Kenyatta and the KAU were behind Mau Mau and the general unrest. It was surely a rather drastic conclusion to make after a single brief tour of Central Province. He refused to confer with Kenyatta or any other African nationalists, having concluded that they were guilty. The assassination of Senior Chief Waruhiu convinced him of the urgency of declaring a state of emergency. Waruhiu was generally seen by whites as a moderate and responsible leader striving for interracial harmony within the confines of colonialism. His assassination was therefore interpreted as a rejection of his strategy and a clear declaration of war on the part of Mau Mau. Of course this was not true, but it gave Baring the pretext to petition the Colonial Office for permission to declare an emergency. On 10 October 1952, in a memo marked "Top Secret," Baring informed the Colonial Office that he had arrived at the conclusion that "Kenyatta and his henchmen" must be removed. If this was not done "the chiefs, headmen, Government servants, missionaries among the Kikuyu who still support us, will cease their support and many will be killed," and also "the trouble will spread to other tribes who are more war like than the Kikuyu and who provide men for the Kenya police." Perhaps more crucial for political considerations in Britain was the fear that, unless African nationalists were silenced, "there will be reprisals by Europeans."[59] On 14 October, the Colonial Office under Oliver Lyttelton cabled Baring approving his plans to declare a state of emergency,[60] which he did on 20 October 1952.

Baring and his military advisers, obviously acting emotionally and on very sketchy and unreliable information, hoped that this state of emergency would be short-lived. The basic reason for this unrealistic optimism was that Baring lacked thorough information about the overall extent of the movement in Kikuyuland. Still acting on the mistaken premise that all was well except for the agitation of the KAU, Baring and his advisers imagined that order and tranquility would be restored easily once the Kikuyu leadership had been removed and locked up. They were hopelessly wrong.[61] They had no precise knowledge about the enemy that they had declared war against. In his initial analysis of the organization of Mau Mau, Baring, while agreeing that not every "act of violence has been planned at the centre," still felt that "there is a plan, a rather ragged and a rather African one, but none the less formidable for that."[62] Yet a month after the declaration of emergency, violence had not ceased; if anything, there was a slight increase. This prompted Baring to inform London that he now thought the Mau Mau organization was decentralized to fit the equally decentralized tribal organization of the Kikuyu.[63] All the time the colonial government's aim was to seek to establish that Mau Mau had a central territorial organization under the command of Kenyatta and that it worked through the KAU.

The declaration of emergency and the subsequent arrest of about 187 KAU officials took the movement by complete surprise.[64] It occurred at a time when there was a rapid evolution in the movement from what could be termed mere solidarity to armed resistance. But plans and strategy for such armed resistance had not yet been arrived at. There was also continuing tension between the KAU executive committee and the movement's Nairobi leadership, Muhimu. However, Muhimu continued to function as a supersecret underground leadership of a multilayered and loosely organized resistance movement that was nameless and largely uncoordinated in its activities. It is quite possible that with the passage of time Muhimu would have declared its independence from the KAU and the KCA and formed a radical, armed-resistance party. This however had not occurred by October 1952, and as a result there arose confusion in Central Province because of the layers of leadership demanding loyalty and devotion of an enraged and embittered people.

The country's elite African leadership under Kenyatta certainly stood against violence, but yet they found that oaths had produced violence and intimidation and a class of leadership previously unknown but now of considerable consequence by virtue of its connection to radical militancy. A crisis of leadership had arisen in Kikuyuland once again. This was true in spite of Kenyatta's eminent position. This prominence left him, nevertheless, without authority over the multitudinous oath-taking ceremonies spread out in Central Province and beyond and shut off from the secretive activities of Muhimu. Kenyatta's supremacy in African politics by 1952 appears to have been general rather than specific. He was the prominent symbol of African nationalism, but he had no power over the militants who now had a firm grip on most of the population of Central Province, even if this grip was uncoordinated and therefore essentially fractious.

The mood of the times in the African population of Central Province and Nairobi and parts of Rift Valley was tense, giving rise to uncontrollable, almost unstoppable fury against the colonial state and its allies. The traditional symbols of colonial power quickly lost their authority and ability to control the deteriorating situation. Chiefs, headmen, and their messengers were frightened, intimidated, and occasionally assaulted. They could not restore law and order in their locations. The district commissioners could not rely on threats, pomp, "show of the flag," or even witch doctors to restore law and order. The government had by 1952 effectively lost its grip on the colony. As it struggled with various options for regaining control, the settlers pushed for and demanded more drastic measures to deal with "the natives." In one instance, a white settler urged mass shooting of the Kikuyu,[65] thereby illustrating in a dramatic way how far removed the settlers had become from normal civil practices in their dealings with Africans.

The colonial government was a prisoner of its own past prejudices against Africans. By refusing to acknowledge the existence of economic and political problems and frustrations that Africans faced, the government ruled out the need for negotiations, which alone would have led to a peaceful resolution to the unrest. The government refused to acknowledge that the colonial settler enterprise was a failure. To admit that settler colonialism was an economic failure and a political embarrassment would have been an uncharacteristic admission that indeed the basis of all colonial policies in Kenya was wrong. Yet the declaration of a state of emergency clearly illustrated that settler colonialism had been a failure after all, and now it demanded massive extra help from London to survive. But for how long? After the military phase of the conflict, which started in earnest in 1953, the settlers found that the answer to this question would be determined in London, not in Nairobi.

PART TWO
The Military and Ideological Phase

FOUR

BRITISH MILITARY
STRATEGY

In a general way the British army's drive against Mau Mau guerrillas was influenced by its past experience against similar revolts in various parts of the empire. John Pimlott has observed that the relative success of the British army against insurgents since 1945 can in part be attributed to experience gained from the "imperial past."[1] Lessons learned from colonial wars of conquest and "punitive expeditions" and armed revolts against colonial imposition, all came to form an invaluable source of information that was readily available to the army in subsequent engagements. Pimlott points out that lessons from the "imperial past" can be a military liability if they are rigidly adhered to irrespective of circumstances. He points out the French *guerre revolutionaire* doctrine, which proved to be of limited value in France's post–World War II campaigns against nationalist revolutions in Vietnam and Algeria.

According to Pimlott the "flexibility of response," together with accumulated knowledge from the past, has been the chief reason for the British army's relative success against insurgency since 1945. It is interesting to note that some of the key strategies used against the Malayan guerrillas and Mau Mau had been employed before against the Boers in South Africa.[2]

It would be wrong to imagine that this accumulated knowledge made the British army's task easy and comfortable. On the contrary, the war against Mau Mau clearly illustrates that counterinsurgency operations were bloody, protracted, and ruthless. The success of such operations depended heavily upon proper coordination between the military and administrative branches of government. This is always vital to ensure that the political goals of the campaign are not jeopardized by the way the war is prosecuted. In the British army's war against Mau Mau it was evident from the start that both branches of government were agreed that "Mau Mau had to be suppressed; political negotiations were totally inconceivable."[3]

After the declaration of the state of emergency, it soon became clear that the colonial government had no overall strategy for dealing with the revolt and unrest. The governor had requested and obtained British troops as well as African troops, known as the KAR (King's African Rifles). These combined troops were composed of the First Lancashire Fusiliers from the Canal Zone, the Fourth KAR from Uganda, the Sixth KAR from Tanganyika, and the local KAR battalions. Many other KAR units were engaged during the course of the campaign against Mau Mau. In their initial assignments, these troops were engaged in random searches and expeditions of harassment that came to be called general sweeps. Up to May 1953, these troops, together with a fast-expanding police force, struggled to contain the unrest by conspicuous demonstrations of force through the affected reserve and the White Highlands. The British troops were assigned to the White Highlands, while the KAR troops patrolled the reserves of Central Province.

"Until the end of 1953," the colonial government later recorded, "the sweeps in reserves were on a small scale, designed principally to surprise and round up Mau Mau meetings and oath ceremonies in progress; also, in combination with a few special demonstrations to show the flag, to accord protection and strengthen the morale of resistance groups in training."[4] These activities were far from efficient and lacked proper coordination, even after the appointment of Major General Hinde as director of operations in January 1953. Since 1952, the emergency had been co-ordinated by "Situation Report" and later by the Colony Emergency Committee,[5] but in each case it was evident that the strong views on security by the ever-contentious settlers were drastically affecting the task of formulating a coherent policy. This was further complicated by the fact that the governor, Sir Evelyn Baring, had no military experience whatsoever and was new in the colony and desired to have an amicable relationship with both the provincial administration and the settlers.[6] He was also generally weak, sickly, and often seen as indecisive.[7]

The situation by early 1953 revealed that the troops had failed to isolate and eliminate the Mau Mau guerrillas. The troops had failed to dislodge Mau Mau not only from the reserve but also from Nairobi. The Crown's military activities in Nairobi at this time are an illustration of how frustration led to indiscriminate brutality directed at the Kikuyu and later Embu and Meru peoples due to the troops' failure to deal Mau Mau a decisive blow.

Throughout 1953, Nairobi remained a contested territory between the government troops and Mau Mau. Unable to locate large open concentrations of guerrillas and activists, the government instead focused its efforts on harassing Africans in their residential areas (locations). The usual practice was to launch raids on markets, round up as many Kikuyu as possible, screen them and deport a large proportion of them to the reserve. Night raids also became common. In these raids, troops descended on African locations or slums, kicking doors open and generally harassing and beating the residents who would then be herded together for screening.

On the night of the 22nd/23rd March, a Nairobi City Council Report states,

a large raid on Pumwani was carried out by the Police and Military. Between eight and ten thousand Kikuyu males were screened by teams from their up-country districts, and the raid resulted in large numbers of men being repatriated, either because their documents were not in order, or because they had been picked out as being wanted in their home districts for Mau Mau activities.[8]

In the absence of a coherent military/political strategy against Mau Mau up to 1953, it is fair to state that these several raids were a strenuous effort by the government to be seen to be doing something. The government was keen to appear tough and decisive against the unrest, even if the enemy remained elusive and hidden. In a further demonstration of administrative toughness the government enacted in 1953 several decrees that severely restricted the movement and commercial activities of the Kikuyu, the Embu, and the Meru people in the city. Motor cars (especially taxicabs) were forbidden from carrying "more than one member of the Kikuyu/Embu/Meru tribes" without permission.[9] In October 1953, members of these ethnic groups were forbidden from selling charcoal, and in a further step of isolation certain estates were declared out of bounds to them. As a result, "it was decided to ban the Kaloleni and Ziwani locations to all Kikuyu/Embu/Meru and to make Bahati and Kariokor the main locations for members of these tribes."[10]

Lack of information frustrated the government's military and political action from the start. No amount of bullying tactics could compensate for the lack of intelligence about Mau Mau which affected the government by 1953. It was against this background of frustration and near despair that the British government appointed General Sir George Erskine as commander-in-chief of the colony's armed forces in May 1953.[11] He had been selected for the job personally by Sir Winston Churchill and had therefore the political backing and professional experience to undertake a major campaign almost indifferent to the peculiar military wishes and instructions from the vocal settler community. Energetic, big, and flamboyant, Erskine was self-assured and decisive, and in this he differed quite markedly from the governor. He pointed out to the settlers that the struggle against Mau Mau was also political. It was an observation which failed to endear him to the settlers. Throughout his tour of duty he was tolerated but never liked.[12]

In his analysis of the problem in Kenya, four months after his arrival, Erskine informed the colonial secretary that "from evidence coming forward from screening teams and the improved intelligence services, it is now clear that Mau Mau is wider spread and deeper rooted than was thought possible even six months ago."[13] Because Mau Mau was so widespread, Erskine told London that "the campaign will be longer than originally thought." The duration of the campaign would depend on the fruition of his strategies, which he started to implement toward the end of 1953.

Erskine's new strategies did not immediately supplant all the efforts at rudimentary organization that had been instituted prior to his arrival. The system of emergency committees was left in place, and through these committees at the provincial and district levels the orders of the military were implemented. This system of local committees had been utilized before in the military campaigns against the Malayan guerrillas.[14] Through this system, the provincial administration and the military became closely coordinated in their counterinsurgency efforts. The cooperation was not always harmonious, but at least order was brought to bear on what had been a fairly contentious aspect of the emergency operation. Alongside this was an improved system of intelligence-gathering and evaluation. Since 1953, there was a noticeable expansion of the Special Branch under the direction of British intelligence officials.[15] Military intelligence expanded through the work of Field Intelligence Assistants (FIA) coordinated by British army officers.

Intelligence information was acquired principally through interrogation. As Erskine's strategy of systematically battling one district after another began to impose intolerable pain on the local population, many people were rounded up and thoroughly interrogated, a process which yielded valuable information for the government. Perpetual harassment and infiltration by trained spies and informers further weakened the protective cover of Mau Mau adherents. Then there were the dreaded screening teams. These teams had been given a particularly foreboding quality by parading arrested persons before hooded loyalists who pointed out Mau Mau activists for the colonial security forces. It was a device developed by Kitson, a British military intelligence officer, who went on to make a career out of counter-insurgency operations in the British army.

Intelligence information also came from the Home Guards (paramilitary units of African loyalists) and the confessions of the captured guerrillas. By the end of 1953, the colonial government had detained thousands of people who had confessed before the screening teams.[16] The information gathered was evaluated and effectively utilized in assessing the spread of Mau Mau and also in identifying the local activists who were immediately arrested.[17]

This information still remained largely incomplete. It was singularly lacking in details about the organizational structure of the Mau Mau forces. Many of the people who had confessed were minor functionaries in the movement and had no access to the more sensitive information about the strength of the guerrilla forces in Aberdares and Mount Kenya. Without this crucial tactical information, it was impossible for the British army to plan an effective offensive against Mau Mau.

This position changed drastically with the capture of Waruhiu Itote (General China) on 15 January 1954. He was the most senior Mau Mau guerrilla leader captured by the government since the declaration of the emergency in 1952. Other than the propaganda bonanza that was bound to be made from the capture of the commander of Mau Mau forces on Mount Kenya, the government was more interested in the intelligence harvest to be scored. After a brief hospitalization for treatment of wounds suffered during the military encounter leading to his capture, General China was declared fit for interrogation. The interrogator was a Kenya-born white superintendent of police, the son of a local coffee farmer. His name was Ian Henderson.[18] Among his key credentials for this job of interrogation was the fact that he was Kenya-born and spoke the Kikuyu language fluently, a rare accomplishment for colonial administrative staff. General China was interrogated for a total of sixty-eight hours at the office of the Special Branch of the Kenya Police.[19] Henderson found General China to be a "complete fanatic," who was convinced he would be hanged.

Although initially very careful not to reveal any sensitive information, it is clear that as the interrogation dragged on, he gave the colonial government and its army the most detailed insight yet into the organization of the Mau Mau forces. He revealed his sphere of influence[20] in the reserve and the location of his headquarters on Mount Kenya. Perhaps more damaging were the details that he offered about his forces' command structure stretching from the reserve to Mount Kenya.

He revealed, for example, that "the supreme body governing both militant and passive wings in the Mount Kenya sphere is the MOUNT KENYA COMMITTEE which consists of twenty leading militant personalities drawn on the following basis: Nyeri District, 6; Embu, 6; Meru, 6; Chairman, 1; and Secretary, 1."[21] Details such as the names of representatives on this committee were revealed by General China. He also offered information about the different layers of organization of Mau Mau and the functions of each committee.

As for the seventy-five hundred forces he commanded on Mount Kenya, General China revealed that they were organized in nine independent units,[22] with names ranging from "Hika Hika Battalion" to "The Ruku Battalion, Meru." For each of the nine units, he gave details about the unit's leadership, organization, and areas of operation in the reserve. He mentioned other fascinating military details; for example, details and the location were supplied of a factory and work done by the "Engineers Group," a unit that was specifically charged with the responsibility of "obtaining arms, ammunition, and material for the manufacture of home made weapons." He confirmed the colonial government's suspicion that Nairobi was the center of Mau Mau activity. Henderson recorded that General China had stated that "many hundreds of recruits have been sent from Nairobi to Mount Kenya sphere, not to mention the Aberdares, and Nairobi continues to be the terrorists' chief source of supply, both in material and in finance."[23] Of special interest to the army were details about the arms possessed by the guerrillas.

Mau Mau guerrillas on Mount Kenya possessed, according to this interrogation, 14 automatic rifles; 361 rifles/shotguns; 4 grenades; 1 Bren gun; 23 revolvers/pistols; and 1,230 homemade weapons.[24] There was an acute shortage of ammunition, which hampered the operational activities of the guerrillas. Food was principally supplied by the "passive wing" in the reserve, and "no food stuffs are grown by the terrorists in the forest." It was also revealed that there was very little active cooperation between the Mount Kenya forces and the Aberdares forces under Kimathi. The two armies were largely independent of each other.[25]

These were extraordinary revelations. Henderson managed to convince General China to arrange for peace talks between the government and the Mount Kenya Mau Mau forces aimed at leading to the guerrillas' mass surrender. General China promptly agreed, having been given the tentative promise that his life would be spared as a reward for the efforts.[26] The "China Peace Overture" lasted three months, and at the end of it mistrust and ill will led to the collapse of what would have been an unprecedented mass surrender of Mau Mau forces.[27] For the efforts, General China's life was spared, and he was detained at Lokitaung prison together with Kenyatta. But the exercise had not been a waste of time for the British army.

The three-month lull in the fighting was used by the intelligence branches to gather extensive information on the passive wing of Mau Mau in the reserve. Many of these people had been pointed out as a result of General China's disclosures.[28] The magnitude of the breakthrough in intelligence for the British army can be seen in the fact that after the collapse of the "peace talks," more than a thousand terrorists and supporters lurking in the reserves were picked up in three days."[29] The British army was starting to score crucial blows at Mau Mau not only militarily but also in the intelligence-gathering area. This was fatal for Mau Mau. The guerrillas could not survive for long if they were not assured of local, moral, and physical support in the reserves and, more crucially, in Nairobi. The arrests and detentions of suspected Mau Mau supporters increased tremendously after 1954, and the reserves for the first time became a dangerous arena for the guerrillas. Less than a month after the collapse of the "peace talks" the army launched one of its most extensive operations against Mau Mau's passive wing. The location was Nairobi and the target: all members of the "Embu/Meru/and Kikuyu tribes."

Operation Anvil commenced on 24 April 1954 after weeks of planning by the army with the approval of the War Council. The operation effectively placed Nairobi under military siege as the army and police combed the city for "undesirable Kikuyu/Embu/Meru people." In its execution, Operation Anvil worked from the premise that all Kikuyu/Embu/Meru were guilty of supporting Mau Mau, and each member of these tribes had therefore to prove their innocence. Of course Operation Anvil was not the first paramilitary offensive against Mau Mau in Nairobi. It was, however, the most extensive and also the most brutal. With Nairobi cordoned off by a military screen, in every section all African

> inhabitants were assembled and the Kikuyu, Embu and Meru among them were separated from the rest, . . . and moved to Langata. There they were searched, screened more thoroughly and documented. From there they were taken under military guard by rail to the distant camps at MacKinon Road or Manyani.[30]

This indeed was "shock treatment with a vengeance," and many families lost property and belongings in the confusion that arose. Families were separated as husbands unable to prove their innocence were herded to Langata enroute to detention camps, and wives and children were dispatched to congested reserves with no prospects for survival.

Operation Anvil caused a tremendous setback to Mau Mau. Its major activists and urban strategists were detained, and the movement could no longer count on support from its adherents in African locations and slums. A close administration of these residential areas was enforced and immediately "Pumwani was declared a prohibited area to Kikuyu/Embu/Meru, and some 1,800 people from this village were allocated quarters in Bahati which had been vacated by detainees."[31] Nairobi remained under military siege for the rest of the year, and periodic, minor Anvil-like raids occurred in African locations.[32] The movement of Kikuyu/Embu/Meru people in Nairobi was further controlled by issuing passbooks to men and women who remained resident in the city. These were either government employees or employees of private companies, of the city council, and of churches, and other private concerns, who had successfully demonstrated their innocence and dissociation from Mau Mau. They did not form a pool of support that Mau Mau could ever hope to rely on. Besides, the continuous paramilitary operations made any effort toward supporting Mau Mau infinitely hazardous. But were all those detained as a result of Operation Anvil supporters of Mau Mau?

Operation Anvil led to the removal of about thirty thousand members of Kikuyu/Embu/Meru tribes from the city to reception camps.[33] Not everyone of the detainees was a Mau Mau activist or urban strategist. Indeed in the months following Anvil, the government was inundated with complaints from relatives, employers, or lawyers of the arrested people, who all vehemently denied any involvement with Mau Mau. It could be argued that these complaints and protests do not in themselves demonstrate the nonparticipation of the detainees in Mau Mau prior to their arrest. But yet it should be remembered that the government itself realized that Operation Anvil had netted a lot of innocent people. As a result it grudgingly set up at Langata Camp a complaints officer to listen to some of the representations. In its acknowledgment of possible error, the government said, "It is reasonable to suppose that in spite of careful investigation a large number of genuine mistakes may have been made; in an operation of the scope of Anvil it could scarcely be otherwise."[34]

A policy pronouncement on Anvil complaints stipulated that cases that merited investigation were as follows: the detention of a person who is not a member of the specified tribes; the detention of a juvenile; the detention of persons who it is not in the public interest to hold in custody; and obvious injustices.[35] But because the government relied heavily on the "hooded screening teams," it was reluctant to release many detainees in spite of complaints.

It is interesting to note that a major proportion of written complaints to the government came from European employers of detained people, many of whom had in general supported the "cleaning up of Nairobi." Many employers vouched for the loyalty of their former servants. This did not always lead to releases. In her submission, Mrs. M. G. Edwards vouched for her servant Gathuru who had served her "well for the past six years and I personally have no reason to doubt him."[36] Big companies also filed for the release of their employees. The chairman of Dialclem Products Ltd. complained about his employees being rearrested after having "passed the Langata test."[37] The churches were also involved. In fact, it turned out that a detainee stood a better chance of being released if church dignitaries vouched for his loyalty.

The Church of Scotland Mission argued that "screening in the great majority of cases is conducted on a basis of snap judgement by the screeners."[38] There were many people detained because they "looked suspicious" or because of false and unsubstantiated rumors or accusations. It would be fair to say that many people ended up in detention camps without having been active supporters of Mau Mau, and it would be wrong to automatically link detention with Mau Mau activism.

In the reserve of Central Province the British army stepped up its offensive against Mau Mau after Operation Anvil. This was the strategy of "clearing up" one district after another.[39] This offensive was aided by several factors. The most crucial factor as already mentioned was increased intelligence information acquired through confession, spying, and interrogation. In Kiambu district, an organized system of confessions began in August 1954 and involved "the individual in a complete confession of all Mau Mau activity recorded on a form and subsequently repeated in public *baraza*. The idea was to break the power of Mau Mau oaths, and to give those who wanted to give up Mau Mau an opportunity to do so, while at the same time obtaining invaluable information."[40] There had also been a phenomenal expansion of the police force and administrative staff, leading to closer control of the population than had been the case before 1952.

By 1954, for example, Nyeri district was more closely administered than before the emergency. It had "no less than 16 D.O.'s and 18 motor vehicles as opposed to 3 D.O.'s and two vehicles before the Emergency."[41] The police force in the district had "grown from two police stations and 35 men before the Emergency to 28 police stations and 500 men."[42] The emergency had therefore led to the expansion of the state and its instruments of control in the reserve. This remained one of the emergency's more enduring legacies in Kenya.

The British army's Thirty-nine Corps Engineering Regiment arrived in Kenya in October 1953 and was used principally to construct roads right into the Aberdares and Mount Kenya. This had important military significance. "Where before a patrol had taken two days to reach a position selected as a patrol base and two days to return from it they now reached it in a matter of an hour or two, arriving fresh, to expend all their energy on the patrol instead of on the patrol march."[43] The net effect of all these factors was that Mau Mau activists and guerrillas were edged out of the reserve and driven into the forests. The forests were also no longer safe bases, as the army and other paramilitary forces launched offensives right into Aberdares and Mount Kenya. Meanwhile the Royal Air Force, using "both the Harvard trainer, and, later the Liberator bomber,"[44] harassed the guerrillas from the air.

The "eviction" of the Mau Mau guerrillas and activists from the reserve was the most protracted aspect of the war. It would not have been accomplished without the active support of a determined section of the Kikuyu/Embu/Meru population. This section came to be known as the Home Guards (or the loyalists).

Active resistance to Mau Mau had been from the start the domain of chiefs and devout Christians.[45] A government survey published in 1954 with overt propaganda intentions observed that

> when a state of Emergency was declared in October, 1952, loyalists among the Kikuyu belonged to two main classes—Government servants such as chiefs, headmen and tribal policemen, and staunch Christians who loathed the abominations of Mau Mau oath-taking.[46]

In its attempts to analyze the composition of the Home Guards, the government report insisted that all ranks of the Kikuyu/Embu/Meru population were represented. "Its ranks include members of practically every occupation and faith . . . traders, artisans, school teachers, chiefs and headmen . . . but the majority of its members are simple peasant farmers."[47] The implication of this description is to project loyalists as simple men whose support for the government was motivated principally by common decency and abhorrence of Mau Mau oaths and not by any self-interest. It further seeks to establish that no economic class distinction based on landownership played a role in the decision to support the government against Mau Mau. This is however a simplistic and misleading characterization of the Home Guards.

> In his study of the Loyalists, B. A. Ogot pointed out that three major groups of Loyalists are discernible. There is the group that was loyal to law and order; there is the

second group of traditionalists that were loyal to age-old traditions and customs; and
there is the large group that seems to have been loyal to nothing but Mammon. . . .
The fourth group of Loyalists were the Christians who were loyal to their faith.[48]

Loyalists were therefore not uniform in origin although they remained uniform in
aim: to defeat Mau Mau. The realization of their diverse interests was contingent
upon the defeat of Mau Mau by the colonial government. Another factor to be borne
in mind is that the leadership of the loyalists tended on the whole to be large
landowners,[49] whose opposition to Mau Mau was out of self-interest to preserve
their property against the demands of landless peasants who actively supported the
rebellion. "It would not be an exaggeration," Sorrenson has observed of the loyalists, "to state that their loyalty to government was at least tinged by their concern
for the protection of their property."[50] As the war continued, promises of land[51]
and other economic incentives by the government swelled the ranks of the loyalists.

The Roman Catholic Missions in Kikuyuland started the Home Guard movement. Its spread as a paramilitary organization owes much to Chief Njiri of Fort
Hall (Murang'a). He "was the first to set about organising his own Home Guard"[52]
with government encouragement. The idea spread to other districts and became an
integral part of the military/political offensive against Mau Mau. Initially poorly
armed and organized, the Home Guards received a boost in May 1953 when they
were officially recognized "as a branch of the Security Forces" under the command of Colonel P. A. Morcombe. He was an Australian with "a background of
experience in fighting the Malayan Communists."[53]

The Home Guard strength grew from about eight thousand men[54] in 1953 to a
formidable figure of twenty-five thousand men[55] in 1954. Why were they so important in the war against Mau Mau?

In military and political terms, the Home Guards represented armed opposition
against Mau Mau. Since 1951 when the movement came to impose a shaky supremacy in the reserve, it had not yet been challenged by an armed local counterforce.
The military operations by the British army and the KAR and the police were all
viewed by the population as government coercive intrusions and helped in the hard-
ening of attitudes. But the formation of the Home Guards, clearly most loathed by
Mau Mau, provided the effective base around which opposition to Mau Mau could
be organized by the government. In this counterinsurgency strategy the government
never forgot that external military actions alone could never defeat Mau Mau. The
Kikuyu/Embu/Meru population had to be divided in order to be subdued.

As the army intensified its campaigns against Mau Mau the Home Guards were
instrumental in providing key intelligence information and in controlling the local
population to ensure that Mau Mau influence was minimized or completely
stamped out. David Galula has observed that in counterinsurgency operations dis-
persal of insurgents by purely military action cannot ensure victory. "If it is possible to destroy the insurgent political organisation by intensive police action, it is
impossible to prevent the return of the guerilla units and the rebuilding of the political cells unless the population cooperates."[56] Naturally this cooperation by the
population is not by every segment of society, but rather by a sizeable minority who
through coercion and propaganda manage to neutralize the influence of the rebels.

"The technique of power consists in relying on the favourable minority in order to rally the neutral majority and neutralise or eliminate the hostile minority."[57] The importance of the Home Guards in this war can be seen in the fact that "they had by the end of the Emergency killed no less than 4,686 Mau Mau, which amounted to 42% of the total bag."[58]

They prevented Mau Mau from maintaining supremacy over the reserve and through their spy network and punitive measures, enforced with particular brutality at the local level, made it impossible for the "passive wing" to maintain contact with guerrillas in the forests. That this was crucial to the outcome of the war can be seen by observing Algeria, where the French failed to build a formidable Home Guard movement against the FLN.[59] Even after the brutal "Battle of Algiers" beginning in 1956, the French realized their victory was hollow.[60]

In Kenya on the other hand, the Home Guards "prevented the Mau Mau revolt from spreading, and also limited the insurgent attempts to intimidate the populace"[61] by representing "on the ground a local force stronger than Mau Mau, which prevented the insurgents from dominating areas and hindering insurgent recruiting."[62] The government decision of "putting Kikuyu people into villages"[63] greatly increased the power of the Home Guards in the reserve.

The villagization policy began as a punitive measure against areas suspected of being solidly behind Mau Mau,[64] but later it was applied to all Kikuyu and Embu areas as a strategic measure. Protected by Home Guards and administered by chiefs under the supervision of military commanders, these villages represented a rather extreme measure of controlling the civilian population. It is a method which had been tried with success in Malaya and was later to be used without much success in Zimbabwe during *chimurenga* (the war of liberation).[65] By early 1955 over a million Kikuyu had been settled in these villages.[66]

In Kiambu district over eighty thousand huts were hurriedly constructed to accommodate over 300,000 people.[67] The inhabitants of these villages were engaged by force in the construction of a wide trench around the forest zone that effectively separated the guerrillas in the mountains from the reserve.[68] The thrust here was to deny guerrillas access to information and also food. Throughout the emergency, food denial remained a key objective of the British army. Several times the War Council restated the folly of any tendency toward "relaxation or cessation of these restrictions," which had played "an important part in the country's campaign against terrorism."[69]

To ensure that these objectives were realized, the government instituted very restrictive decrees that controlled the movement of the Kikuyu/Embu/Meru people throughout the country. As far as possible they were to be isolated for effective control. In part this was for war requirements, but also as a deterrent measure. The restrictions applied to the "rebellious tribes" were intended to serve as a warning to the "loyal tribes."

In 1953 the government declared that

No adult Kikuyu/Embu/Meru shall:
   i) leave his district of origin within the Kikuyu land unit or;

ii) be or remain within any district of the Central Province other than his district of origin; or

iii) travel by train, motor-vehicle, or bicycle or other means of conveyance from any place in the Central Province to any place in such a province, except within the boundaries of a Municipality or Township . . . or;

iv) if employed upon any farm or in a forest area or if dependent on any person so employed, leave such farm or forest area; unless he is in possession of a permit issued to him by an Administrative Officer or Police Officer.[70]

More often than not such permission was granted upon the favorable recommendation of a Home Guard. What these restrictions did was to make life a nightmare for Mau Mau activists and sympathizers. Survival was now precariously linked to loyalty toward the government. There can be little doubt that these restrictions made people revise their position of loyalty to Mau Mau. Survival has a way of forcing people to compromise their positions or beliefs.

Similar decrees were enacted to control the movement of Kikuyu/Embu/Meru in Rift Valley Province[71] and also in Coast, Nyanza, and Northern provinces.

Alongside these penalties the government instituted a number of incentives to weaken people's support for Mau Mau. Many of the restrictions would be relaxed if a village was judged by authorities to be loyal. Once loyalty had been established, the villagers would be eligible for "amenities, sugar allocations, medical supplies, vitamins for children, etc."[72] These were basic essentials for survival, and many families sympathetic to Mau Mau must have experienced immense mental agony as they weighed their survival against adherence to the rebellion. Finally, the government looked at development at this time as a reward for loyalty and so it put "development with staff into good areas" and withdrew it "from bad areas."[73]

Throughout the emergency, government support for the Home Guards remained strong. In a circular to all administrative officers in Nyeri district in 1954, the D.C. enumerated the reasons for the British military and political campaign against Mau Mau. He said, "First and foremost the fight is for good against evil, for right against wrong, for Christianity and all it stands for. We are also fighting for the loyal Kikuyu leaders."[74] With this in mind, the D.C. urged his administrative staff to ensure that the Kikuyu tribe accepts the "leadership of the Kikuyu loyalists, from the Assistant DO down to the junior headmen."[75] It is a commitment from which the British never wavered, believing as they did that it was the loyalists and especially the Christians who "may be the rock upon which the tribe may be built."[76]

One of the first problems that Erskine had to attend to immediately after assuming command of the security forces was to strive to halt the brutality of the armed forces against the civilian population. Indeed the chief characteristic of the war against Mau Mau was brutality. Since 1952 the security forces seemed convinced that every means was justified in the drive against the rebellion. The armed forces viewed themselves as agents of law and order pitted against murderous and sadistic rebels and felt no constraint whatsoever in their brutal suppression of the revolt. Ironically, however, the forces of law and order did not believe in the rule of law.

Erskine issued a directive to the security forces in June 1953 warning them that he would "not tolerate breaches of discipline leading to unfair treatment of anybody."[77] He informed them of his disapproval of "beating up" the "inhabitants of this country just because they are the inhabitants."[78] Erskine was not alone in recognizing the wanton violence of the armed forces against the civilian population. Other groups with more intimate knowledge of the daily struggle for survival in the reserve made similar observations.

Canon Bostock, archdeacon of central Kenya, observed that, "There are far too many instances of cold-blooded murder by members of the Security Forces, and of beating, for which it seems impossible to obtain redress."[79] These murders were committed by white and black members of the armed forces who "stand by one another, lie, cover up things" and as a result no justice could ever be "secured in these cases."[80] In a private letter to the governor, the moderator of the Church of Scotland in East Africa pointed out that his church could not "accept without protest the instances of brutality which, under the cloak of justice, law and order, the forces of the government have indulged in to an inordinate degree."[81]

The standard response by the armed forces was that they were fighting a war and could not escape "instances of brutality." In a war of this sort, so the argument went, it would be impossible to prevail "without a margin of inhumanity."[82] The trouble was that this "margin of inhumanity" by the armed forces remained particularly wide and was widened each year with vigor. Erskine's warning was not immediately heeded nor was the governor's directive in 1954 in which he felt "considerable disquiet at the number of instances which have recently come to notice in which members of the Kikuyu Guard have abused their position either to pay off scores or to assault persons in their captivity."[83] The governor, the War Council, and the provincial administration must in the end be held responsible for the conduct of the security forces.

Sir Evelyn Baring's strongest desire was to prosecute the war with firmness, and as a result he felt compelled to support those members of the administration accused of brutality.[84] This was particularly frustrating to Colonel Arthur Young, the newly appointed commissioner of police, who found that the administrative officers had overwhelming power over police duties.[85] Colonel Young eventually resigned,[86] having failed to convince the governor that the security forces were using unjustifiable measures to combat Mau Mau.[87]

The security forces had no trust in the "justice" of law courts. The attorney general's insistence that all Africans arrested be brought before the courts presented a severe obstacle to the armed forces' desire for summary justice which would "teach the natives a lesson."[88] But they found a comfortable loophole in the law to allow them to torture and murder "suspected terrorists." Under the state of emergency, protected areas had been declared over "military installations, prisons and power stations in danger areas,"[89] while the majority of "administrative districts in the Central and Rift Valley Provinces" were declared special areas.[90] In protected and special areas, members of the armed forces could shoot anyone who failed to stop when ordered to do so. And so naturally, this became the most common cause of shootings of Africans in Central Province by the security forces. Thousands were shot "while attempting to escape."[91]

Although all branches of the security forces were associated with brutality, the charge was particularly strong against the Kenya Regiment (KR), the Kenya Police Reserve (KPR), the General Service Unit (GSU), and the Home Guards.[92] The KR was a "territorial battalion of the colony composed of white settlers,"[93] as was the KPR. In his assessment of the KPR, Colonel Young was "apprehensive of their obvious independence of command and the combination of their somewhat carefree enthusiasm and their lack of consideration for the African."[94] The KR and KPR represented therefore the armed expression of settler outrage, fears, and hatred. It is significant to note that these units operated in the closest proximity to African areas and thus had ample opportunity to implement their excessive hatred against Africans through torture, murder, and thorough beatings.[95]

The KR and KPR troops as members of the Electors' Union would have been aware of the organization's memorandum of November 1952 about Mau Mau. "In the case of subversive leaders," this memorandum declared, "it is quite clear that steps must be taken in some way for their neutralisation or liquidation."[96] Their conduct alongside that of other security forces introduced an unparalleled reign of terror in the reserve. This led some observers to conclude, in obvious anger, that "the English Settlers were a morally dead and intellectually rotting breed" who meant to "liquidate all young Kikuyu and will do so unless the whole world rises in defence of these helpless men."[97]

As the emergency progressed, the law provided for the death penalty for a variety of offenses which easily lended themselves to abuse through false accusations.[98] The most notable of these offenses were "consorting with terrorists" and "supplying and aiding terrorists." It is the Home Guards who reported such cases to the government and often provided the only evidence against accused persons.

Other than torture and killing of "suspected terrorists," the Home Guards were also accused of extortion, corruption, and sheer greed in the execution of their duties. "Throughout the Emergency," Carey Francis wrote, "Africans in the Security Forces have taken bribes and looted: when houses are searched money and valuables commonly disappear."[99] The Home Guards looked at themselves as local enforcers of law and order who were mandated to carry out their duties by the colonial government. In most cases they were overzealous. This was partly due to a desire on their part to appear useful and thereby to justify their presence to the government. There were also personal reasons. Many in the Home Guards looked at the emergency as an opportunity to enrich themselves by preying on the defenseless civilian population.[100] In Ngugi wa Thiong'o's novel *A Grain of Wheat* (1967), Karanja represents the crafty and ruthless individuals who joined the Home Guards for self-interest. "When Mau Mau breaks out, he betrays his people, confesses the oath and is made a chief, collaborating fully with the settler government to persecute his own people."[101]

The white colonial officials who supervised the Home Guards generally defended them so long as they hunted down Mau Mau guerrillas and sympathizers.

This was so in spite of the fact that the corruption and brutality of the Home Guards had reached scandalous proportions by 1955. As already noted, the white colonial officials and troops were equally guilty of brutality against civilians. William W. Baldwin, an American drifter who served in the GSU in Kenya during the emergency, offers a vivid picture of the general government disposition toward the Home Guards at this time. He writes,

> We . . . did not delve too deeply into some of the minor illegalities practised by the Home Guard. So long as we did not find one conniving with Mau Mau, we left them pretty much alone. . . . The indiscretions of the Kikuyu Guard were a small price to pay for their tremendous contribution toward quelling terrorism.[102]

Inquiries from London and questions in the British Parliament forced the government to curb somewhat the behavior of the Home Guards. But on the whole the government resisted pressure to prosecute them, and police investigations in this direction were frustrated.

The government's general fear was that prosecution might "lead to a disastrous fall in Kikuyu Guard morale and desertions"[103] and thereby retard the progress of the war against Mau Mau. By 1955 the government devised a scheme that both absolved the Home Guards from any impending prosecution and offered Mau Mau guerrillas a chance to surrender. This was the government amnesty of 1955.

This amnesty was preceded by protracted "peace talks" between the government and Aberdare-based guerrillas.[104] Unlike in 1953, this time the guerrillas were on the defensive, and some of them were quick to acknowledge that the reserves were now dangerous and that they had "suffered many losses as a result of ambushes on the way to and from the reserves."[105] The collapse of the "peace talks" on 20 May 1955 left the guerrillas on the Aberdares in disarray, splintered by internal squabbles.[106] About one thousand surrendered under the amnesty, before[107] the government embarked on its last offensive against the guerrillas in the mountains. At the same time the Home Guards' fear of prosecution had been put to rest, for this amnesty also covered them.

After 1955 the most effective weapon used by the government against Mau Mau was the "pseudo-gangs" composed largely of former guerrillas. As already noted, Frank Kitson had developed this technique[108] to pinpoint Mau Mau hideouts for the military and also to venture into the forest under the guidance of former guerrillas on "seek and destroy" expeditions. But up to 1955 these "pseudo-gangs" had always been led by whites, "from the Kenya Regiment, all picked men and mostly from Kenya homes."[109]

When Lieutenant General Sir Gerald Lathbury took over from Erskine as commander-in-chief in 1955, he enthusiastically supported the use of pseudo-gangs and in fact saw them as the ultimate weapon against Mau Mau in the last phase of the war. Under the supervision of Ian Henderson, pseudo-gangs, now renamed Special Force Teams, were organized as an independent unit of the police. The difference between the Special Force Teams and earlier pseudo-gangs was that Henderson groomed these new teams, composed only of Africans and mostly former guerrillas, to go into the forests unsupervised by whites to kill their former comrades. It was an extraordinary development. There were hardly any defections by these former guerrillas to Mau Mau, even though they were armed and basically on their own in the forest. Several explanations have been offered.

The colonial troops that worked closely with these former guerrillas believed that Mau Mau guerrillas owed their "loyalty to an individual rather than to an idea or an abstraction" and that "the individual officer who had interrogated them . . . was one to whom they would give their allegiance, not to anything as intangible as government."[110] The implication of this view is that the guerrillas had no loyalty to the aims of Mau Mau in general but rather to its leaders. This is speculative and must have been an explanation which satisfied the deeply held view by the British that it was the force of magic and tyranny of the leaders which sustained the rebellion.[111] Lathbury himself attributes this development to Kikuyu adaptability "due to a peculiar streak in their psychological make up. . . ."[112]

What is not mentioned by these explanations is the volume of threats and the effects of sustained interrogation on the guerrillas, who must have been aware by 1955 that the tide had turned against their rebellion.[113] Many of these guerrillas had known former comrades who had been hanged for "consorting with terrorists." Besides, the improved intelligence network of the security forces and Special Branch had a lot of information on many of these guerrillas. The threat to use such information against them or their relatives must have proved an unsettling prospect. Kitson provides us with some sketchy information on how he managed to "turn around" some of these guerrillas.

He relates an incident of a captured guerrilla named Kamau who was made to realize that "whatever else happened the Mau Mau were obviously not going to beat the Kikuyu Guard, backed up by the Police, and British army."[114] After further interrogation and "grooming," Kamau agreed to make himself useful in order to "avoid being hanged, which was the penalty for being a gang member."

A deliberate system of brainwashing followed by horrid threats was effectively used in the development of pseudo-gangs. The general principles of making "a man shift his allegiance" were later elaborated upon by Kitson. To be able to accomplish this task, a man "must be given an incentive that is strong enough to make him want to do so; then he must be made to realise that failure will result in something unpleasant happening to him. . . . He must be given an opportunity of proving both to himself and his friends that there is nothing fundamentally dishonorable about his action."[115] In the context of the general events in Kikuyuland by 1954, there were thousands who had renounced their oaths and allegiance to Mau Mau, actions which the pseudo-gangs knew and most probably used as a rationale for their actions. In the interrogation of captured guerrillas, the military and Special Branch officials fooled the prisoners by pretending to know more than they did.[116] This technique was successfully exploited to frighten the prisoners into "cooperation."

The stories of these captured guerrillas are indeed incredible, and they will remain so until the actual guerrillas who fought against their comrades choose to write their own stories. Such a prospect is unlikely to occur soon, given the unenthusiastic reception such accounts would receive. Also, it is my contention that these former pseudo-gang members were affected more than is readily acknowledged by the official process of rehabilitation during the emergency.

What is clear is that the use of former guerrillas in the war effort was a propaganda coup for the government and an economic strategy by the army. The government had effectively turned Mau Mau against Mau Mau in a duel made uneven by the Special Force Teams' superior firepower and its support by a formidable army. The outcome was predictable.

Mau Mau casualties increased considerably in 1955, when only two thousand guerrillas were still active in the mountains. The policy of food denial was tightened by "requiring that cattle be kept in guarded enclosures during the night and prohibiting the peasant cultivation of food crops within three miles of the forest."[117] This led to starvation of the guerrillas, many of whom subsequently lost their lives by being shot as they attempted to reach the reserves for food. Shortage of ammunition and lack of food considerably reduced the fighting capacity of the guerrillas, who were now being hunted deep into the forests by their former comrades. At this stage captured guerrillas were, in Henderson's uncharitable phrase, "lean and verminous";[118] they were weak, exhausted, and hungry. Government estimates show that by 1956 only five hundred guerillas were still at large.

These were for the most part a leaderless and undisciplined fighting force, a fact extensively exploited by the security forces.[119] The pressure on the guerrillas was never relaxed. Why didn't the government forget about the five hundred guerrillas in the mountains? The answer lies in the government's fear of them as a symbol of resistance and especially one of their major leaders, Dedan Kimathi.[120]

The capture of Kimathi now became an obsessive concern of the Special Force Teams under Henderson, for it was believed that so long as he remained free, he represented the unbeaten spirit of the rebellion. And so he had to be captured and eliminated to signify the ultimate defeat of Mau Mau. He was captured in Nyeri on 21 October 1956, and with that solitary event on the edge of the forest, the military offensive against Mau Mau had essentially come to an end.

It had been a violent and ruthless offensive. Afterwards the government supplied the following statistics: 11,503 Mau Mau killed,[121] 1,035 captured wounded, 1,550 captured in action, 26,625 arrested, and 2,714 surrendered. The rest of the statistics are as follows:

Security Forces Casualties	Killed	Wounded
European	63	101
Asian	3	12
African	101	1,469
Loyal Civilians		
European	32	26
Asian	26	36
African	1,819	916

Source: *Historical Survey of the Origins and Growth of Mau Mau* (The Corfield Report) (HMSO, 1960), p. 136.

With regard to Mau Mau, these figures are silent on the question of thousands of civilians who were "shot while attempting to escape" or those who perished at the hands of the Home Guards, the KPR, and other branches of the security forces. All these eventually came to be classified as Mau Mau.

FIVE

PROPAGANDA AND THE OATHS

The major aim of the government propaganda offensive against Mau Mau locally and internationally was to discredit African nationalism as being basically a criminal endeavor. The government also sought to show a direct linkage between Kenyatta, the most prominent nationalist leader, and Mau Mau. In the famous Kenyatta trial of 1952/1953, he was accused of managing an unlawful and secret criminal society. Also, Kenyatta had visited the Soviet Union between November 1932 and September 1933 and thus was automatically suspected by the colonial government and especially by the local white settlers as a communist. The settlers saw in Mau Mau a communist plot to take over the country using violence and intimidation. Occurring against the general background of the cold war between East and West, it was easy and expected for the settlers and their supporters to see communist plots behind every form of nationalist agitation.

The trial of Kenyatta, Oneko, Ngei, Kaggia, and Karumba officially opened on 3 December 1952 at Kapenguria in Rift Valley Province. To the colonial government, this trial was seen as a forum in which to demonstrate categorically that the recently declared state of emergency was justified. It was therefore a political necessity that Kenyatta and his associates should be found guilty and given long sentences. But before this could happen, the government had to mount a case against them. This was not easy. The difficulties lay in the fact that no solid evidence had been produced to link the accused to criminal activities or even to the main charge of managing Mau Mau. In desperation the government resorted to using the police to assemble as many "witnesses" as possible to testify against Kenyatta. Kaggia notes that Henderson, the notorious police officer, "was the man who collected all the prosecution witnesses during the three weeks before the trial and it was he who was responsible for assembling the prosecution evidence. He schooled the witnesses and chose about one hundred to come to Kapenguria,"[1] to testify.

These "witnesses" were not only schooled but also bribed. The governor notified the colonial secretary that "every effort has been made to offer them rewards and to protect them,"[2] although he wondered what would happen "when they are confronted in court by Kenyatta's formidable personality." The attorney general as Member for Law and Order was in constant communication with Ian Henderson about the hunt for witnesses and the "rewards" they would be offered. At some point before the trial, when assembled "witnesses" needed some guarantee of cash payment, he wrote to Henderson confirming that "cash grants will be paid to the witnesses immediately after the trial at Kapenguria."[3] The most celebrated case of bribery involved the Crown's principal witness, Rawson Macharia. Macharia was offered a package that involved two years' study at a British university and then subsistence for himself and his family plus the promise of protection and a government job upon his return to Kenya. "The value of the offer amounted to over £2,500."[4]

It was not only African witnesses that needed to be schooled and bribed. The trial judge had to be selected with care and with the understanding that he would convict Kenyatta and his associates. The government chose Ransley Thacker, a settler and a recently retired high court judge. He engaged in what were later described as "irregular activities" during the trial and stayed in Kitale Hotel in the White Highlands where he freely fraternized with fellow settlers. The judge also engaged in shady dealings with the governor, seeking to extract some financial reward for his services. Desperate to obtain a conviction, the government gave Thacker "an ex-gratia payment of £20,000 . . . drawn against some special Emergency fund on Evelyn's own instructions."[5] Quite simply, this was a bribe. In spite of all these efforts, the government failed to "cut Kenyatta to size" or to impress upon the Africans that these arrested political leaders were mere gangsters.

The evidence produced by the government was "pretty thin."[6] Few would dispute that Kenyatta, like most Africans and especially the Kikuyu at this time, sympathized with the general spirit of Mau Mau and its quest for political freedom and economic reforms. But at the same time it would be a gross overstatement and misrepresentation of facts to declare Kenyatta the leader of Mau Mau. "On all the evidence available then," Guy Arnold states, "and still more in terms of what has come to light later, Kenyatta was not the organiser of Mau Mau and was not responsible for it."[7] The government's frantic efforts to find incriminating evidence in the papers and books taken from Kenyatta's home during the arrest proved fruitless, nor were the police able to produce any evidence in spite of continuous surveillance of him since 1947.[8]

The Kapenguria trial was given immediate and significant international publicity through the defense lawyers retained by the KAU with the help of Fenner Brockway and Leslie Hale, British members of Parliament. It was a formidable team led by D. N. Pritt, Q. C. Pritt, a former member of British Parliament, was about the most widely known lawyer practicing in England in the 1950s.[9] He was supported by Diwan Lall from India, a personal friend of Nehru and a former Indian ambassador to Turkey, and H. O. Davies from Nigeria. Davies was the only black member of the defense team. Local talent included A. R. Kapila, F. de Souza, and Jaswant Singh. The world press was bound to show interest in a case that such formidable talent had been retained to defend. This international attention caught the government unawares.

From the start, Pritt's basic line of defense was that there was no criminal case to answer, that his clients stood accused as African nationalists, and that therefore this was a political case, with African nationalism on trial.[10] This point generated many heated exchanges in court and provided the press with ample material for coverage. Throughout the proceedings the Crown denied that this was a political trial, insisting that it was a criminal case: "Queen against Kenyatta and others for what is a crime."[11] The Crown argued that "it would have been the same if Queen against Kenyatta were for a felony or for picking a pocket!" In his sentencing of Kenyatta and his associates to seven years' imprisonment with hard labor, Thacker returned to this point of drawing a distinction between a political and a criminal case. He argued that although the accused had "engaged in politics over a number of years," this did not "make the trial a political trial." Rather, it was "an ordinary criminal trial on ordinary criminal charges."[12] This statement, however, did not assuage all doubts that had been cast over the trial by the African population and international sympathizers of African nationalism.

Pritt's reputation, stature, and defense strategy frustrated the government's aim of making the trial a quiet affair in a miserable courtroom in some isolated corner of Kenya. The court proceedings greatly increased Kenyatta's stature as leader of African nationalism in Kenya. The world press had put Kenya in the spotlight, and the government found it impossible to ignore it. In fact, the Crown in response to these new realities greatly adjusted its position on the case. Toward the end of the trial the Crown's counsel had altered its emphasis of merely branding the accused as leaders of a criminal society to describing in detail the atrocities allegedly committed by Mau Mau and the threat that it posed to Christianity and law and order.[13]

On the whole, however, the limited, positive publicity which African nationalism as organized under the KAU enjoyed during the Kapenguria trial, did not extend to Mau Mau. Kenyatta and his associates and their defense team all dissociated themselves from Mau Mau.[14] This dissociation haunted Mau Mau throughout the emergency. Even those external friends of African nationalism found it necessary to make a scrupulous distinction between Mau Mau and nationalism. Fenner Brockway, for example, found the origins and nature of Mau Mau profoundly disturbing.[15] Why was it necessary to make this distinction? The reasons lay for the most part in what the government, through its spies and missionaries, and the press reported about Mau Mau oaths, which were said to be central to the revolt's political and military offensive. "It cannot be denied," Fenner Brockway wrote, "that many of the practices of Mau Mau represent a reversion to a primitive barbaric mentality" and added that "this has shocked, perhaps most deeply, those of us who have cooperated in the political advance of Kenya Africans."[16]

Some of these "profoundly disturbing" aspects of Mau Mau emerged suddenly on the local and international scene in March 1953, before judgment was passed in the Kapenguria trial. On the night of 26 March 1953, Mau Mau guerrillas raided Naivasha police station in the Rift Valley and managed to overwhelm "the small garrison, released about 150 prisoners and captured a number of rifles and automatic weapons and a great deal of ammunition."[17] It was a brilliantly executed offensive, and the colonial forces felt humiliated and enraged. On the same night in Central Province in the village of Lari, there occurred perhaps the single most bloody episode against civilians in the war. According to official reports ninety-seven people in the village were killed, twenty-nine wounded, and forty-six reported missing.[18] Mau Mau was blamed for the massacre, although its activists have insisted since then that their target at Lari was Chief Luka and his family and fellow loyalists, not innocent civilians.[19]

In the tangled story that emerged, it would be an almost impossible task to divide the casualties accurately between Mau Mau and the government forces. What is undeniable is that Mau Mau murdered Chief Luka and his family and known loyalists in the village, leaving alone homesteads of nonloyalists.[20] In the ensuing battle that raged throughout the night, government forces no doubt enraged by Mau Mau attack engaged in bloody reprisals that led to more casualties. Even a pro-Home Guard government publication agreed later that "the number of terrorist casualties in the battle and pursuit after the massacre far outnumbered those of the loyalists and security forces combined."[21]

On the morning of 27 March 1953, as the local and international press converged on Lari in the smoldering ruins of the village, the destruction and massacre were presented to the world as the work of Mau Mau. It could be argued that the government welcomed the Lari massacre for it afforded it perhaps the most powerful propaganda issue yet against Mau Mau and its alleged barbarism. "The news of this atrocity," Michael Blundell later recalled, "had a profound effect in Great Britain and on the international scene." Specifically, Michael Blundell felt that "it largely eliminated sympathy for the Mau Mau movement" and also that "the concept of the noble African fighting for his legitimate rights against the wicked imperialists was difficult to sustain when the bodies of the Kikuyu women hacked to death and battered skulls of their children cried out the contrary."[22] What was not highlighted in the graphic tales about the Lari massacre was that the tragedy was linked to a land feud that had its origins in the land alienation schemes for settlers[23] and therefore that land continued to be the main drive behind the Mau Mau revolt. After 1953, the government propaganda offensive emphasized the barbarism of Mau Mau and its "bestial and pagan oaths" with the obvious aim of portraying the guerrillas as mentally deranged and morally debased beings.

Official propaganda was given considerable boost by the British parliamentary delegation to Kenya in January 1954, which later published a White Paper on its visit. In the report, the delegation characterized Mau Mau as "a conspiracy designed to dominate first the Kikuyu tribe and then all other Africans and finally to exterminate or drive out all other races and seize power in Kenya."[24] In the delegation's view, Mau Mau was a secret society which used terrorism and foul oaths to secure obedience. But it is the oaths that were crucial here. Their details and true nature were found to be so nauseating and objectionable as to be "unfit for general publication."[25] Leaving the details unpublished was just as effective as publishing them, for the public was left to indulge in extravagant imagination as to how foul these oaths really were and also to believe any stories and rumors that sounded incredible.

In London, the colonial secretary stuck to his opinion that Mau Mau was a secret society that was not "the child of economic conditions." According to him it was essentially "an anti-European, anti-Asian and anti-Christian" movement that committed the worst crimes "you can imagine."[26] If the revolt was not "the child of economic conditions," then the settlers and the government were not to be seen as the heartless villains whose policies had triggered the revolt but rather as victims of unprovoked barbarous assault by Africans under the spell of magic and foul oaths. This somewhat unrealistic and obviously false posture was adhered to by the government in open forums as it sought to steer the spotlight away from its policies to the oaths which the press covered extensively after 1953.

The administration of Mau Mau oaths can be divided into three stages. The first stage consisted of the unity oath administered throughout Central Province and among the Kikuyu in Rift Valley Province after the crucial meeting in 1950 of Kikuyu leaders at ex-Senior Chief Koinange's home. The second stage involved a modified form of the original unity oath and more crucially the introduction of the warrior oath, the Batuni oath, from about the middle of 1952. The pace of administration of this oath to many young would-be warriors increased tremendously after the declaration of the emergency in October 1952. The third stage consisted of what came to be known as the "advanced oaths" which referred to oaths beyond the Batuni oath. On the whole it would appear that these "advanced oaths" were introduced after 1953 and were generally administered to the forest fighters.

The unity oath was the general oath, administered extensively to as many Kikuyu as possible with the obvious intention of secretly uniting, disciplining, and fostering political consciousness among them.[27] It was a recruitment drive, secretly extending political consciousness and commitment to the nationalist struggle. It was executed secretly for fear of government reprisals. As a general rule, those who had taken the oath were expected to induce their friends to take it also.[28]

The ceremony itself was conducted under the cover of darkness in a hut by a designated oath administrator who was helped and protected by several armed men.[29] If possible an arch of banana leaves[30] was at the site of the ceremony, and all those to be initiated passed under it and passively responded to instructions from the oath administrator. These instructions generally started with the order to remove shoes, coins, watches, and other metal items. Each ceremony utilized meat and blood from a dead goat, and the initiate usually took the oath while holding "a damp ball of soil against his stomach with his right hand . . . a symbol of the person's willingness to do everything in his power to assist the association in regaining and protecting the land belonging to the Kikuyu people."[31] By 1952, increasing tension and rapid expansion of the oath-taking activities had led to a modification of this oath to the extent that its details were not uniform throughout Kikuyuland. However, the holding of a dampened ball of soil and the employment of meat and blood from a dead goat remained the standard. Also by 1952, the initiates were expected through this ceremony to be blood brothers,[32] and so they licked each other's blood or ate a piece of meat on which each initiate's blood had been smeared.[33] As much as the details of this oath may be fascinating, it is what the initiates swore to do that was of political importance.

The unity oath bound the initiates to obey the movement's leadership, to help recruit new members, and through subscriptions to pay sixty-two shillings and fifty cents to the movement. Initiates also swore never to reveal the details of the oath, never to sell land to Europeans or Asians, and to be of general use to the movement's leadership and to blood brethren when called upon. By 1953, according to Njama's account,[34] the initiates were expected to be of exemplary moral standards, refraining from intercourse with prostitutes and not abandoning a woman after making her pregnant. But they also swore by this time to defy specific colonial laws and policies, for example the Beecher Educational Report recommendations and government educational policy. The penalty for breaking or disobeying the oath was death. On one level death was expected to mysteriously overcome the disobedient initiate, for the oath was solemn and supposed to have semireligious and magical attributes. On a more immediate level, those who betrayed the movement and the oath would be killed by Mau Mau. As Njama and his group of initiates were reminded, "If you reveal this secret the Government will imprison you and we will kill you for the breach of the oath you have taken today."[35] The alternatives were clear: obey or perish.

The Batuni oath reemphasized the need for unity, but more specifically the initiates swore to kill on behalf of Mau Mau. They swore never to be afraid of waging war against the white man to recover "stolen lands." Secrecy again was insisted upon as crucial for the security of Mau Mau. Those initiated were expected to demonstrate considerable courage in action by, for example, participating in raids or bringing in "the head of an enemy."[36] These raids were to be directed against loyalists, resisters, betrayers, and of course Europeans and their property. It is significant to note that the definition of the enemy was wide enough to include "father, mother or sister"[37] if these were on the "other side."

Like the unity oath, the Batuni oath was administered by designated oath administrators in small huts in secret locations guarded by armed men. The contents of the two oaths differed substantially however. In the Batuni oath the rituals were more elaborate and more awe-inspiring. The initiate had to be naked, and for the first time a Mau Mau oath involved sexual symbolism and acts. Specifically, the initiate put his penis through a hole in the thorax of a skinned goat and repeated the vows of the oath.[38] He held the thorax of the goat with his left hand while with his right hand he took "seven small sticks, one at a time" and rubbed them into the thorax of the goat while he repeated the vows of the oath.

The Batuni oath was the second or advanced oath. It was administered to those who had already taken the unity oath and who were seen by the local Mau Mau leadership as likely to make good warriors. Not everyone who took this oath went to the forest[39] or brought in "the head of an enemy." Yet the very act of taking it demonstrated a higher sense of commitment to the cause of Mau Mau.

In its initial propaganda and calculation of strategy, the government looked at the unity oath as savage but relatively harmless. It acknowledged that some chiefs and a great number of Christians had been forced to take the unity oath against their will by "Mau Mau adherents . . . exerting economic-cum-social pressure on the non-Mau Mau by boycotting their shops, failing to contribute to customary communal assistance in hut building, etc."[40] In addition were Mau Mau's threats of physical violence for noncompliance, an effective practice while Mau Mau dominated the reserve areas of Central Province. Still, the unity oath was deemed harmless by the government because "it did not require the initiate to do anything, it merely demanded his silence and sympathy."[41]

The situation changed completely when the existence of the Batuni oath was reported in mid-1952[42] and when acts of violence by Mau Mau adherents directed against loyalists, Europeans, and their property became common. Settlers' fears were especially aroused by the Batuni vow urging the Kikuyu to fight and recover "stolen lands": the settlers interpreted this as a war cry to drive them out of Kenya. This was not only objectionable to them but intolerable. From then on, everything associated with the oaths became vile, savage, and decidedly criminal. Settlers felt that by introducing the Batuni oath, Mau Mau had become an intolerable danger and that its practices were no longer "mere exciting conspiracy," but rather the movement had been transformed into a "planned licentious venery."[43]

Subsequent government propaganda, while acknowledging the existence of these two stages of Mau Mau oaths, nonetheless dwelt on the "advanced oaths." The reasons are simple. These "advanced oaths" were generally held to be particularly foul and therefore likely to arouse the anger and disgust of the local and international audience against Mau Mau. The calculation was to emphasize what was seen as the worse aspects of Mau Mau and its oaths in a bid to deny it sympathy and allies.

The existence of these "advanced oaths" has always been a matter of controversy, especially among African nationalists. Prominent Mau Mau leaders either kept quiet about the subject or denied the oaths' existence, leaving open the suggestion that these oaths were either a creation of malicious imperial propaganda or isolated acts engaged in by desperate and unruly guerrillas. In his autobiography, *Mau Mau General* (1967), General China does not deal with these oaths nor does he give any details about the type of Batuni oath he took. H. K. Wachanga in his memoirs[44] gives details about the unity and Batuni oaths that closely correspond to those given by Karari Njama and J. M. Kariuki in their books. But he does not give any details about the advanced oaths or even his opinion about their existence or nonexistence. This is strange considering he acted as the Mau Mau general secretary in the forest.[45]

Kariuki asserts that the unity oath and the Batuni oath were the only "legitimate ones," although he does not categorically deny that the "advanced oaths" existed. He is correct, however, in remarking that "the 'evidence' containing these stories was largely compiled from confessions made in statements given either immediately after physical torture or in knowledge that such torture was possible and indeed imminent."[46] But this itself is not sufficient proof that all the information given under interrogation was false and fictitious. Indeed, most of the information about Mau Mau was obtained in this fashion; through torture, interrogation, spying, bribery, and general intimidation. It needs to be emphasized that it is the information obtained from confessions and interrogations that ultimately broke the supremacy of Mau Mau in the urban and rural areas of Central Province.

Mutonyi, one of the original members of the Mau Mau central committee believes that "if such oaths did exist, they must have been invented by individuals without authority of *Muhimu*, and possibly with active inducement from the colonialists who sought to discredit us."[47] It is clear from this statement that even some Mau Mau activists regard these "advanced oaths" as something to be ashamed of, and herein lies the controversy. The emphasis has been shifted from the utilitarian value that these oaths might have had during the emergency to whether they are acceptable today in circumstances of noncombat tranquility. It is clear that the existence of these oaths was not a creation of the central committee. But this is not by any means a unique occurrence in the revolt. Several facets of Mau Mau were not created or invented by the central committee; an example in point is the organization of the guerrilla forces in the Aberdares and on Mount Kenya.

The controversy about these oaths revolves around sexual symbolism and acts. Sexual symbolism in oaths was not new to Kikuyu culture. It was usual for certain "sexual taboos to be broken" when taking particularly important oaths. In Barnett's study he found out, for example, that "a person accused of killing through witchcraft had to submit, if he maintained his innocence, to a public oath in which he swore, while inserting his penis in the vagina of a sheep, that he did not commit the crime in question and calling on the wrath of Ngai (God) to destroy him if he were lying."[48] Barnett further notes that in a related case, "if a man were accused of having impregnated a girl and he denied it, he would have to swear publicly, while biting a piece of sweet potato or a tip of a bunch of bananas which had been inserted in the girl's vagina by an old woman, that if he had ever had intercourse with the girl, the oath should kill him."[49] Subsequent employment of sexual symbols and acts in the Batuni oath or the "advanced oaths" could be said to have occurred within the traditional cultural context of the Kikuyu people. These oaths administered during the emergency were not replicas of similar traditional oaths but rather were creative employment of traditional symbols and rituals in extraordinary and often bewildering war situations. It is therefore unlikely that these "advanced oaths" were "a European invention altogether," for as Rob Buijtenhuijs has observed, "The detailed descriptions in literature do correspond rather well to our current knowledge of Kikuyu culture."[50] Indeed, in a recent television interview Joseph Theuri, a former forest fighter, revealed that some forest fighters took these "advanced oaths."[51] These, according to Theuri, included eating meat which had been inserted in or rubbed against genitals, and even the drinking of human blood.

The details concerning "advanced oaths" were obtained, as already indicated, through interrogation, confessions, and information from government spies. Details obtained by confession teams were then delivered or leaked to the press, especially to the international press gathered in Nairobi. Churches also gathered such information and had access to government information about these oaths. In due course, Mau Mau became associated exclusively with advanced oaths, so much so that no government publication or article of the press or church communication during the emergency ever failed to mention the "foul oaths and barbarism" of Mau Mau.

Most of the information gathered from confessions or interrogations was apparently part of the numerous documents destroyed by the colonial government on the eve of independence. It has been alleged that this massive destruction of documents was part of the official strategy to protect the identity of informers and key loyalists from possible reprisals by the independent African government.

As it happened, no such reprisals were envisaged or carried out by the African government, and thankfully information on Mau Mau survived in private collections of colonial officials or of eminent church personalities who were involved with Mau Mau during the course of their duties. Officials whose private collections contain details about the Mau Mau's advanced oaths are Sir Frank Loyd and Rev. Canon Peter Bostock. Sir Frank Loyd was the D.C. in Nyeri in 1948, the D.C. in Fort Hall from 1949 to 1953, and the D.C. in Kiambu from 1954 to 1955. He later served as the P.C. of Nyeri from 1956 to 1958. Bostock served in Kenya for a long time as a missionary and official of the Christian Council of Kenya.

Bostock obtained information on the Mau Mau oaths from W. Scott Dickson, acting general secretary of the National Christian Council of Kenya. This information was circulated to all churches affiliated with the council. The aim was to let the churches have a relatively uniform version of the "advanced oaths."[52] This information was to be utilized in the churches' spiritual struggle with Mau Mau and also for propaganda purposes, specifically to demonstrate to the congregations the depravity of those engaged in armed revolt. Bostock's information,[53] which is basically the same as that of Sir Frank Loyd, was apparently "supplied by the Naivasha Screening team from information received from confessions."[54] According to this piece of information, Mau Mau had eight oaths.

The first and second oaths resemble the unity oath.[55] The third oath marks the beginning of what probably constituted the "advanced oaths." In the third oath, "a piece of meat is placed in the anus of an old woman and taken together with the oath." The fourth oath was, according to this information, the oath of captains in the armed revolt. During the ceremony, "the administrator waves his hand over the head of the 'victim' seven times. The eyes of the human head are then pricked seven times, and the fingers of the right hand of the dead man are bent seven times." Majors took the fifth oath in which "the brain of a dead man (African) is bitten and eaten seven times." The sixth oath was for colonels, and each initiate had "to drink the blood of menstrual discharge seven times." Brigadiers took the seventh oath in which "the brain of a dead man (European) is bitten and eaten seven times." The last oath, according to this information, was the eighth oath. It was taken by generals. The initiate had to "drink the urine of a woman during menstruation seven times." Also "the wrist bones of the left hand of a body are broken up and mixed with excreta and earth and blood, and are taken seven times."[56] Apparently no intercourse between the initiates and animals occurred, as was rumored.

Other versions of these oaths that have been retrieved do, however, point out the extensive use of women and sexual acts between them and the initiates[57] during the oath-taking ceremonies. It would be fair to say that these oaths, like the unity oath and the Batuni oath, were not uniform in details throughout Kikuyuland. Lack of uniformity suggests that improvisation or local circumstances determined to some degree the text of these oaths.

The administration of the so-called advanced oaths was limited to a small group of people—the forest fighters. Only a few Kikuyu had taken the Batuni oath before the declaration of the emergency, and after 1952 the fraction of those who eventually took it remained far smaller than that of those who did not take it. Indeed, by

1953, some oath administrators of the unity oath had not taken the Batuni oath themselves.[58] From this relatively small number, an even smaller fraction took the "advanced oaths." The aggregate number of such people is difficult to gauge, but it can be safely assumed that these oaths were administered after the tide started to turn against Mau Mau in 1954.

Isolated and besieged in the forests by an aggressive and persistent enemy, the forest fighters must have felt the need for more extreme oaths to demonstrate their courage and to rededicate themselves to the revolt. As defections increased after 1954, and confessions from former comrades revealed the secrets of the movement, it became necessary for those remaining in the forest to subject themselves to an even higher form of courage, dedication, and discipline. This was principally to prevent defections and surrender to the enemy, a strategy not particularly successful as subsequent defections, confessions, and pseudo-gangs amply demonstrated.

The forest fighters who took these oaths were desperate beings operating in a particularly hostile and trying environment. They turned to oaths for inspiration and endurance. Were they mad or perverted? Kariuki suggested that the few who took these oaths were "perverted individuals driven crazy by their isolation in the forests."[59] This is not accurate. Many of these forest fighters were not mad but rather beleaguered, and they resorted to local idioms through which they could find sense and meaning in their desperate position. The more desperate they became the more they "invented" extreme oaths to offset dwindling confidence and also probably to instill fear in their enemies. Outside the forest, however, these oaths were seized upon by the government and the media to discredit Mau Mau and the whole nationalist movement. No other aspect of the revolt was as discussed as these oaths.

The portrayal of Mau Mau in the foreign press, especially in Western countries, tended on the whole to emphasize the alleged "atavistic nature" of the movement. In its issue of 10 November 1952, *Time* magazine devoted two pages of pictures to Mau Mau. On one page was the picture of a dead cat "left hanging from a bent sapling in a forest clearing" which bore a threat "written in blood that any person who works for whites will be destroyed by the power of this oath."[60] The magazine also suggested without proof that Mau Mau were in the general habit of "nailing headless cats to their victims' doors."[61] This was seen as evidence of callousness and cruelty by the rebels, who reportedly also employed magic. *Life* magazine informed its readers that in Kenya, "natives use violence and voodooism to terrorize the British" and that although "Mau Mau embrace modern concepts of national independence, they go back to a primitive voodooism to gain their ends."[62] The foreign press characteristically concentrated on how the Mau Mau were rebelling rather than on why they were rebelling. Without discussing the reasons behind the revolt and exposing the British government's ruthless response, Mau Mau appeared to the world as a revolt without cause, except for the desire of Africans to kill, maim, and terrorize. The world was confronted with a murderous movement guided by voodooism and without cause or aim, "except to kill and disembowel as many whites, chiefs, headmen and non-Mau Mau Kikuyu as possible."[63] Portrayed thus, it was difficult for Mau Mau to be liked or tolerated.

The foreign press did not stop at merely showing that the revolt was senseless. Most coverage about the revolt consistently described, with emotive and graphic imagery, the killings attributed to Mau Mau. It was not enough to state that Mau Mau had killed people. As far as possible the stories never failed to mention that the victims had been "hacked to pieces." This tendency toward emotive and graphic imagery was particularly employed if the victims were white.

Throughout the emergency only thirty-two settlers were killed by Mau Mau, although the general impression created by the press and government propaganda seemed to suggest that the "highlands were strewn with eviscerated bodies of white settlers."[64] In those cases where settlers' murders were reported, emphasis was placed on the particularly cruel way in which these had been carried out, "usually with help from trusted servants." Settlers were depicted as betrayed benevolent employers. The Mau Mau were seen as striking not only "from their jungle hideouts" but also from the kitchen. "There is no way to be sure," Robert Ruark wrote, "that a servant is not a member of the secret terrorist society. The news may come some dark night when he opens the door to his fellow Mau Mau, who will chop you into small bits."[65] To be sure, there were servants who turned on their employers or facilitated the entry of Mau Mau into homes of their employers. But this was a relatively small number, and many Kikuyu house servants continued to work for settlers and other Europeans at the height of the emergency with no dramatic incidents. It would therefore appear that the general fear which "affected the European community was largely psychological."[66] All the same, stories spread by the press and other avenues of official propaganda were enough to create a large and vigorous pool of sympathizers for the settlers.

For the Western audience, it was easy to sympathize with their kith and kin in Kenya who were living in "lonely gimcrack homesteads"[67] and surrounded by rebellious Africans. The war against Mau Mau could not, however, be won if all the effort was directed at converting international opinion against the aims and strategies of the revolt. It was on the home front that the physical war would have to be fought and won. The government's propaganda machinery was mobilized to facilitate this military objective.

Immediately after his appointment as director of operations and chief military aide to the governor, Major General William Hinde recommended the establishment of a powerful propaganda machinery under central control.[68] This was to mobilize public opinion against Mau Mau by emphasizing government strength, power, and benevolence and highlighting the barbarism of the guerrillas. Hinde wanted government propaganda to turn women against Mau Mau and ultimately to get the Kikuyu people on its side.[69] The government agency charged with this responsibility was the African Information Service.

The information service in its strategy aimed both to frighten and encourage its audience. Propaganda, we must remember, is of little use unless it induces people "to behave in a specific way."[70] In this case, the information service wanted its audience to hate Mau Mau or at least be nonresponsive to its messages. This could be achieved only if the alleged atrocities of Mau Mau were widely publicized. After the Lari massacre in March 1953, this was done. The information service prepared what it called a "horror book" full of pictures of mutilated and horribly burned bodies that were said to have been victims of Mau Mau.[71] This horror book was "designed for tribes other than Kikuyu," although the Lari massacre was extensively and repeatedly used by the government propaganda machinery. In most of the leaflets about the massacre, there were lots of pictures of dead bodies that had been specifically chosen because of their potential to shock and disgust all those who looked at them. Having shocked its audience, the information service would then present government troops in a positive light as guardians of peace, refraining as far as possible from mentioning atrocities committed by these troops or the Home Guards. The aim was to show that in spite of its ruthlessness, Mau Mau was "being defeated rapidly."[72]

Other than leaflets and horror books, the government also utilized radio. The radio, not reliant on literacy to convey its messages, became a formidable tool and was used to spread official propaganda to far more people than would have been otherwise possible using the written word. As in all wars where the radio has been utilized, the government's objective was "to dominate rather than enlighten the public mind."[73] But lengthy commentaries on the evils of Mau Mau, however effective, could not be relied upon to sustain the interest of the listeners. And so the government radio resorted to appealing to what Hinde referred to as "the African sense of humour," although he thought that "in the case of the Kikuyu, it is not as strongly developed as in other tribes."[74] In a separate document, a government minister on the War Council elaborated on how and why radio drama and satire were to be turned against Mau Mau. "From the very beginning of the Emergency," the minister wrote, "it has been obvious that if we could make the Mau Mau movement a matter of ridicule, especially to other tribes, we should be taking a great step forward towards its elimination."[75] He cautioned that military offensive alone could not uproot Mau Mau from the hearts and minds of the Kikuyu. He recommended that the government should institute methods of "laughing the Mau Mau out of the African peoples' system."[76] This was to be done by utilizing the remarkable talents of a popular African radio comedian known as Kipanga.[77]

Kipanga's duty was simply to "make the Mau Mau movement a matter of laughter and ridicule to all Africans." He was to "get other African tribes laughing at the mumbo jumbo of sheeps' eyes, banana skins, drinking of blood and some of the nastier practices of Mau Mau,"[78] and thereby help to achieve what was referred to as "a psychological victory over the power of the movement." As he entertained, satirized, and laughed at Mau Mau, Kipanga was supposed to be preparing a general "frame of mind in which the African and the Kikuyu in particular, says to himself, 'I took the oath, I drank the blood, but of course it did nothing to me.' "[79] Kipanga's radio drama and satire was supposed to demystify the power of the oath and portray Mau Mau as an object of ridicule. Civilian hatred of the revolt was important in denying the guerrillas local "passive support" and in reinforcing the activities and power of the Home Guards. Propaganda erected a barrier between the civilians and the guerrillas and their messages. As much as this was an important military strategy, the actual fighting depended, of course, on the soldiers and the Home Guards, and these were not exempt from official propaganda.

Soldiers, it has been said, do not define the enemy; they leave this task to the politicians.[80] It is the politicians who isolate particular groups of people and communities and instruct their military forces to attack and destroy. Sam Keen correctly argues that ''as a rule, human beings do not kill other human beings'' and therefore ''before we enter into warfare or genocide we first dehumanise those we mean to eliminate.''[81] In war situations, propaganda takes on the responsibility of dehumanizing ''those we mean to eliminate'' in order that they may be killed without producing guilt in the soldiers or their civilian bosses. In the war against Mau Mau, all soldiers, and especially the British soldiers, were given a summary of the ''causes of the revolt'' by the government. But more importantly, these soldiers were given information about the guerrillas' use of foul oaths. As expected, the ''causes of the revolt'' emphasized that educated Africans had cunningly used their ignorant brethren to launch a murderous campaign against a lawfully constituted government. The emphasis, however, was on the cruelty of the guerrillas acting under the spell of foul and unspeakable oaths.[82]

Many of these British soldiers arrived in Kenya with very little information about Mau Mau. Frank Kitson, who later played a crucial role in the formation of pseudo-gangs, recalled that as he waited in Britain for his flight to Kenya, he read a few newspaper stories about Mau Mau. Now it will be recalled that many of these stories were part of the negative portrayal of the revolt in the international press. He remembered seeing the picture of Kenyatta as ''the leader of the revolt.'' ''Unfortunately, he had appeared in an animal skin carrying a spear,'' so Kitson had ''a distorted idea of the rebellion from the start.''[83] After his arrival and the subsequent talk by his superiors about the revolt, Mau Mau became associated in his mind ''with all that was foul and terrible in primitive savagery.''[84] Official propaganda therefore succeeded in dehumanizing the guerrillas and ensuring that the soldiers saw them not as people but as agents of evil. In killing them, the soldiers were killing an evil idea; thought had been paralyzed. This is a common practice in military psychology where ''the enemy is not merely flesh and blood but devil, demon, agent of the dark forces.''[85] William Baldwin's views on Mau Mau clearly reinforce this point.

William Baldwin arrived in Kenya with no knowledge at all about the country or the background of the revolt. An American drifter who was broke, he was forced to join the GSU (General Service Unit) to finance his eventual journey to the United States. After only a few months in Kenya, he had formed a negative impression of Mau Mau. ''The Mau Mau had given ample proof that they meant to destroy what Europeans had created in Kenya.''[86] Baldwin thought that ''there were enough backward areas in the world without allowing a group of ignorant, murdering lunatics to add one more to the already formidable list.''[87] He was fighting Mau Mau in order to save civilization.

On one occasion, Baldwin and his group chased some Mau Mau guerrillas reported to have killed a mother and her child in particularly horrible circumstances. When they found them, the guerrillas were ''dressed in filthy rags and covered with sweat and blood,'' and ''they looked like wild beasts of the forest.''[88] After killing them, Baldwin reflected on his feelings.

I tried to analyze my emotions toward the dead men. Hate? A bit, perhaps. Anger? Some. Disgust? Yes, more so than hate or anger. But more than anything I looked upon them as diseased animals, which if left alive, were a constant menace to the community. Only in death was a cure possible.[89]

He had killed the men to save them from their own foul deeds and the community from the menace of these "diseased animals"! It is this need to justify murder, torture, harassment, and general intimidation of the suspected rebels which was behind the government's propaganda to dehumanize Mau Mau guerrillas. If the world and the local audience were convinced that the military forces were fighting cruel agents of evil, then any military effort to defeat the enemy, however extreme, would probably be excusable as a regrettable necessity.

It was clear during the military offensive against the revolt that the government's propaganda among the soldiers had been successful. As the troops fought in the forests they looked at their operations as a "big game-hunt, the Kikuyu as a particularly clever species."[90] General Sir George Erskine had issued instructions to his soldiers emphasizing that "the qualities which must be developed in troops engaged against the Mau Mau are . . . those required to track down and shoot shy game."[91] It should be remembered that a basic point of dehumanization is to give the victims of hatred and propaganda a new, almost nonhuman identity. This has been true in many wars in the past and even present times. During the Second World War, for example, "before the Japanese performed medical experiments on human guinea pigs . . . they named them *Maruta*—logs of wood."[92] In the war in Kenya, Mau Mau guerrillas were looked upon by the government and the military forces as "beasts of the forest."

On another more speculative and opportunistic level, the government and the settlers freely floated the idea that the leadership of the revolt, identified as Kenyatta and his associates, was either communist or communist-inspired. This was a speculation that was taken seriously even by the Colonial Office. The suspicion, of course, lay in the fact that Kenyatta had visited the Soviet Union and was therefore assumed to have imbibed the "red gospel." Less than a month after the declaration of emergency, *Time* magazine informed its readers that Kenyatta had spent the 1930s in Moscow "as a student guest of the Kremlin" and had later returned to Kenya "to spread the Red gospel."[93] Although the article provided no proof of its allegations, it was, however, bound to register considerable impact on an audience living under the international tension of the cold war between East and West in the 1950s.

The Colonial Office in London finally addressed itself to the question "Is Mau Mau communist-inspired?," on 7 July 1953.[94] Mau Mau could only be communist-inspired "if the leaders . . . followed the doctrine and practice of any Communist Party" or if the "movement was supported or sustained by Soviet or satellite organizers and arms."[95] The Colonial Office concluded that there was "no evidence for any of these beliefs." Mau Mau was "set in a purely African idiom," and although its ritual (oaths) had "drawn further and further away from known Kikuyu practice," this had been in "the direction of savagery, not of Marxism."[96] In this document, the Colonial Office also determined that although Kenyatta had visited Moscow in the 1930s, there was nothing since then "to suggest any link with communist theory." These conclusions did not stop the rumors or the suspicions which the settlers and government officials clung onto fervently without proof. The Colonial Office document was an internal secret memo that was never publicly announced. The chief civilian and military officers were informed of these conclusions but allowed the suspicions about communism to linger in hopes of using them as yet another damming weapon against the revolt. Such strategy is characteristic of most propaganda campaigns, which not only are biased and deceptive but also rely on "misinformation and indifferences to truth."[97]

This "indifference to truth" continued many years after the declaration of the emergency in statements by officials of the local administration in Nairobi and even by former Colonial Secretary Oliver Lyttelton. In his memoirs, Lyttelton insisted that Kenyatta was "a daemonic figure with extreme left-wing views"[98] and that Mau Mau guerrillas received support and money from the Soviet Embassy in Addis Ababa, Ethiopia.[99] This is surprising, considering that the Colonial Office document that discounted links between communism and Mau Mau or Kenyatta had been written while Oliver Lyttelton was the colonial secretary.

The propaganda campaign against Mau Mau must rank as one of the most concerted and excessive assaults against a nationalist movement in post–Second World War Africa. The roots and causes of the revolt were submerged under tons of official and nonofficial propaganda. It is the killings attributed to Mau Mau that graced newspapers, official reports, and Sunday sermons. In the end, Mau Mau was equated with the devil. After restating that "the Mau Mau oath is the most bestial, filthy and nauseating incantation which perverted minds can ever have brewed," Lyttelton concluded that he could not recall any instance when he had felt the forces of evil to be so near and so strong as in Mau Mau."[100] "As I wrote memoranda or instructions," Lyttelton recalled years later, "I would suddenly see a shadow fall across the page—the horned shadow of the Devil himself."[101]

It can hardly be denied that the major objective of this negative portrayal of the revolt was to deny it any legitimacy or respectability. Consistently, Mau Mau was portrayed as a criminal, ruthless, secret society whose members were savages that committed the "worst crimes you can imagine." But the constant reference to Mau Mau being "anti-Christian and anti-white" suggests that the authors of this propaganda had specific knowledge of their audience and their prejudices and biases. In propaganda campaigns, "the audience must not only be capable of receiving information or opinions, but it must also possess the potential ability to respond in a manner desired by the propagandist."[102] The propagandist therefore seeks to capitalize on the residual fears, biases, and prejudices of his target audience. In the campaign against Mau Mau, much capital was made of the revolt's alleged assault on civilization, culture, and of course Christianity. The excesses attributed to Mau Mau were given as an example of the revolt's savagery, callousness, inhumanity, and lack of consideration of others. By being cast as anti-Christian, Mau Mau became the archetypal enemy usually perceived as "atheist and barbarian, a denier of

God and the destroyer of culture."[103] This message obviously struck a responsive cord in the Western audience.

The agents of propaganda during the revolt came from Western countries and shared their Western cultural values, prejudices, and biases. It can therefore be safely argued that their relative uniformity of hatred against Mau Mau must be traced to this common cultural heritage together with the selfish interest of wishing to maintain settlers in power over Africans.

To be sure there was racism and bigotry, for "as a rule of thumb, since the Industrial Revolution the technological nations have tended to view any peoples who did not have electricity, machine tools, and indoor plumbing as morally inferior and somehow lower on the scale of human evolution."[104] But above this, there was a cultural bias and intolerance against unfamiliar practices of non-Western people whose actions were condemned especially when they threatened white dominance. Oaths, especially those involving sexual symbolism and acts, were immediately condemned as the work of the devil. What was particularly fatal for the revolt was the linkage of Mau Mau to "advanced oaths." This linkage stifled any rational, objective discussion of the revolt. The focus on oaths was sensational and damning to Mau Mau.

Mau Mau did not have a comparable propaganda machine to challenge the distortions that were actively spread about it or to explain its practices. It relied on the oaths to "spread the word," but this proved ineffective against a well-orchestrated modern propaganda campaign. Later revolutionary movements in Africa like the MPLA of Angola, FRELIMO of Mozambique, and PAIGC of Guinea-Bissau had overseas offices and representatives who engaged in their own propaganda campaigns. Mau Mau did not have any external office or indeed an internal office to plan its publicity and propaganda offensive. Abroad it relied on sympathizers of African nationalism, but in no time these sympathizers, including prominently Fenner Brockway, made a clear and determined distinction between nationalism and the revolt. They condemned Mau Mau practices as barbaric and harmful to the nationalist cause.

SIX

MAU MAU MILITARY AND POLITICAL STRATEGY

During Kenyatta's trial there had been a faint hope that with the help of his powerful lawyers he might be released and resume his political activities. This hope was dashed on 8 April 1953[1] when he and his associates were given long prison sentences. In Central Province, the White Highlands, Nairobi, and other areas with large Kikuyu populations, the mood of the people was immediately transformed from guarded optimism to desperation. This desperation heightened as the government embarked on its counterinsurgency operations in 1953. It is in these conditions of desperation, fear, panic, and anger that the widespread, open Mau Mau revolt was born.

Indeed there had been oath-taking for action, even armed action, but before the emergency there had not been a general revolt of the Kikuyu against the British. In this regard, it may be accurate to argue that "the final resort to violence was provoked by the Emergency, rather than the cause of it; that only the arrival of troops, the arrest of political leaders, and the imposition of harsh emergency measures (including forced repatriation of squatters) drove the Kikuyu into open revolt."[2] Partly in desperation and partly in angry defiance, the Kikuyu refused to be subdued by "an increasing settler fury."[3] The Kikuyu demonstrated this angry defiance by withdrawing to the forests where Mau Mau then launched its armed revolt. It is the groups that withdrew to the forests, sometimes willingly, sometimes through coercion or fear and for varied periods of time, that the British armed forces fought from 1952 until 1956.

The entry into the forest was not an orderly or organized activity. Other than the initial entry of Dedan Kimathi, Stanley Mathenge, General China (and their initial followers), the rest of the people who became guerrillas entered the forest in a haphazard, uncontrolled manner. This entry into the forests of Mount Kenya and the Aberdares was, as Donald Barnett has stated, "a reaction to external stimuli rather than the unfolding of a well-laid plan for revolutionary action or guerrilla warfare,"[4] and hence there was no mechanism for controlling and directing the entry of the youth and other militants to the mountains. This stage of the revolt was further complicated by the fact that not all those who entered the forest did so with a view to waging war against the British.

The overwhelming majority of the forest guerrillas came from the reserves of Central Province.[5] Some of them were landless peasants or peasants with small holdings, and many were young men. These young men had taken the warrior oath and had been active in oath-taking activities in the reserves prior to the emergency. As the British began to tighten their grip on the reserves, these young men, eager and motivated, drifted to forests adjoining their home areas to seek refuge from British brutality. Their entry into the forest was therefore a mixture of a commitment to fight and a desire for "safety and protection traditionally afforded by the forest."[6]

Not every youth entered the forest voluntarily. Some were coerced by the local underground Mau Mau committees or by representatives of groups already in existence in the forests. These youths "were captured by force to fight"[7] with the guerrillas. Naturally, it was this group that fell prey to offers of surrender from the government and who, together with other reluctant recruits, became members of pseudo-gangs as the revolt entered its most difficult stage after 1954.

The squatters from the White Highlands swelled and fueled the ranks of the guerrillas, for the forests offered them protection and food. They drifted into the forest angered by the loss of their land in the Highlands or in Central Province and aware that in the initial stages of the revolt the forest was a much safer place than the reserves. The urban centers also contributed a substantial number of guerrillas, though far fewer than the reserves of Central Province.[8] Many of these urban dwellers were "first generation urbanites who had recently left the reserves"[9] and were therefore essentially peasants. But why did all these groups drift to the forest?

For the militants, forests were to be their chief base area from which to organize guerrilla activities against the enemy. The forest has been identified as the best base area for guerrilla warfare.[10] It is generally impenetrable, dark, and if accompanied by rugged mountains, it affords a superior barrier against enemy attacks. It allows the guerrillas the security they need to build and organize their forces away from enemy interference and harassment. In Central Province from 1952 to 1956, the forests of Mount Kenya and the Aberdares were the only areas that offered natural protection from the British security forces. The peasants withdrew into them as a tactical retreat and felt safe for a while from enemy attacks. But as already stated, not every peasant drifted into the forests to fight. Some "were not much motivated by idealistic or political considerations, but rather were escaping from Government repression in the Reserves"[11] and did not realize that "the struggle might last two or three years."[12] It is therefore not surprising that many of these people, although residing in the forest, "continued to place primary importance on personal safety and survival."[13]

Initial organization of the forest forces was largely a reflection of the manner in which these various groups had drifted into the forests. As individuals, or small groups of friends or kinsmen, they withdrew and wandered through the forests often without knowledge of the existence of other groups. From October 1952 to May 1953, the various groups of guerrillas had no organizational framework by which to link their military and political activities with groups in other parts of the forest or to formulate concrete short- and long-range political goals. The result was seven months of random, intimidating violence and general confusion.

These initial groups relied on their relatives in the reserves for information and, more crucially, for food. They established camp in forests near their home areas and reacted to events in their home areas with more interest than to those in outlying areas. So, although there was a state of emergency throughout Central Province and the Highlands, for the individual guerrilla there was a tendency in the first seven months to particularize the impact of the emergency to events in his village, location, or division. Activities by guerrillas at this time, therefore, tended to be influenced by a more personal assessment of the immediate locality. In determining, for example, who the enemy was, they could not look for and identify enemies beyond their immediate environment. It was the chief or headman of their location or village or a notorious Home Guard who was their immediate target.

Organizational structure of these early groups was essentially simple and rudimentary, characterized by a loose union of small groups of often related individuals from the same area. As for the qualities of the leader, a premium was placed on the individual's personal reputation. This, however, was not an accurate way to determine the military and political capabilities and creativity of the individual. The leader had to organize raids into the reserves for food, clothing, and information and to institute discipline and coherence in his group. Under such circumstances the various groups throughout the forests developed different organizational structures, some groups being more coherent than others. The military training, activities, and preparedness of these groups also tended to differ.[14]

A significant change in the organization of the forest groups occurred starting in March 1953 when the initial small groups "began to give way toward . . . more tightly organized groupings concentrated within a number of large, permanent camp-clusters."[15] The reasons for this change were grounded in survival. Small independent groups realized they lacked adequate ammunition and could not withstand enemy onslaught alone. There was the inevitable acknowledgment that these groups were fighting the same enemy. The formation of these permanent camp-clusters was a voluntary act on the part of the groups, and the leaders that arose from these unions formed the first real military leadership of the forest guerrillas.

Members of these larger groups, like those of the initial small ones, were either relatives or originated from the same sublocation or location. The basis of their union was either area of origin or kinship ties. In May 1953 this change in the organization of forest guerrillas led to the formation of the first district-wide military unit: the Utuma Ndemi Trinity Council and Ituma Ndemi Army (the Nyeri district council and army), which chose Stanley Mathenge as chairman and head of "Ituma Ndemi Army," and "the rank of General was issued to six major camp-cluster leaders."[16] This was the first attempt to give coherence and order to Mau Mau forest forces since the declaration of the emergency. It had taken seven months for this to occur, and even then this was still limited to Nyeri forces alone. Meanwhile, the various independent and semi-independent forces had been waging war in the form of raids with varying degrees of effectiveness in the reserves. The Mau Mau movement in the forests would forever be haunted by events of the first seven months of the revolt. A spirit of unregulated independence had emerged among the various camp-clusters, whose leaders were jealous of their independence and would later resist any efforts to unduly regulate or diminish their power and prestige.

There was also the uncomfortable fact that no single individual or organization in the forest had directed the entry of the various groups to the mountains, and therefore no one among the leaders could claim automatic preeminence over the others. In spite of these obstacles, the need for a more unified response by the forest groups to British counterinsurgency operations continued to be felt. It is this need that gave rise to the Kenya Defense Council.

Through the initiative of Dedan Kimathi, the Mau Mau forces in the Aberdares convened the now famous Mwathe meeting in August 1953. After eight months of general revolt, it had become obvious to the several camp-cluster leaders that some form of unified strategy was needed to enable them to confront British forces effectively. The Mwathe meeting brought together military leaders who had led their independent units for about a year and were unwilling to surrender this independence even if the need for unity (especially military unity) was recognized as a desirable ideal. These independent units had established organizational and structural patterns which probably would have to be dismantled or considerably altered if the Mwathe meeting ever hoped to achieve meaningful unity. This drastic need was side-stepped and instead "the Kenya Defense Council and the formal military hierarchy it created, . . . tended to legitimize rather than alter the positions previously held by the guerrilla leaders."[17] The meeting, however, formally recognized eight Land and Freedom armies, "their commanders and area of operation," and attempted to formulate a general military strategy.

It was immediately apparent that the Kenya Defense Council did not have power or command over the behavior of various sectional military leaders and their still independent Land and Freedom armies. Besides, not every guerrilla unit had been represented at this meeting. The Mount Kenya forces under General China, although formally recognized as just another of the Land and Freedom armies, operated in practice as a separate military unit from the Aberdares' forces. Mount Kenya forces under General China did not feel themselves to be subordinate to the Aberdares' leadership.

Perhaps more damaging to the envisaged unity was the lack of "an administrative and enforcement machinery" by the Kenya Defense Council. Without an "enforcement machinery" it was impossible for the council to ensure that its resolutions and directives were uniformly adhered to and implemented. Much was left to the goodwill of the various leaders to interpret and enforce the council rulings and directives as they deemed appropriate. This was a voluntary military union whose directives could be disregarded with impunity and with few, if any, penalties. There were also smaller but still significant units that were not represented at the meetings. Their activities did not benefit from even the ritual endorsement of the council nor did they feel obliged to seek its recognition. The Kenya Defense Council did not have the authority or power to dislodge any military unit from a particular geographical position or to order its disbandment. The fortunes of the council were further complicated by the refusal of Mathenge to attend this meeting.

Mathenge felt that Kimathi had overstepped his authority by convening the Mwathe meeting, for he regarded Kimathi as his clerk.[18]

The unity thus created by the meeting was symbolic and not effective. It provided a desirable framework within which to work toward a credible, effective unity in the forests. In the absence of "enforcement machinery," Kimathi was quick to recognize that any semblance of unity would have to be solicited through diplomacy. It is with this in mind that he toured the several armies in the Aberdares to establish personal relationships with individual leaders who would then give him their loyalty. This loyalty could be withdrawn at any time, and furthermore Kimathi did not gain the loyalty of individual guerrillas independent of their leaders. He did not have independent access to the guerrillas and spoke to them only through their leaders.

By the end of 1953 it had become sadly apparent that the Kenya Defense Council was not as effective as originally desired. It had difficulty convening meetings partly because of its large membership and also because its members were so widespread in the forests and difficult to contact at short notice. Problems of communication remained even with the aid of couriers. It is against this background that Kimathi and other forest leaders made yet another attempt to organize for unity. The new body was called Kenya Parliament.

Kenya Parliament was formed in February 1954 and was composed of thirteen members, many of them from Nyeri district. This small and restricted leadership enabled Kenya Parliament to meet more often than the Kenya Defense Council but yet denied it widespread authority over those forest armies outside Nyeri district or even from North Tetu Division in Nyeri. Barnett found that of the thirteen members of this new body only six came from outside the North Tetu Division of Nyeri district.[19]

Among the council's tasks was "reinforcing unity and developing objectives"[20] of the revolt. It also specifically hoped to place Land and Freedom armies under its control,[21] in order that politics might control the warriors and their weapons. On a more ambitious level, Kenya Parliament saw itself in 1954 as a body that would eventually evolve into a "legitimate interim African Government of Kenya."[22] The name of the body was symbolic of the hope rather than the fact; certainly it could not lay claim to any national representation in its ranks. There was an urgent need to expand the revolt outside the Kikuyu "cauldron," and Kenya Parliament as a name was deliberately chosen to appeal to the national sentiment.

The effectiveness of Kenya Parliament, although greater than that of the Kenya Defense Council, was again hampered by the independence and power of the various forest leaders. Submission to its directives was voluntary and could only be secured through diplomacy and appeal to a personal loyalty that each of the "cooperative leaders" had toward Kimathi. Its eventual fate was sealed by the refusal of some key Aberdares military leaders to submit to its authority or recognize its significance. Prominent among these defiant leaders were Mathenge, Kahiu-Itina, and Kimbo.[23]

By the end of 1954, unity among the forest guerrillas had not been realized. There had been several valiant attempts to this end, but none had managed to avert or nullify problems of personality, ego, jealousy, power-rivalry, and kinship ties that continually stood in the way of a united front. Neither the defense council nor the Kenya Parliament had led to any "greater coordination of activity." As for Kenya Parliament, it certainly "represented the ideal of a central organisation, rather than an effective legislative and executive body,"[24] and it would therefore be wrong to look at it as representing the golden era of unity in the forest.

In spite of failure to achieve unity of command and coordination, forest guerrillas, in small and large groups, managed to wage ferocious attacks on government forces in the reserves, principally in Central Province but also with isolated attacks in the Highlands and the urban areas. These attacks eloquently illustrate not only the courage and creativity of the forest guerrillas but also the limitations of their strategic initiatives.

"Guerilla warfare," Gerard Chaliand writes, "has consistently been the choice of the weak who oppose the strong" because "it enables them to avoid direct decisive confrontations and rely on harassment and surprise."[25] The story of guerrilla warfare is one of surprise attack, ambush, and withdrawal to a safe base. The weak resort to guerrilla warfare because of their inability, at least in the initial stages of the conflict, to "present organized army opposition"[26] to better-armed and organized forces of the enemy. Yet these "ill-armed, ill-trained and ill-clad bands" have sometimes succeeded "against superior forces led by professionals."[27] Mau Mau guerrillas although unable in the end to triumph militarily over "superior forces led by professionals," relied on harassment, surprise, and ambush in their battle against government forces.

A consistent strategy of Mau Mau guerrillas was to harass and intimidate the non-combat population into active support for the cause or into neutrality. Most of their efforts were expended on neutralizing the effects of resisters or betrayers as they quickly came to be known. The betrayers had to be eliminated to ensure that they did not gain converts and threaten the viability of opposition and armed resistance. This was a strategy which Mau Mau militants had employed since 1952 to thwart overt opposition to the oath-taking campaign. Fred Kuabi has recently revealed that at the height of the oath-taking campaign, before the state of emergency was declared, there existed local district liquidation squads who eliminated traitors.[28] Even after the emergency had been declared and guerrillas had established themselves in the forests, elimination of traitors continued to be the chief military objective of Mau Mau guerrillas. The drive for the ever elusive goal of Kikuyu unity in support of militant nationalism and now armed revolt never diminished.

Because the guerrillas operated in their home areas, they were able to isolate traitors and eliminate them quickly. Such eliminations also acted as a deterrent to would-be traitors. But in strategic terms, it was more than this. It was a demonstration of the guerrillas' power to inflict punishment on the enemy. In guerrilla warfare, there is an inescapable need on the part of the guerrillas to demonstrate to the sympathetic or coerced population their power and ability to engage the enemy. Only through such acts of awe-inspiring courage and power can the local population be convinced that the guerrillas are viable and that they can survive.[29] In Central Province the guerrillas held the initiative from 1952 to 1954. What does this mean?

During this period Mau Mau guerrillas operated with little overt opposition from the local population. The government forces had not been deployed to any effective degree in the reserves, and the sheer forceful presence of the guerrillas ensured a shaky supremacy. Now it should be remembered that this was not because the local population uniformly and unanimously supported the revolt. It was far from that. What was apparent was that there were few people to challenge militarily the dominance of the guerrillas. The guerrillas exploited the common and widespread hatred of government insensitivity and failure to grant economic reforms, and especially its failure to address the land problem. This sympathy enabled the guerrillas to be sheltered, fed, and supplied with information. But even during this period when Mau Mau was said to have the initiative, government forces were starting to make inroads into Mau Mau territory. The establishment of the Home Guards, spies, and the expansion of administrative centers and personnel eventually provided a focus of opposition against the guerrillas. This increased the need on the part of the guerrillas to demonstrate their presence and power in the reserves and cities, especially in Nairobi. By 1954, the Kenya police's annual report noted that "murders of loyal tribesmen was almost an every day occurrence."[30] By 1954, the reserves became a severely contested territory between the guerrillas and the government forces.

As for the local population, there was the urge to survive. There were reports of "tribesmen constantly changing sides." Unable to defend themselves against either the guerrillas or the government forces, the local population had to be on good terms with both until one of them established permanent preeminence. "If the Mau Mau bands happen to make their presence in an area felt more strongly than the government forces," Colin Legum observed, "the peasants take new Mau Mau oaths and change their allegiance. As soon as the government forces return in strength, the oaths are solemnly repudiated."[31] Mau Mau had determined that loyalty to the cause would only be extracted and maintained by coercion or threat of violence. The guerrillas never varied much from this general strategy. But it was a strategy which could not be relied on to measure the local population's commitment to the revolt in general or to the particular manner in which it was being executed.

A consideration of Mau Mau military and political strategy clearly shows that the guerrillas failed to link their military exploits to political mobilization. There was an underlying assumption that the local population already knew the causes of the revolt and therefore needed no constant reminder. The unspoken message was that everyone knew why the guerrillas had taken up arms, and now the task at hand was to fight. It is as if the military effort was seen as a step higher than the political effort in the drive toward regaining land and freedom. H. K. Wachanga, one of the major leaders in the Aberdares, states that the oath was their central leader, and that "through it we had a strong unifying force. It bound us together and gave us direction in our struggles and hardships."[32] The oath may have offered the guerrillas inspiration in their hardships, but as subsequent events clearly demonstrated, it was not an adequate substitute for an elaborate politicization campaign before and during the revolt. Guerrilla warfare depends ultimately on the support furnished by the "passive wing," the politicized but not necessarily combatant section of the population. This support is secured through propaganda, education, and organization of the revolutionary movement before the guns become active, before the shedding of blood.

A description of Mau Mau military exploits[33] shows that whenever the guerrillas invaded an area their main emphasis was to eliminate traitors, to collect food, and sometimes to administer oaths. In the hurried circumstances after 1954, these oath-taking ceremonies were usually impromptu activities conducted by a varied group of people whose politicization efforts were never adequate.[34] They were mass baptismal ceremonies agreed to by the local population, not as a demonstration of their absolute commitment to the revolt but as a way of avoiding possible reprisals from guerrillas. When Wachanga led a large raid on Gakindu market in Mukurweini Division in September 1953, his group took "all the goods they could carry and about Shs. 5000."[35] Wachanga and his group did not make any efforts to recruit the shopkeepers to their cause or to seek for their neutrality in the conflict. There was a tendency by the guerrillas to condemn people outright and not to realize that in any guerrilla war people change their positions constantly. Former enemies can change and become great comrades!

Mau Mau guerrillas were unable to exploit to their advantage the contradictions in the reserves among the Home Guards and loyalists. At the start of the emergency there were Home Guards who sided with the guerrillas,[36] but this became rare as the revolt expanded and the government increased its forces. The Home Guards, as discussed in chapter 4, had different origins which were not necessarily congruent. It is possible that these contradictions could have been exploited by Mau Mau to cause a rift in the counterinsurgency operations.

In their relations with African troops, the guerrillas also failed to induce any significant defection of these troops to the revolt. Although as Wachanga says, their methods of torture and killing were developed with a view to frightening the enemy troops,[37] they also made it difficult for these troops to crossover. In all the evidence available, there is no mention of a significant effort to induce defection of enemy troops to the revolt. The little contact made between these two sides that was not hostile was commercial. This involved the buying of weapons from poorly paid African troops, police, and Home Guards.[38] Most of this commercial activity was handled by Mau Mau's passive wing.

In emphasizing the military offensive only, even at a time when they still held the initiative, the guerrillas failed to realize that triumph for them and their cause was impossible if unaccompanied by a political message and a constant politicization of the passive wing. In analyzing a similar problem in Guinea-Bissau, Amilcar Cabral noted that political work was fundamental to the struggle, "so fundamental that . . . every shot fired is also a political act."[39] In the case of Mau Mau there was an unfortunate tendency to regard its work as merely to fight, creating with it a definite militarist spirit. Militarism, as Mao noted, erroneously leads the guerrillas "to regard military work and political work as opposed to each other"; and "to fail to recognize military work as only one of the means of accomplishing political tasks."[40] Guerrilla warfare is essentially a political war, and military efforts are important only as they advance the political agenda. Of course, Frantz Fanon has argued that violence in revolutionary war has extraordinary value to the individual combatant whereby it "frees the native from his inferiority complex and from his despair and inaction" and "makes him fearless and restores his self-respect."[41] But if this violence is outside a political program, or if it is not properly organized or orchestrated, it can degenerate into mere spontaneous violent outbursts that may deter the advancement of the political agenda.

Although Fanon praised violence as an avenue to national liberation in Third World countries, he also condemned spontaneity. He was at pains to emphasize that politicization of the masses was an indispensable component of a successful revolutionary war and that the uncontrolled heroic deeds of the lumpen proletariat or the peasants could not deliver victory. "The scattering of the nation," Fanon wrote, "which is the manifestation of a nation in arms, needs to become a thing of the past" and that the leaders of the rebellion should realize that "even large scale peasant risings need to be controlled and directed into certain channels."[42] Fanon warned, "You won't win a national war, you will never overthrow the terrible enemy machine, and you won't change human beings if you forget to raise the standard of consciousness of rank and file." His conclusion: "Neither stubborn courage nor fine slogans are enough."[43] Measured against such an appraisal, Mau Mau military efforts appear to be spontaneous and lacking in coherence. This is not to say that they were muddled or lacking in imaginative creativity. They were however, a composite sum of separate military initiatives by different camp-clusters that had no adherence to uniform or standard techniques, rules, and regulations.

Some of these separate military initiatives can be seen in the way the war was fought in the reserves, the Highlands and the cities. In Kiambu district there was far less military activity by the guerrillas than in the other districts of Central Province. The explanation lies in the diffuse nature of the guerrillas' organization. Guerrillas from Kiambu, under the leadership of General Waruingi, went to the forests "but they never comprised more than a few hundred fighters and were never integrated into the Mau Mau hierarchy under Kimathi and Mathenge."[44] Their activities were, on the whole, controlled by the local council of the passive wing and elders "who prohibited the killing of loyalists or traitors without council consent."[45] The local council acted to avoid reprisals from "government policy of collective punishments" whose results were seen as having "had a beneficial effect"[46] to counterinsurgency operations.

Nyeri district was, on the other hand, "over represented in the forest"[47]; it had the largest number of guerrillas in the forest. It was therefore inevitable that there should have been more clashes between guerrillas and government forces in Nyeri than in Kiambu. This difference in the level of military activity led the D.C. for Kiambu to remark cynically that during the emergency the inhabitants of Kiambu district had been "more interested in trade, litigation, corruption, intrigue, fitina, and politics than in receiving the crown of martyrdom."[48]

In Murang'a district the guerrillas, although fewer than those from Nyeri, tended to be more "aggressive,"[49] basically because their chief leader, General Kago, operated in the reserves and became a major thorn "in the side of the security forces." After his capture and execution even the colonial security forces conceded that Mau Mau had "lost their most daring leader in the Reserves."[50] These different levels of activity grew inevitably out of Mau Mau's inability to achieve a general military command. The results of this setback were tremendous.

Mau Mau's various military commanders did not respond to events in unison or even after consultation with other commanders but as they saw fit in their areas. The result was that it was difficult to mount a united armed assault on the enemy. Without coordination, these various military initiatives, although deadly, had their general effects minimized by the concerted and overwhelming response from the government forces. One of the few times that Mau Mau planned a united assault from the Aberdares was on 25 June 1953. According to Wachanga, the guerrillas "destroyed many bridges, killed enemies, stole livestock and goods, and burnt many houses" leaving Central Province "silent and sad the next morning."[51] The results of this raid were not as dramatic or effective as Wachanga has alleged. No evidence exists of mass destruction of bridges or of Central Province having been left "sad and silent" after the raid. In fact, Njama's account of the incident is more somber. The raid, according to Njama, who was present at its planning and evaluation, was a failure. It failed because of fear on the part of the guerrillas but more specifically because of the "superstitious beliefs which were being taught by the witch-doctors that if a deer or a gazelle passed across the path of a group that was going to raid, it indicated bad luck and the warriors should abandon the plan."[52] On the way to the reserves, a deer and a gazelle crossed the warriors' path twice, prompting them "to put off the raid."

There was also no agreement as to the area on which to concentrate attacks and harassment. As early as the Mwathe meeting of August 1953, Kimathi had suggested that more raids be directed at the Rift Valley on settlers' farms. This suggestion was never enthusiastically received. Some generals were afraid of starving in an area they did not know well.[53] But there were also personal motives on the part of the leaders for wishing to remain in Central Province, especially around their home areas. Wachanga believes that some of the leaders "enjoyed the company of women"[54] and therefore chose to fight near home where they would have an "easier life." Without agreement as to the area to be attacked, it was impossible to determine or control the level of progress against the enemy. The warriors fought where they chose and maintained their own level of enthusiasm, which no "big leader" would influence to any appreciable degree.

As the revolt dragged on, parasitic and criminal elements in Central Province emerged and took advantage of Mau Mau's diffuse and incoherent organizational structure. These criminal elements were called *komerera*.[55] They operated in small gangs on the edge of the forest and robbed the local inhabitants of their property while masquerading as Mau Mau. Their ruthless methods did little to endear the Mau Mau to the victims who believed that komerera had some connection with the revolt. Some of these criminal elements may well have been "in the pay of the Home Guards,"[56] but many of them were independent entrepreneurs who saw an opportunity to benefit themselves by fishing in troubled waters. Genuine confusion arose when by 1955 Mau Mau guerrillas were raiding the reserves for food and supplies to the extent that the former passive wing became sick of the war and looked at the "Mau Mau movement as evil."[57] In the urban centers criminal elements arose and collected money and supplies for personal profit[58] in the name of Mau Mau.

The "big leaders" could do little to stop criminal activities because they did not know the criminals, and besides, some of their own guerrillas were engaged in komerera-like activities after 1955.[59] This increase in criminal activity by the guerrillas underscored the revolt's inability to define its membership or to control the course of events. The initiative Mau Mau had held up until 1954 rapidly eroded after that and was replaced by desperate acts and efforts to survive in an increasingly hostile forest. In the initial stages of the revolt in 1953, Mau Mau had launched two memorable assaults at Naivasha and at Lari.

The Naivasha raid stands out as the distinctly major military success of the guerrillas throughout the revolt. Captured weapons were sorely needed in the mountains, although there was some squabbling before they were divided among the raiders.[60] The Lari massacre, on the other hand, was a mixed blessing. Although, on the one hand, a prominent loyalist was eliminated, the guerrillas were unprepared to respond to the propaganda offensive that the government launched in the wake of the massacre.[61] It was a great offensive, but it surely must be seen as a tactical blunder, for it failed to take into account the response of both the "fence sitters" and active supporters who may have been affected considerably by government propaganda. Denials and protests by guerrillas from the forest could not compete with a calculated and well-orchestrated official propaganda complete with photographs and "eye-witness" accounts.

In both of these assaults, there was no evidence that they were individually or collectively part of an overall strategy. They appeared to be rather isolated episodes and not the unfolding of an elaborate strategy. Mao warned that in a revolutionary situation, "The plan of the first battle must be the prelude in the plan for the whole campaign and forms an organic part of it."[62] There must be some connection between the first battle and the whole campaign strategy and further that isolated and uncoordinated battles, however heroic, cannot deliver victory. "Even though victory is won in the first battle," Mao observed, "if the battle prejudices the entire campaign rather than benefits it, then the victory in such a battle can only be considered a defeat."[63] It would be unfair to look at the battle at Lari in 1953 as "a defeat," but all the same it unleashed in the conflict issues which Mau Mau was not qualified to handle; it could not handle the repair of its public image tarnished by government propaganda nor could it convince the "fence sitters" who started to go to the loyalists' camp, that the revolt was viable and disciplined.

Loss of initiative by the guerrillas from 1954 was chiefly the result of major government military offensives in Nairobi and the reserves. Operation Anvil in April 1954 disrupted the lifeline between the city militants and the guerrillas. This lifeline, although vital, was not particularly elaborate and organized nor was the relationship between the two factions formal. There does not appear to have been any overall coordinating body that funneled supplies to the mountains. Rather, what was apparent was that relations were at the district or locational level, and it is the locational committees in Nairobi that strove to furnish the guerrillas in the mountains with "arms, ammunition, medical supplies, clothing and money."[64] Lack of overall unity of the militants was evident in both the urban centers and the forests. Operation Anvil severed the link between urban centers and the forests and left the guerrillas with no window to the world and no alternative source of supplies. It was in 1954, then, that the guerrillas were driven to the inner depths of the forests.

The forests initially had been a wonderful base area, but as government troops pursued the guerrillas deep into them, the revolt entered its most difficult stage. Not self-sufficient in food and supplies, the guerrillas were surrounded and hunted. They did not have "a liberated zone" in the reserves, and so their contacts with the passive wing became more sporadic and even hostile. The enemy had brought the war to them, and they could either surrender, fight and drive back the enemy, or fight to "the last man." The entry of government forces in the forest completely disorganized Mau Mau's tentative though problematic steps toward unity. Large camp-clusters generally were disbanded, and most guerrillas returned to their initial small groups now dispersed throughout the forest. The preoccupation of these groups became survival, with the hunt for food a major preoccupation. Suspicion in guerrilla ranks increased tremendously as former comrades "turned-coat" and led government troops to the forest. The animosity among leaders, which the Kenya Defense Council and Kenya Parliament had tried but failed to resolve, rose to the surface. It was therefore inevitable that extraordinary methods would have been tried to save the revolt from utter collapse and also to revitalize the military offensive. Chief among these extraordinary methods was the use of witchcraft in military matters.

Magic and witchcraft formed an integral part of the traditional Kikuyu military organization. It would appear that every armed unit had magic powders and potions dispensed by *mundu mugo wa ita* (The army's medicine man).[65] The medicine man was also the chief military consultant, for apparently no war could be initiated by warriors without consulting him. Among other things, he advised them on "which routes they were to take and what omens to avoid."[66] The subsequent employment of witchcraft and magic by Mau Mau guerrillas must therefore be seen as rooted in their traditional culture. Embarking on a major revolt in hurried circumstances, most guerrillas naturally resorted to the organization and strategies they knew or had some information about: the traditional Kikuyu organization. It offered them an immediate frame of reference. This is not to imply that their forest organizations were a replica of precolonial Kikuyu patterns. They were, however, like most initiatives of the guerrillas, an improvisation of strategy, an approximation of traditional structures and values under the strained circumstances of the emergency. But if the guerrillas tried to incorporate their cultural structures (and even values) in their organizational patterns and strategies why didn't they receive overwhelming endorsement from Kikuyu leaders? The answer must lie in the impact of colonialism and especially Christianity on the Kikuyu.

In one of the most fascinating comparative studies on African revolutionary movements, Terance Ranger determined that, in the case of Zimbabwe, the guerrillas relied heavily on traditional religion. "Peasant religion," Ranger states, "formed an indispensable part of the composite ideology of the war."[67] This "peasant religion" was manifested through traditional spirit mediums who played a crucial role in the radicalization of the peasants even before the war, because "the mediums symbolized peasant right to the land and the right to work it as they chose."[68] It was the spirit mediums who brought together "peasant elders, who had hitherto been the local leaders of radical opposition" and the young guerrillas who "entered each rural district, armed with guns and ready to administer revolutionary law."[69] The political message carried by the guerrillas had to be crafted with regard to the pre-existing radical disposition of the peasants and created and maintained by a spirit medium whose eyes were fixed on the land. Endorsement of the guerrillas and their goals by the elders gave them legitimacy and the vital help they needed from peasants. The *Chimurenga* (war of liberation) in Zimbabwe was therefore a modern people's war that took care to advance its goals "within the idioms of radical peasant consciousness."[70] This did not happen in Kikuyuland.

There was no formal linkage between Mau Mau and traditional religion because "the Kikuyu had been so profoundly influenced by mission and independent Christianity that they had little but the most marginal religious 'traditions' to draw on."[71] There were no venerable traditional spirit mediums to offer focus to peasant radicalism nor were the "tribal elders" inclined to endorse the revolt. Other than the efforts of Ex-Senior Chief Koinange, at the start of the oath-taking campaign, no "tribal elder" of stature among the Kikuyu endorsed the revolt. It so happened that the "tribal elders" were no longer those who had stuck to their traditional customs, but they were the chiefs, evangelists, the educated elite, and other propertied persons. Power, influence, and prestige had shifted toward these groups away from undiluted traditional institutions. These new "tribal elders" failed to embrace Mau Mau.

In the forests, lonely, harassed and outgunned by the enemy, the guerrillas relied more and more on the predictions of seers and *mundu mugos* (medicine men) and even on witch doctors after 1954. General China had revealed in his interrogation that prophecies of witch doctors influenced Mau Mau war efforts.[72] Kiboi Muriithi talks of Roda, a female seer, who "would warn the forest fighters not to approach a certain spot as the enemy would be patrolling." He concludes that "her predictions were always right,"[73] and many guerrillas relied on her for guidance. Njama was disturbed by the power of the witch doctors and seers on the military conduct of the guerrillas. Many of them believed that the seers were "God's messengers" and to disobey them would be tantamount to violating a solemn religious injunction. Njama also discovered to his painful dismay that Mathenge believed in witchcraft,[74] and thus there was little chance of the revolt's leadership condemning reliance on seers. This reliance on the seers, prophets, and witch doctors becomes all the more crucial when an examination is made of Mau Mau's offensive against the government's transport and communication infrastructure which, in any war circumstances, should have been considered a legitimate military target.

Throughout the revolt no attempts were made by the guerrillas "to derail the trains on the main line of the Uganda Railway, although the route traversed through the Kikuyu Reserve: no roads were blocked; no bridges destroyed,"[75] although all these were vital to the government's war effort. Che Guevara considered that "one of the weakest points of the enemy is transportation by road and railroad," and that "a considerable loss in lives and material to the enemy" can be caused by planting at any point "a considerable amount of explosive charge."[76] Such losses slow down considerably the rate and volume of the enemy's offensive. In the war in Kenya, the guerrillas did not engage in any substantial sabotage, although even the government expected them to do so as part of their military strategy.[77]

During his interrogation, General China was asked by Ian Henderson why Mau Mau had not tried to derail trains. He answered that this was for the same reason the British did not bomb the reserves.[78] This surely is not a satisfactory answer. Earlier on, in October 1953, General China wrote a personal letter to his former boss at the East African Railways Corporation. In the letter he spoke of his many hardships since leaving the corporation's employment, troubles which led him to the forest.[79] He informed his former boss that he had not attacked trains because he did not see "any mistake of the government of E.A.R."[80] He was more interested in what his boss thought of him. "How do you think about me?" General China asked.

Wachanga, on the other hand, states that the refrain from sabotage of the transport and communication infrastructure was because the guerrillas did not want their people in the towns to suffer.[81] Again, this is not a satisfactory answer. The African residents in Nairobi, Nakuru, and other towns did not have electricity in their homes, and so loss of electrical power would have caused minimal hardships. The European and Asian residential and commercial districts would have suffered, but these belonged to the enemy.

There is, therefore, good reason to argue that the absence of any substantial sabotage is attributable to Mau Mau's reliance on seers, prophets, and witch doctors for strategic calculation and planning. These seers failed to realize the military significance of electricity, railways, and roads, and since the guerrillas relied on the seers for guidance they could not embark on unsanctioned exploits. Lack of sabotage must be seen in retrospect as one of the most costly prices the revolt paid for relying on witch doctors. It allowed government troops to move uninhibited on unguarded roads and rails and to extend roads right into the mountains. These roads brought the war too close and allowed government troops to "encircle and annihilate" the guerrillas. Before the final "encirclement and annihilation," guerrilla leaders engaged from 1952 to 1954 in some considerable discussion and correspondence about the political aims of the revolt.

Any discussion about Mau Mau aims in the forests must inevitably pay special attention to the few and scattered writings of Dedan Kimathi. Kimathi, as already indicated, emerged as one of the primary leaders of the revolt and one whom the government propaganda identified as the overall leader, a misleading claim since the revolt never had a supreme leader in the forest. Kimathi was behind the commendable efforts to create the Kenya Defense Council and Kenya Parliament and hoped that these would form the central organs of the revolt. In both efforts he achieved minimal success, and the revolt rumbled along without a supreme commander or organization. If Kimathi was better known than the rest of the leaders, this can be attributed to the fact that many letters were written in his name by Njama and also because his tours to various Land and Freedom armies in the

Aberdares made him the most widely known leader to the guerrillas. There is also the contention by Wachanga that "some actions taken by others were attributed to him" so that, for example, "after a Mau Mau action, many times notes were left, claiming that the action taken had been by Kimathi."[82] As a result, his name became better known than those of the rest of the big leaders. Kimathi became the symbol of the revolt in the forests. But this was a nonexecutive characterization, and however brilliant and commendable his efforts may have been, he must still be seen as only one of the "big leaders," although he may have been "bigger" than the rest of them.

To say this is not to diminish Kimathi's place in the armed revolt, for no one can ever do that, but rather to portray accurately the man and the struggles he endured as he undertook to coordinate and articulate the aims of the combatants and those whom they thought they represented. Indeed, because most of the surviving literature from the forest days is linked with Kimathi, we have a better picture of him than of the rest of the leaders. Karari Njama, considered to have been the most educated person in the forest, ended up as his general secretary and later co-authored a fairly sympathetic appraisal of his former boss. The result is that it is through these writings that we can gain a glimpse into the revolt's aims as they were articulated during the forest days. Other leaders of the revolt do not seem to have held views contrary to those expressed by Kimathi.

One of Kimathi's first letters published in the local press was the one dispatched to *Habari za Dunia*, a Nairobi Swahili newspaper whose editor was W. W. W. Awori, also a member of the Legislative Council and a former official of the KAU. It was published on 28 August 1953. Other than the rather inaccurate claims he made about going "round throughout Africa for three months" and also being a member of the "Defense Council of the whole of Africa, the Kenya Branch, and also being President of all branches,"[83] the letter contained some vital points. He observed that government harassment of people in the reserves had enabled Mau Mau to increase "a thousand times in the forests" and that "young men and women and even old men are in the forests for fear of being killed or badly beaten or being arrested."[84] He also condemned racial discrimination and the lack of an African political organization, factors which made "everyone side with the Mau Mau."

In a recent publication, Maina wa Kinyatti has released *The Dedan Kimathi Papers*.[85] This slim book contains, according to wa Kinyatti, a small fraction of Mau Mau papers, the rest having been confiscated by the colonial government and not scheduled for release until 2013 A.D. Maina wa Kinyatti contends that the letters and papers he translated and edited are "factually accurate and wholly authentic," having obtained them from "Kenyans who had them in their personal libraries."[86] Of course, he does not release the names of these Kenyans nor does he disclose the current location of the original documents. It is hence difficult to wholly endorse the authenticity of these "Kimathi Papers." Some of the letters, especially the Kenya Land and Freedom Army Charter (KLFA Charter) of October 1953[87] come close to being the revolt's manifesto. However, in their study Njama and Barnett found that "unfortunately, the Movement issued no manifesto"[88] during its turbulent life.

Perhaps the revolt's most elaborate aims and aspirations were promulgated in the letters between Kimathi and General China after his capture, when General China sought to induce Kimathi and the Aberdares' guerrillas to accept talks for surrender.[89] The chief reason for the revolt according to Kimathi and Kenya Parliament was land. The war was about land in the Highlands and other "stolen lands" in the reserves. The war could only be stopped if the British government granted full independence "under African leadership and also handed over all the lands to Kenya citizens."[90] On the vital question of reprisals against loyalists and Home Guards after the war, Kimathi's reply was important in light of what later came to happen in the country.

"If we achieve land and freedom," Kimathi wrote to General China, "we would forgive all the *thata cia bururi* (loyalists, traitors, Home Guards, etc.). . . . After all, we are certain that all these loyalists are our real brothers, sisters, parents, in-laws, and our beloved friends."[91] Certainly they were not such "beloved friends" as the war raged on, but Kimathi concluded that "blood is thicker than water," thereby opening the way for a possible reconciliation between the two sides. Land and freedom remained the consistent aims of the revolt. In their letters, Kimathi and General China reflected on the economic basis of the revolt in urban and rural areas and the general disgust over the country's racial discrimination, that could be ended only by attaining political freedom.

The propagation of these aims remained the preserve of Mau Mau's leaders, mostly through the writings of Kimathi (his letters especially) and the resolutions of Kenya Parliament. These meetings of Kenya Parliament were not "tidy, democratic, parliamentary sessions." They were poorly organized gatherings at which the leaders made decisions and presented them to their followers. Such decisions were never questioned by the ordinary *itungati* (soldiers, guerrillas, guards). The guerrillas followed orders.[92] Kiboi Muriithi, a fairly prominent guerrilla during the revolt, recalled discussing his reasons for going to the forest with his mother. He wanted freedom of movement without harassment, freedom to attend European schools, and he also wanted to see "Kenyatta as the Governor" of Kenya.[93] Were these aims different from those expressed by the KAU up to the time of its proscription in 1953? Evidence suggests that the aims of the guerrillas and those of the KAU were more similar than has hitherto been acknowledged.

In principle, the KAU endorsed the idea of political independence for Kenya from as early as 1947. Admittedly, this was not seen by the KAU leadership as an immediate possibility, and even up to 1951 in its last major memorandum "it never asked for independence" but rather for the return of "stolen lands."[94] By 1953 the prevailing wisdom of the KAU leadership was that independence would not be granted soon.[95] The guerrillas in the forest picked up this idea of independence, and in all their communiqués they never failed to mention it. They were simply reemphasizing, with persistence, an idea which the KAU had already embraced.

The guerrillas did not have a program of action aimed at seizing power in Kenya. As their efforts in negotiations indicated, they envisaged that a negotiated compromise would be reached with the colonial government, a compromise that would include the release of detainees, withdrawal of troops from the reserves, and finally the granting of independence.

On the question of land, the guerrillas like the KAU continued to demand the return of stolen lands, which now included the White Highlands. There were differences, however, even in the forest as to who would be entitled to these stolen lands in independent Kenya. These differences can be traced to the power struggle among the forest leaders and also to the role of literacy in the revolt. Kenya Parliament was composed largely of semiliterate leaders and left out illiterate leaders who felt rightly or wrongly that they had been edged out because of their illiteracy. These illiterate leaders, who included Mathenge and Kahiu-Itina, objected to Kimathi's leadership and argued that in the event of independence, the " 'White Highlands' should be returned [sic] over to the Rift Valley squatters and labourers."[96] Kahiu-Itina and his colleagues later formed *Kenya Riigi*, a group opposed to Kenya Parliament, whose focus was a return to old Kikuyu customs. Kahiu-Itina wanted the revolt and independent Kenya to be led by illiterate leaders.[97]

There was thus no agreement as to how land in general and "stolen lands" in particular would be distributed in independent Kenya. Wachanga's belief was that "all freedom fighters in the forest, prisons and detention camps would be given cash compensation and free land"[98] with those who had "suffered greatest" being given "the greatest rewards."

Discussions in the forest about freedom and land were general and not specific; they do not represent clear-cut policy pronouncements but rather general wishes. In their ideological orientation, guerrillas in the forest had not advanced beyond the general positions held by the KAU nor had they formulated any program of action to be followed in independent Kenya. Because they did not liberate any area during the revolt, they were denied the necessary laboratory to try out their ideas about freedom and social and economic organization.

What must never be forgotten is that the guerrillas and their splintered leadership never looked at themselves as supplanting the KAU leadership in detention or prison. They never laid claim to the nationalist political leadership. It would be accurate to look at them as interim militant bearers of the nationalist spirit. In all their songs in the forest,[99] there is no denunciation of the old KAU leadership and its aims. In fact, in the songs categorized as "detention songs" they sang with praise about their national heroes who had been detained on 20 October 1952 and specifically of their leader who was, of course, Kenyatta.[100] A general mistake would be to look at the guerrillas as a party or group of people who aimed to provide leadership with aims and objectives radically different from those endorsed by the KAU.

In their unsuccessful negotiations with the government, the guerrillas and their leaders never presumed they could negotiate the future of the country or even the terms of a cease-fire without the endorsement of "their leaders." Kimathi and Kenya Parliament informed General China to let the government know that before any agreement could be reached Jomo Kenyatta and other nationalist leaders had to participate in the negotiations.[101] When Wachanga and his group engaged in the last protracted negotiations with the government, they immediately demanded to meet "their political representatives" who included Mathu, John O'Washika, and W. W. W. Awori, all members of the old KAU leadership.[102]

In spite of its problems and setbacks, the Mau Mau revolt had several strong points and could be said to have scored some significant indirect victories. At the outset it must be mentioned that the guerrillas fought against tough odds. For over three years they fought the government security forces with unflinching determination and unaided by any external source; indeed they were shut off from the rest of the world. If "the existence of a sanctuary just over the border is almost essential and always highly desirable"[103] for a successful guerrilla war, then Mau Mau must stand out as one of those few struggles in modern times to have functioned without such an outlet. The revolt functioned entirely without external friends or influence nor did it receive any arms from outside the country. No correspondence existed between any external body or government and the guerrillas; indeed they were never recognized as a legitimate liberation movement by any government or international organization. Theirs was a lonely struggle fought in the reserves and mountains.

At the start of the emergency the government thought it would crush Mau Mau in a short time. The tenacity of the guerrillas made this impossible. What is remarkable is that they fought with very few modern weapons. The guerrillas were outgunned throughout the duration of the revolt. *Pangas* and *Simis* (long, sharp double-edged knives) and occasional pistols were no match for Bren guns and automatic rifles. This mismatch in weaponry ultimately broke Mau Mau's effectiveness, for it became obvious that firepower must be matched by firepower to score a victory. Mau Mau was found lacking in this department.

If Mau Mau fought with no overall coordination nor grand strategy, their ability to harass and intimidate government forces and Home Guards must surely be seen as remarkable. Even when raiding for food, the guerrillas managed to cause enough insecurity in the reserves that no one felt safe. In fact, the level of insecurity in the reserves was their other unheralded weapon. They attacked small Home Guard posts continually and generally established an aura of ruthless courage. Their attacks may have been small and isolated, but they were continuous. The stationing of the armed forces in the reserves up to 1956 is clear testimony of this fact.

The courage of the guerrillas in battle was never doubted. Even Ian Henderson, perhaps the revolt's most prominent enemy policeman, praised what he called their "bush craft," which he thought had reached "a superlative standard." He mentioned the guerrillas' ability to run in the forest "at staggering speed."[104] They had learned to evade enemy attacks so well that when the army launched its massive attacks in 1955 the results were disappointing. By 1954, the guerrillas were at home in the forest; they had learned how to survive. Life in the forests, as all guerrillas will testify, was difficult.[105] The Mau Mau guerrillas had little food, no source of clothing or medicine, and when the security trench was dug around the forest edges, they were literally cut off from the world. That some of them survived in these adverse conditions is evidence of their remarkable courage and resourcefulness. "They trapped wild animals" for food and also "caught trout with which the Europeans had stocked the mountain streams."[106]

Up to 1954, the revolt, although never universally popular nor supported by all Kikuyu, had "captured their imagination as a 'liberation force' which, despite its ruthless methods, seemed to promise some prospect of obtaining new lands for the land hungry peasants."[107] It represented a possibility of success, a possible breakthrough in the perennial struggle for land and economic reforms. As a method it was of course ruthlessly suppressed by the government with the aid of the Home Guards, but questions about its causes went unanswered. The government eventually had to address itself to the grievances that had sparked the revolt. This was done in spite of Oliver Lyttelton's untenable thesis that Mau Mau was "not the child of economic conditions." This could be seen as the revolt's ultimate success: it forced the colonial administration to listen to African complaints and to set out to institute reforms. These reforms were part of the government's rehabilitation program.

British financial expenditure and military commitment to combat the revolt led to a rethinking of the whole colonial situation. This expenditure, calculated at £60 million,[108] was intolerable if it meant an infinite commitment to maintain the settlers in power. It persuaded even "influential Conservative political figures in Britain to bow to the wind of change in Africa."[109]

Meanwhile, events occurring outside the forest started to drastically undermine Mau Mau's effectiveness from 1955 on. In 1955 limited political activity by Africans was again allowed in Kenya. Africans could form district-based organizations, although "at this time'. . . among the Kikuyu, the Embu, and the Meru of the Central Province, only an advisory council composed of Loyalists" was permitted.[110] Nonetheless, this was seen as a significant step toward possible change in the future. Dominated militarily in the reserves, the inhabitants of Central Province had no alternative but to watch the unfolding of yet another avenue to reforms. At this time they had lost the inclination or perseverance to support an armed revolt.

In the urban areas, the trade union movement under Tom Mboya had emerged, after the proscription of the KAU in 1953, as the only political forum open to Africans. Although Mboya condemned the violence of the "terrorists" and firmly dissociated his union from Mau Mau activities, he all the same resisted pressure to denounce it in unqualified terms.[111] He and his union had emerged as the African "voice," and he denounced colonial policies and called for economic reforms—increased wages, better housing, a halt to squatter evictions. He denounced "collective punishments of villages" and "confiscations of cattle."[112] It is not surprising that these developments, alongside government economic intervention in Central Province especially through a massive land consolidation program,[113] weakened considerably the support the revolt initially enjoyed.

These developments had tremendous repercussions in the guerrilla ranks. Government amnesty for surrender in 1955 came at a time when the military effectiveness of the guerrillas had largely been nullified by the successes of the security forces. Morale was low, organization further splintered. Many guerrillas had either surrendered or been captured as they entered the reserves in search of food. Many had been killed in clashes with government forces that now penetrated deeper and deeper into the forest with former guerrillas leading the way. It was in this tension-ridden situation that the last attempt at coordination of the guerrilla forces was made in the Aberdares in March 1955. At this meeting, Kimathi was given the title of prime minister, with the understanding that Mathenge or Kimemia (another "big leader") would assume the title of field-marshall. Mathenge did not participate in the meeting, nor were the now much-splintered guerrilla forces brought any closer after this exercise.

The split widened with the formation of Kenya Riigi, the organization under Mathenge and Kahiu-Itina that stood opposed to Kenya Parliament and Kimathi. Kenya Riigi, composed largely of illiterate leaders, wanted to negotiate surrender terms with the government. Kimathi stood opposed to these negotiations because, according to Wachanga, he wanted to "lead the negotiation himself."[114] The lowest point in guerrilla strategy was reached when Kimathi ordered the arrest of Kenya Riigi leaders.[115] They were caught but eventually escaped and continued the negotiations until they broke down in May 1955.

Throughout 1955 internal squabbles intensified in the forest as guerrillas found themselves on the defensive and fighting for personal survival. All organization broke down, and the need for more effective leadership was sorely felt. When Kimathi was shot and captured in 1956, the war in the forest had largely come to an end. The guerrillas had been militarily defeated, and untold misery had been inflicted on the people of Central Province. However, the need for reforms had been urgently pointed out by the revolt. These reforms, as already mentioned, came to constitute the government rehabilitation program.

PART THREE
Rehabilitation, Independence, and Legacy

SEVEN

REHABILITATION

It was clear from the start that the government's rehabilitation program in Kenya would be significantly influenced by British experience in the rehabilitation of communist guerrillas in Malaya. Rehabilitation efforts in Malaya offered a technique that, with due adjustment, could be effectively utilized in Kenya. T. Askwith, a commissioner for community development, was dispatched to Malaya to study and observe this process.[1] The ''Malaya pattern'' of rehabilitation was, in turn, broadly based ''on the system successfully used with communist prisoners in Greece.''[2]

Rehabilitation of former Mau Mau guerrillas, detainees, and prisoners proceeded from the official premise that the Kikuyu had been ''tainted with terrorist doctrine'' and therefore had to be ''decontaminated.''[3] They had to be made to renounce not only violence but also Mau Mau and its aims. The government was outspoken in its aim to create a new Kenya, a new society in which violence and support from Mau Mau would be completely absent. It was the official view that if the rehabilitation process proved a success, then the formula could ''be applied to the whole tribe of 1,500,000 Kikuyu and other tribes.''[4] The African population in general, and the Kikuyu in particular, had to be educated on the benefits of alien rule. Now one would have hoped that after the revolt the colonial government would have ceased singing the glories of imperial domination. This did not happen. On the contrary, the cornerstone of the rehabilitation program was that Europeans were friends of the Kikuyu (and Embu and Meru) and were ''trying to seek the good of all races in Kenya.''[5]

At all times emphasis was placed on the mistakes the detainees and Mau Mau had committed. The guilty party in the revolt and the cause of the suffering inflicted on the people of Central Province was, according to the government, Mau Mau and the Kikuyu people themselves. It was therefore essential for them not only to admit this guilt but also to renounce their past ''evil ways'' and promise to be loyal, law-abiding subjects upon release. But rehabilitation also served an immediate military purpose.

The rehabilitation program was an essential part of government counterinsurgency operations. Victory over Mau Mau would have been much more difficult without government promises of economic and political reforms aimed at undermining the legitimacy and purpose of the revolt. Detentions, communal punishments, and confessions weakened considerably the peasants' resolve to support the revolt. In its strategy, the government did not wish to alienate the Kikuyu, Embu, and Meru peasants permanently. It would have fought a much more protracted war had this happened. To avoid permanent alienation and sympathy for the revolt, the government initiated the rehabilitation program almost as soon as the war started. Reforms, however minor they were, and the vast rehabilitation program were instituted in 1953 while the fighting was still raging on. Prominent settler publications urged modest reforms.[6] These reforms, of course, called for minor adjustments in the status quo, for no settler in 1953 seriously entertained the idea of dismantling the system to accommodate the legitimate aspirations of Africans.

The government's position was that it offered the Kikuyu and all Africans in Kenya a much more attractive future "than that promised by Mau Mau." This future could be open to them once they showed they had reformed. "It is important to give them real hope of advancement in the future," Dr. Mary Shannon wrote, adding that "doors will be opened to them as soon as they show themselves fit to enter."[7] Of course, it was the government's chief duty to determine how fit any person was "to enter" its doors.

The rehabilitation program had many facets, but the major one was what came to be called the "pipeline." It involved the passage of detainees from transit screening camps to work camps and finally to open camps in their villages.

All detainees were classified under one of three general headings: "black," "grey," or "white." The "blacks" were those considered by the administration to be so deeply involved in Mau Mau that it seemed improbable they would ever give it up.[8] These were the "hard core," those considered to be key leaders of the revolt either as oath administrators or as guerrilla commanders. The majority of the detainees were classified as "grey." These were people whom the government felt had been affected by Mau Mau in a general way and could "in the course of time, be induced to give it up completely."[9] They were held in detention under suspicion of involvement in Mau Mau or because they were alleged to have committed acts for which it was difficult to obtain evidence for conviction in court. It was toward the "grey" category that "the government's rehabilitation programme was mainly directed."[10] The "whites" were those cleared of involvement in Mau Mau after screening or found "clean" after undergoing the rigorous rehabilitation process in the pipeline.

The first official effort at rehabilitation was initiated at two detention camps, one at Kajiado and another at the Athi river. The lessons of the experiment at these two camps later proved an invaluable source of knowledge and were duplicated at almost all of the detention camps, with varying degrees of success.

A few months after the establishment of the Kajiado camp, P. W. Foss, O.B.E., visited it as a government consultant.[11] In his observations, he felt the detainees had been gripped by an evil ideology and that if they were ever again "to be useful citizens, this ideology must be supplanted by a better and more powerful ideology."[12]

The detainees had to be induced, conditioned, or forced to renounce the "evil ideology" of Mau Mau. To facilitate the realization of this objective, Foss suggested a two-stage process. In the first instance, detainees' "existing cohesion and morale" had to be broken down. This then would be followed by the "intensive plugging of a superior idea." He realized that it was not going to be easy to undermine and break down the "cohesion and morale" of the detainees, and so he suggested they be subjected to an intensive barrage of announcements designed to induce intense self-doubt. The detainees had to be made to feel that their relatives, loved ones, and society at large had abandoned them and despised them. Foss suggested that the announcements proceed along these lines:

1. You have been fooled.
2. You are lost and forgotten.
3. Your families, your women, your people despise you.

The announcements were to be made in the Kikuyu language and repeated frequently. They were, in the end, destined to have "a cumulative effect."

The detainees' privacy was to be invaded continually, thereby denying them the opportunity for internal organization. This violation of privacy, carried out by Kikuyu spies, ensured that detainees would not easily trust each other. Solidarity among detainees was not allowed to develop, for it was reckoned that it was easier to deal with individuals than with a group.

Music was employed in this psychological warfare. Foss recommended that before announcements "music should be played to the detainees to hold their attention and soften them so that the broadcast announcements have greater force and are less easily shut out."[13] This, then, was to be a deliberately planned rehabilitation program that employed tactics of terror and psychological warfare for the purposes of behavior modification toward a predetermined goal: to produce loyal, law-abiding subjects of the Crown. It was the view of Foss, and indeed of many officials, that Mau Mau guerrillas and their supporters needed a spiritual rebirth, an immersion into a religious faith that would rid them of their past "evil ways" while at the same time ensuring that they would not revert to the "evil past." Foss was forthright in his recommendations on this issue.

The "superior idea" was to be Christianity, and to this end, he felt, there should be "an intensive campaign of religious revivalism of a non-denominational character carried out by Kikuyu."[14] Kikuyu evangelists were to be attached permanently to the camp and given a free hand in their operations. Any detainee who responded positively to the religious message had to confess before a priest and have this confession written down. But more than this, such a detainee had to admit to the priest and to a government official that he had sinned by taking the oath. He would then be charged with the responsibility of "spreading the word" to his fellow detainees, and for this he would receive a substantial remittal from his sentence. It is not, therefore, surprising that Kajiado camp remained a place for intensive rehabilitation and that many detainees were transferred there for the purpose of "turning them around."[15]

Rehabilitation work at the Athi river detention camp started in July 1953. It was, like Kajiado camp, a well-organized affair, drawing closely on the Malayan experience.[16] The camp had an overall administrator under whom worked several assistants. Perhaps the most interesting aspect of the camp administration hierarchy is that the deputy camp commander was a priest whose title was "ideological training officer."[17] Rev. H. J. Church and a team of African evangelists and ministers were responsible for training and reorienting the minds of detained persons. Life at the camp was not an endless session of religious instruction however. Detainees lived under a "regime of Spartan discipline and hard work,"[18] and like in Malaya, they were taught some industrial crafts[19] that were supposed to be useful to them upon release from detention. The main focus of the camp, however, remained the drive for the detainees' denunciation of Mau Mau and armed resistance. Strict discipline in camp administration, of course, entailed a lot of physical violence toward the detainees to induce confessions or to alert the detainees of the necessity of such confessions.

The ideological training officer was quick to realize that he could make substantial progress only if key Mau Mau detainees confessed and if such confessions were broadcast repeatedly to other detainees, not only at Athi river but also in other camps and even in the reserves. To this end, some of the detainees who confessed found themselves enrolled for ideological training duties, thereby breaking the detainees' solidarity.[20] In confinement, living under a hostile regime, it was difficult for many to hold out after some of their key comrades had confessed. This is not to suggest that all detainees at the Athi river camp confessed; it would be fair to say, however, that a substantial majority did, leading the government to designate the camp a "psychological warfare training centre."[21] The camp was used to train both African and European personnel involved in rehabilitation work in other camps.

At both the Kajiado and the Athi river camps, religious instruction never failed to insist that Mau Mau was an atavistic movement that had killed women and children and disrupted social and economic progress. Detainees were not exempt from the government propaganda offensive launched in the reserves and towns. Mau Mau, the detainees were again and again reminded, was wholly evil and therefore had to be abandoned.[22] To encourage detainees to accept Christianity, the ideological staff spent a lot of time "refuting the idea that Jesus was a European and that Christianity was a purely European invention."[23]

The camp staff were convinced it was their duty to prepare the detainees for reentry into society after ridding them of the reasons which led to their arrest and detention. Influenced by the Malayan experience, the rehabilitation program aimed to retrain the detainees, change their attitudes, and in the process, "remake Kenya by changing the leaders of Mau Mau."[24] If this were to happen, then the rehabilitation program would have to be extended to the many camps and prisons that held several thousand other detainees. This was done, and the story of the pipeline and its effects started with the detainees assembled at Manyani and MacKinnon Road screening camps.

Detainees were sorted out and categorized at these two massive camps. Those considered to be dangerous, "immersed in Mau Mau ideology," were immediately labelled "black" and dispatched to special detention camps, like Mageta Island in Nyanza Province. The detainees classified as "grey" were dispatched to the more than forty-five work camps (detention camps) scattered throughout Central and Rift Valley provinces and elsewhere in the country.[25] This was the first stage in the long process of rehabilitation on the pipeline.

Detainees were held in detention camps under strict semimilitary conditions. The official view was that idleness would hinder rehabilitation, and so under this pretext detainees were set to perform heavy manual work.[26] The new airport at Embakasi in Nairobi was constructed using Mau Mau detainees' labor.[27] They cleared numerous forests, participated in land terracing and digging canals for irrigation.[28] Heavy manual work was deemed an appropriate exercise for inculcating communal living and development of self-respect and public spirit.[29] In truth, however, the government was exploiting cheap labor, for although the detainees were technically paid, the amount was ridiculously small. For a day's work, a detainee received 80 cents, with foremen receiving Shs. 1/60.[30]

Also in detention were those Kikuyu repatriated from Rift Valley Province, Tanganyika, and other parts of Kenya for "security reasons." They were treated like "grey" detainees and went through the "pipeline," although there was little evidence, if any, to link them to Mau Mau. Their families were dispatched to the reserves, the government having abandoned an early idea of detaining families together.

Those Kikuyu in the reserves who were loyal to the government but landless were held under semidetention and mobilized as what came to be called "ALDEV gangs" (African Land Development). They were employed for low wages to perform manual agricultural work in their districts and divisions under the supervision of chiefs and the district administration.

If camp officials were satisfied that a detainee had demonstrated acceptable flexibility and was willing to confess, they transferred him to detention camps within his own district. This flexibility was determined by the assessment of loyalists from his district or village who toured detention camps as government employees. They interrogated him to determine how committed he might still be to Mau Mau. Once he had made an initial denunciation and had performed manual work satisfactorily, he would be transferred nearer his home. At each stage, detainees were subjected to Christian religious services in which they were urged to reform themselves by denouncing Mau Mau. The government provided funds to the churches for this work.[31] The emergency provided a golden opportunity for the expansion of Christianity, a sort of government-sponsored mass evangelism.

Scrutiny of each detainee intensified after being transferred to his home division. In Nyeri district, for example, screening teams composed exclusively of loyal Kikuyu were employed at each camp and screened each detainee monthly.[32] However, it was not enough merely to confess to the screeners. Each detainee before moving on through the pipeline had to confess publicly before his fellow detainees, repeating what he had said in private to the officials. The Ministry of African Affairs provided a standard format to be followed in such a ceremony. The priest had to satisfy himself that any detainee about to confess, "realises the sinfulness of partaking in Mau Mau oaths, that he has repented, and that he desires to have the forgiveness of Christ." He should also have "undergone a short course on the Christian theme of sin, repentance, atonement in Christ . . . and is genuinely anxious to receive further instruction in the Christian faith."[33]

Living conditions in the camps were rough and brutal. Throughout the rehabilitation process there were numerous reports of atrocities committed by prison and camp staff against detainees. Sam Thebere, a former detainee, has recently stated that these brutal conditions included frequent beatings, psychological terror, and the carrying of buckets full of feces.[34] Any complaints by detainees were either suppressed or neglected. The Colonial Office in London was aware of these complaints and conditions but chose to ignore them. Will Mathieson, a former senior official at the Colonial Office, has revealed that the colonial secretary issued no communiqué to the governor to stop violence in detention camps.[35] There was no official effort from London or Nairobi to halt brutality in these camps.

The governor took the view that rehabilitation could not be free of violence and, moreover, that the detainees were loathsome, dangerous criminals who could not expect to be treated kindly. On top of this was the inescapable fact that the Colonial Office and the government in Kenya had an intrinsic attitude and view that an African's life was not as important as a European's life.[36]

This official callous attitude was passed on to the African prison and camp warders, the majority of whom had little or no training. In 1953, when detention camps were introduced, there was a phenomenal growth in prison population. The prison department did not have the necessary trained staff and so was forced to undertake massive recruitment of warders, cooks, and other support personnel. In 1953 alone, "the subordinate staff increased by 108%," and the new recruits were given minimal training, in some cases lasting only one month.[37] Other warders were appointed locally where camps had been established and proceeded to work with no training at all; some of them were later absorbed into the prison's department staff.

These untrained or ill-trained warders were let loose on detainees who, the warders had been made to believe, were enemies of peace and stability. Anxious to prove their worth, many of them treated the detainees brutally, confident that their European supervisors would generally support them; and in most cases they were right. They were to maintain discipline, a highly sought after behavioral disposition throughout the rehabilitation period. Like in Malaya, discipline was defined as a "spirit of cheerful obedience."[38] Detainees had to be obedient, submissive, and cheerful through it all! Camp commandants interpreted disobedience and defiance from detainees as a threat to the rehabilitation process. This was particularly true in those camps that housed the "hard core" detainees. In these camps, every effort was made to break the detainees' solidarity, compel them to work, and change them from "black" to "grey." It was the forced labor, however, that led to the tragedy at Hola detention camp in 1959.

Hola camp was established in the Coast Province to house those detainees classified as "hard core." By January 1959 the camp had a population of 506 detainees of whom 127 were held in a secluded "closed camp"; these were the uncooperative ones. They were seen as uncooperative because they refused, despite persuasions and threats of force, to join in the rehabilitation process; they refused to perform any manual work or to obey orders. Naturally the camp officials felt their authority was threatened and feared that such defiance might spread to the "cooperative" detainees and even to the other camps. These hard core detainees had to be broken.

The camp commandant, acting on a plan drawn up by the prison department, set out to force the detainees to work on 3 March 1959.[39] The results were tragic. Eleven detainees were clubbed to death.[40]

The government tried unsuccessfully to cover up this obvious case of brutality. The initial statement on the matter mentioned that the men had died "after they had drunk water from a water cart which was used by all members of the working party and their guards."[41] The implication was that the men had died after drinking water in the hot sun. That such an incredible explanation was released clearly illustrates the degree to which the government felt no need to be accountable for its actions to the public or to the detainees. A subsequent official inquiry confirmed that the detainees had died from excessive violence. The government pathologist determined that the men died from "acute pulmonary oedeme caused by shock" due to violence.[42]

In light of the wide publicity given to this tragedy in both Kenya and Britain, and in spite of the fact that the British House of Commons debated the issue, it is surprising that no official was held responsible and punished for it. Sullivan, the camp commandant, was retired "from the Service without loss of gratuity."[43] The Hola incident, however, proved a turning point in Kenya's history; the British government found it impossible to remain indifferent to the internal events in Kenya, for the publicity given to them was causing political problems for Prime Minister Harold Macmillan.[44] For Kenya's African population, the Hola tragedy remained the most prominent example of government brutality toward detainees. It was seized upon by African politicians, as will be seen in chapter 8, to demonstrate the need for an end to the emergency and the attainment of independence.

In the reserves of Central Province, African residents were subjected to their own form of rehabilitation. Like in detention camps, mass evangelism was encouraged, the government having concluded that Christianity would inculcate good manners in Africans.[45] For those who were not inclined to accept Christianity, the sensible thing to do was to avoid being vociferous in their opposition. Many of them needed official permits to travel outside their villages or districts. They had to show their loyalty certificates before attaining such permits. As far as possible, loyalty certificates were issued only after an individual had confessed any personal connection to Mau Mau and renounced the revolt. It helped if an individual had positive recommendations from a priest and a Home Guard.[46]

Home Guards and loyalists, in general, gained power by the role they played in the massive land consolidation program in Central Province, a program conceived as part of the government's counterinsurgency operations. The government hoped that the products of land consolidation would form an integral part of the "carrot" in the war against Mau Mau.

The decision to consolidate landholdings in Central Province was an essential part of the Swynnerton Plan, which recommended that communal land ownership should give way immediately to an individual land tenure system. Such a system, Swynnerton argued, would give an individual "security of tenure through an indefeasible title," and encourage him "to invest his labour and profits into the development of his farm."[47] Although there had been some land consolidation before the emergency, it was low key and limited to small areas. Suspicion of intentions which characterized the relationship between African peasants and the government made it difficult for this program to expand. The emergency and the consequent increase in powers of the provincial administration and the removal of peasants into villages made implementation of the Swynnerton Plan easier.[48] Starting in Nyeri district under Hughes, land consolidation spread quickly to Murang'a then to Kiambu.

Throughout this exercise, the provincial administration, which had a more vested interest in the matter, was guided by political consideration. Hughes and even Johnston, the special commissioner for Central Province, felt they had to take advantage of the emergency to implement what to them seemed like an agrarian revolution: the pooling together of fragmented landholdings to produce one piece of land under individual tenure. It was their belief that unless they pushed hard, more detainees would be released and probably disrupt the program.[49] There were other considerations. Looking to the future, Johnston and his district commissioners believed that land consolidation would produce a specific class of landed gentry in Central Province and that this class "based largely on loyalists . . . would become a bulwark of conservatism, having no truck with Mau Mau or any other Kikuyu 'nationalist' manifestation."[50] Even in Britain there appeared influential writings calling for the creation of an African middle class which was seen as essential for future stability.[51] The European community was warned that if it wanted to avoid "a repetition of Mau Mau in the future . . . every effort must be made now to create a class of Africans whose interests are identical to their own."[52]

Land consolidation was supposed to produce this conservative middle class. Even Swynnerton envisaged the rise of such a class of what he called "able and energetic Africans." It was never clear from 1955 to 1958 just how many such "able and energetic Africans" would be produced by land consolidation. What was evident was that the rest of the population looked at this exercise as an opportunity to acquire individual title and security of tenure to their land.

Initially, the government wanted to use land consolidation as a punitive measure against Mau Mau activists and guerrillas. Land belonging to individuals identified as Mau Mau leaders' was seized and placed in a pool of common land. Key loyalists urged the government to pursue this policy of land seizure aggressively, believing as they did that "forfeiture of land is the severest punishment that can be inflicted upon any Kikuyu." These loyalists, who included Harry Thuku, Rev. Wanyoike Kamawe, and chiefs Njiri Karanja, Eliud Mugo, and Muhoya Kagombo, argued that land seizure would "do more to stop the Movement (Mau Mau) and prevent a similar movement from ever starting again, than any other action."[53]

These land seizures were not so widespread and extensive as rumored, but the fact that they happened quickly spread fear and anxiety in detention camps. Those detainees who had land feared they would lose it to loyalists during consolidation or that they would be given barren and unproductive pieces. This was a matter that demanded their presence in the reserves, and they knew they could not leave without convincing the camp commandants, rehabilitation staff, and loyalists they had reformed. Land consolidation, therefore, had a direct influence on the pace of movement by detainees along the pipeline.

The government halted the seizure of land in 1955, privately acknowledging that it was impossible to exclude all former Mau Mau sympathizers, for even the elders on land committees were probably former members of the "passive wing."[54]

If the loyalists did not succeed in seizing all land belonging to Mau Mau guerrillas, they still had tremendous power over the reentry of former detainees into the reserves. It was the loyalists who supervised detainees in the open camps to which they were released from the work camps. These open camps formed the last stage in the rehabilitation process. Conditions in these camps were not as restrictive and brutal as in other camps on the pipeline. Detainees at this stage were allowed contact with their family, who also fed them. But it was the loyalists who eventually had to agree to their release. "The golden rule with regard to the release of detainees," A. N. Savage observed, "is that no release is effected without the agreement of local loyalists."[55] Once released, their conduct and adjustment was monitored by probation officers who worked closely with chiefs and other loyalists. At no point could an ex-detainee assume that he was not under scrutiny.

The same scrutiny was applied to women detainees, all of whom were held at Kamiti Prison in Nairobi.[56] Invariably congested and often disease-ridden, the Kamiti Prison detention camp was as brutal and ruthless as other detention camps. Upon release, women ex-detainees were also monitored by probation officers. Other nonofficial agencies actively extended the rehabilitation program for women into the reserves. Chief among these was the women's organization *Maendeleo ya Wanawake,* whose activities included "working towards loyalty [and] cooperation" and the teaching of various handicrafts and domestic hygiene.[57] This organization, alongside East African Women's League, prepared female ex-detainees and African women, in general, for domestic work.

These organizations clearly sought to steer female attention and energies away from politics and onto "cooking, sewing, [and] mother craft," activities viewed as nonthreatening to the status quo. Young girls who had been detained were released after extensive religious instruction, for the government was of the opinion that Mau Mau had extensively undermined their morality.[58]

Young men and boys who had not been detained were viewed as vulnerable to the corrupting influence of Mau Mau and were therefore not exempt from general rehabilitation. For them the government felt the Scout movement would be the ideal vehicle for rehabilitation. As early as 1953, Sir Geofrey Rhodes, commissioner of Scouts, wrote to the governor to suggest various ways in which scouting could be of assistance during the emergency.[59] Rhodes was convinced that an "extension of Scouting in all the Reserves will do much to prevent similar outbreaks" and for this endeavor he demanded official support. Government response was favorable. It noted the differences in attraction to scouting between a European and an African boy. But still, it was the general official view that scouting offered "opportunities for diverting the average African boy's mind away from sex and politics."[60] Scouting was therefore actively exploited as both a counterinsurgency weapon and a vehicle for rehabilitation. Its activities were organized in schools throughout Central Province and beyond.[61]

Was the government rehabilitation program a success? In regard to the immediate political and administrative concerns of the provincial administration, this program was seen as a success. District commissioners were generally pleased with its results. In Kiambu district, in 1956, the district commissioner reported the results of a police survey which had revealed that ex-detainees "are better behaved than the rest of the population." He added that ex-detainees were generally "more reliable and hard working employees than the loyalists," whom he thought found it hard to "give up the excitement of the gun or spear for the shovel and jembe (hoe) of prosaic peace."[62] By 1958, the D.C. was still confident of the positive results of the pipeline, stating that "there was continued evidence that returned detainees were less inclined to crime, either of a violent or subversive nature, than the 'normal' citizen."[63]

In Nyeri district, the situation was similar to that in Kiambu. The administration was full of praise for the pipeline and especially for the Kikuyu screeners. In 1956, the D.C. in his annual report noted that no trouble had been experienced with returned detainees, whom he thought were in many cases, "better citizens than some of the lucky ones who have never been detained."[64] In 1957, of the four thousand detainees released in Nyeri, "only six had to be returned to a camp," reflecting in the administration's view, the success of the pipeline.[65] By 1958 there was no Mau Mau activity at all, and all active counterinsurgency operations had ceased in Nyeri;[66] while in Kiambu the district pipeline had ceased to exist by March 1958.[67]

Detainees were released to an altered environment. Alongside counterinsurgency operations in the forests, the government had expanded considerably its intelligence operations in the reserves. There were several thousand spies (official and unofficial), supported by vigorous Home Guard units that had immediate links to reinforced police and army units. It was therefore difficult for ex-detainees to revive Mau Mau in the reserves. Many of them were tired, bruised physically and mentally from the rehabilitation process. The experience had been painful and so punitive that many ex-detainees dreaded the prospect of being returned to Manyani or to any of the other camps.

On an individual level, each released detainee was aware of the fact that to be set free he had had to confess and reveal the secrets (if he knew any) of Mau Mau. Whatever may have been the extenuating circumstances, it was clear that at a personal level confession signified a form of betrayal of the revolt. The resultant guilt must have weighed heavily on the detainees as they trooped back to their home areas, which now were dominated by loyalists who loathed Mau Mau. In the changed circumstances, detainees were not returning home as war heroes but as people who had gone astray and had to be reformed and brought back to the mainstream as defined by the victors. In detention camps they had denounced Mau Mau oaths as a sin, and many had agreed, as a condition for release, to be good Christians. They had been made to feel ashamed of their past activities in Mau Mau and especially of the oaths. This may have been one of the most serious aspects of the pipeline. By making detainees feel ashamed of Mau Mau, and especially of the oaths, the pipeline ensured that ex-detainees would avoid associating themselves with similar revolts.

Indeed, in detention camps the concern of many detainees was not to rekindle Mau Mau upon release but to be reunited with their families, safeguard their land during land consolidation, and generally try to pick up the pieces. In Ngugi wa Thiongo's novel *A Grain of Wheat*, Gikonyo confessed, in part, because of his strong desire to see his wife, Mumbi, again.[68]

There was, however, an effort by some ex-detainees to organize an underground movement in Central Province called *Kiama Kia Muingi* (Council of the Masses). Its existence was reported in 1955 in Kiambu district. The Special Branch believed it was an offshoot of a Mau Mau underground organization that had not been destroyed during counterinsurgency. Government intelligence officers believed that Kiama Kia Muingi had three main objectives: To achieve compensation either from the loyalists or the government for any losses suffered by Mau Mau adherents, to take revenge on the loyalists, and to continue to agitate for land.[69] Kiama Kia Muingi was a small, loosely organized, informal association that did not condone or advocate violent confrontation with the government. Although it enjoyed some growth in Murang'a, it did not manage to become a threat to the government rehabilitation process in the reserves. By 1958 it had suffered defeat in Kiambu and most of Central Province.[70]

On the economic front, government efforts were on the whole a failure. The Swynnerton Plan of 1954 was supposed to create a vibrant agrarian economy in the rural areas based on cash-crop farming and increased earnings.[71] Specifically, land consolidation was supposed to produce large landholders who would employ labor, for the administration knew that consolidation would result in landlessness for some. Somehow the administration did not look at this development as negative. On the contrary, Swynnerton looked at landlessness alongside "energetic and able Africans" who owned a lot of land as "a normal step in the evolution of a country."[72] Some members of the provincial administration speculated that a landowner with three acres would employ about three laborers when his land was fully operational.[73] Based on this idle forecast, the administration envisaged a future in which there would be almost full rural employment, with laborers engaged in cash-crop farming and living in peace and prosperity under the watchful eyes of a conservative gentry. As it happened, the future did not evolve according to this plan.

In the first place, the administration failed to take into account members of a landholder's family who would stay on the land and provide necessary labor. The family would also need to be fed, and so there would be an immediate need for food crops as opposed to cash crops. Population explosion in Central Province was such that most of the consolidated plots were small, many of them fewer than three acres each.[74] Such small acreage was insufficient to produce cash crops and food crops to support a hungry population.

To alleviate some of this congestion in Central Province, the government pursued an active policy of reexporting labor to the Rift Valley to work on European farms. As early as August 1954, the provincial commissioner for Rift Valley notified Nairobi and his colleague in Central Province that settlers had started to express an interest in rehiring their dismissed Kikuyu laborers.[75] In most districts, it was hoped that original employees who had been rehabilitated or had served as Home Guards would be returned to their original employers. The reexport of labor to Rift

Valley would reduce the number of detainees in the camps and thereby lower government costs during the emergency.[76]

It was not until 1957 that the first pilot schemes to rehire labor into Nakuru district were initiated.[77] By the end of 1957, about sixteen hundred heads of families had been allowed into Nakuru district. Together with their families and other laborers, there were about ten thousand Kikuyu in this district alone by the end of the year. Demand for Kikuyu/Embu/Meru labor on settlers' farms unfortunately decreased sharply as many more ex-detainees were released and reexported to the Rift Valley. Unemployment among ex-detainees seeking agricultural work was reported by the end of 1957 and increased in 1958.[78] Rift Valley, therefore, did not have the ultimate solution to landlessness and unemployment in Central Province.

In Nyeri district, the D.C. noted an increase in petty thefts in the townships. These thefts, the D.C. pointed out, were committed by gangs of unemployed youths trying "to keep body and soul together."[79] By 1958, the unemployment situation had not improved in Nyeri, and the administration feared that a significant number of landless ex-detainees had nothing to do.[80] The options open for landless ex-detainees in Nyeri were to go back to Rift Valley, to be resettled in the newly opened irrigation schemes like the one at Mwea-Thebere or on the land near the forests.[81] These schemes, however, could not absorb all unemployed ex-detainees.

In Kiambu, a similar problem existed, leading the D.C. to suggest that all unemployed and landless ex-detainees should continue to be engaged on work gangs (under ALDEV) as a temporary solution.[82] Other temporary solutions included issuing permits for Kiambu residents to take up manual labor in Nairobi.[83] For Central Province as a whole, there existed significant unemployment during this period. Always aware of the threat that this situation posed to the rehabilitation program, the administration kept coming up with short-term temporary solutions. Some of the unemployed people were engaged as laborers in the building of the massive British army base at Kahawa, just outside Nairobi, and in the building of the Nyeri-Sagana road.[84]

The situation in urban areas was just as difficult and precarious. Throughout the tense period from 1946 to 1952, African politicians and trade unionists called on the government to build more houses for Africans in towns. In 1953, obviously in response to the tremor caused by the revolt, the government negotiated for £2 million for African urban housing.[85] In the same year, the Nairobi city council built 2,889 houses for Africans and set aside an area for individually constructed housing by Africans. These were, however, late gestures and certainly inadequate to meet demands for housing from African urban residents. Racist attitudes about Africans' filth and dirt, of course, persisted to interfere with these plans and projections. Bishop Walter Carey, a white missionary, wondered aloud how an African could be prevented from turning these new houses into slums.[86]

The Carpenter Report was yet another direct outcome of the immediate impact of the revolt. This report, issued in 1954, was concerned with low African wages and salaries, another perennial complaint of African politicians and trade unionists. In its recommendations, the Carpenter Report sought to stabilize African labor in the urban areas. To achieve this, the report argued for a higher salary "sufficient to provide for the essential needs of the worker and his family and also the provision of a house in which the worker and his family can live."[87] The Carpenter Report finally recommended that the base wage level of adult males should be changed "from one which takes account of only the needs of a single man to one based on the needs of a family unit."[88]

Government response to this crucial recommendation was not enthusiastic. While accepting, in theory, that the basic adult minimum wage should be assessed at two and a half times the basic youth minimum wage, the government rejected it as unwise and far too expensive.[89] Instead, the government considered it "a sounder policy to aim at an adult wage based on what is sufficient to maintain a man and his wife, but not his children."[90] At a future unspecified date, the government hoped the adult wage would be increased to cover the expenses of a man, his wife, and only two children.

Government reforms failed to solve the original economic problems that had, in large part, sparked the revolt. In fact, some of the problems became more critical as a result of rehabilitation; particularly landlessness. Individual titles to land made it impossible for the ahoi and other landless peasants to subsist in rural areas. Individual titles reduced, if not abolished, the influence of the muramati and grossly diluted any remaining kinship obligations toward landless kith and kin. Now that the government was actively encouraging the growing of cash crops (in itself a significant change over previous policies) land came to acquire a profound monetary value. It had been the hope of the administration that ahoi would be accommodated as laborers on newly consolidated farms. But as already pointed out, this did not happen, and those farmers who employed labor were far fewer than originally envisaged. There were, as a result, hungry, impatient, unemployed laborers.

Not surprisingly, land consolidation was opposed by the ahoi and all those who had lost out in litigation over land disputes.[91] They wanted a piece of their own land to be able to benefit from the new opportunities at cash-crop farming, opportunities which were certainly making a few large landowners wealthy and powerful. Land consolidation, which apparently had come to stay, failed to provide any long-term "safety net" for the ahoi and other landless peasants.[92]

What was needed was land outside the reserves. Unfortunately, the government was not keen to undertake any reformulation of the country's long-standing agrarian policy which reserved the White Highlands for European settlers. In theory, the ownership of land along racial lines had been condemned by the Royal Commission of 1953 to 1955.[93] The government had also issued a sessional paper making it legal and therefore possible for land transfers "from a person of one race to a person of another race" to take place.[94] In practice however, the acquisition of land by Africans in the White Highlands was not viewed as a viable possibility or a serious option during this time.

All of these official, isolated solutions born out of desperation and expedience far from answered the economic problems facing Africans. There was an urgent need for a comprehensive solution that would rely for its success on the initiation of fundamental reforms in the country's political and economic policy. This had not occurred when the state of emergency was officially ended in January 1960.

The end of the state of emergency predictably increased the anxieties and fears of prominent loyalists.[95] For over seven years they had wielded considerable power in the country and even benefited materially from their services. They had fought with determination, lost a number of men and members of their families, but more crucial for the future they had been instrumental in the defeat of Mau Mau. What did the lifting of the state of emergency restrictions mean to their future?

They had always feared the coming of such a moment, and that is why the most prominent among them had appealed repeatedly to the government never to release the hard core Mau Mau detainees and prisoners. In 1953 several petitions were submitted to the governor by loyalists appealing for permanent exile of Mau Mau leaders.[96] Led by chiefs Muhoya Kagombo, William Mathangani, and Magugu, described as very influential in the Githunguri area of Kiambu district, prominent loyalists reminded the governor that the hardships in Central Province were the result of people following "the wicked leadership of Jomo Kenyatta, Peter Mbiu and their numerous lieutenants."[97] The governor, together with the provincial administration, agreed with the loyalists that permanent exile from Central Province for prominent Mau Mau leaders was necessary. The Colonial Office, however, had reservations about the idea. In its view, it was not proper to engage in "any undertaking that these people would never be allowed to return even in the distant future."[98] The eventual return of all those described as hard core was therefore not ruled out, even if, for the moment, such a prospect was deemed unlikely due to "national security."

This is not to underestimate the considerable power and influence of loyalists in the post-emergency period. Many had been recruited by the army, police, and the civil service and as such were far closer to the instruments of power than former Mau Mau activists. Their worry was over the intentions of the rising African politicians. Would they cooperate with them or treat them as adversaries?

There were worries also among the ex-detainees and guerrillas. There were those who had actively supported the government and killed their former comrades. What would be their fate? Would they be singled out at some future date for revenge? There were, of course, a few detainees in prison and detention camps in 1959 who, after the Hola massacre and the controversy surrounding it, were let out without having confessed or gone through the pipeline.[99] What was going to be their relationship with those who had confessed?

Settlers also had their moments of insecurity and fear. Although the British government and its local allies had won the war and still maintained a large military force in the country, settlers were not assured that they would continue to be the dominant race. Indeed, two key constitutional amendments were introduced during the emergency period that had substantially increased African representation on the Legislative Council.[100]

By 1960, the country's political and economic problems demanded a resolution to the question of the country's political future. Rehabilitation had managed to defeat militancy and mass radical activism. It had created a landed gentry, few in number but quite significant. For the moment, this landed gentry with its allies in the civil service held power. Their dominance was, however, threatened by mass unemployment, landlessness, and racial tensions.

EIGHT

TOWARD INDEPENDENCE
Political Parties and Decolonization

When the Kenya African Union (KAU) was banned in June 1953, Africans were left with no formal political organization to articulate their demands to the colonial authorities. Although the KAU had been largely ineffective in averting the emergency, its presence represented an alternative avenue toward resolution of the crisis. In its absence, the burden of being spokesman for Africans and their multifaceted demands fell on the trade unions, especially the Kenya Federation of Labour. It was the only body in the country able to step in and assume the political role previously discharged by the detained leaders.[1] Led by Tom Mboya, the trade union movement continually harangued the colonial authorities on matters related to the emergency as well as on the traditional labor matters. The spirit of nationalism was kept alive by Mboya and the trade unions. This was important because, although the trade unions never supported Mau Mau, they continually pointed out the economic basis of the revolt and the need for African political parties through which Africans could channel their fears, frustrations, and hopes.[2]

Mboya's rise to prominence is linked to his activities during these years of emergency. His incisive and continuous criticism of the government on behalf of the African population showed him to be an astute politician who clearly stood above ethnic identification. As he later stated in his autobiography, he was one of the few African leaders whom the Kikuyu "and other affected tribes" spoke to "freely and discussed their intimate problems."[3] It would be unfair to charge him with usurpation of national leadership at this time. Together with the trade unions, he provided an invaluable service of speaking out against colonial policies when it was neither safe nor easy to do so.

One of the early targets of Mboya's criticisms was the Lyttelton Constitution of 1954, proposed by the then colonial secretary. In response to the Mau Mau revolt, although never acknowledging it as such, the British government imposed this constitutional reform to allow for a limited multiracial government in Kenya. The calculation was that this step would be praised as positive by the Africans and thereby diffuse the tensions in the country. Under this new constitution, an African was "brought into the Council of Ministers for the first time, as well as increasing to six the number of Africans in the Legislative Council."[4] The trade union movement vehemently opposed these provisions, arguing that there had been no direct African elections and hence African views were still unrepresented. The lone minister was also seen as powerless and ineffective. He was there to show multiracialism at work when, in fact, reality was that Africans were still dominated and exploited as before. This constitution also provided for elections on a limited franchise by Africans to elect representatives to the Legislative Council.

In 1955, official approval was given for the formation of African political parties. It had been two years since the banning of the KAU, and now, using emergency powers, the government hoped to control the political evolution of Africans in Kenya. It was to be a slow process that would avoid the "militancy" of the KAU, and instead foster the "growth of responsible opinion" and moderate politicians. To be able to achieve this, African political parties would be allowed only at the district level, and later, on an unspecified date, a national convention of district associations would be allowed. Political organization was supposed to be a gradual process whose pace would be determined by the government.

The various district associations formed between 1955 and 1957 predictably centered around specific ethnic groups and their unique problems.[5] The most unfortunate result of this stage in Kenya's political development was the emergence of powerful personalities associated with and linked to specific districts and ethnic groups. The colonial government's policy, by insisting on district associations, gave rise to ethnic spokesmen, men who became more identified with their ethnic groups than with national politics. There were, of course, exceptions like Mboya, but many politicians during this time could be said to have arisen to national prominence because of their power base at the district level.

In the elections of March 1957, some of these "local bosses" entered the Legislative Council (Legco) in the first elections in which Africans ever voted in colonial Kenya. Many of them were new to politics in general, let alone to national politics. Other than Mboya and Oginga Odinga, none of the new representatives, who included Ronald Ngala, Arap Moi, and Masinde Muliro, could claim any significant exposure to national politics. They had made their debut in politics at the local level and had had minimal contact with other African leaders. In this respect, Odinga is correct in saying that the newly elected African representatives were virtual strangers to each other.[6] They had been elected, however, on a platform largely fashioned by the trade union movement in Nairobi and its local branches. The platform "stipulated that candidates should only be supported if they condemned the Lyttelton Plan in general and pledged themselves not to take part in government and be used by the British."[7] When they arrived in Nairobi, these representatives, therefore, were aware of the need to subvert the functioning of the Lyttelton Constitution even if they had been elected on its provisions.

To avoid possible defection from the general elections' pledge, Mboya organized the new Legislative Council members into the African Elected Members Organisation (AEMO) of which he became secretary and Oginga Odinga its chairman. The AEMO coordinated these members' activities, especially their parliamentary thrust, which at all times was to criticize the colonial government for its policies. Eagerly exploiting their parliamentary immunity, these representatives, until re-

cently, hardly known outside their districts, spoke with determination against colonialism, racial discrimination, and the pain of emergency restrictions. With their
speeches and contributions covered in the local press and through their own public
meetings, these representatives reached more people than the KAU had been able
to even at the height of its power. Still, they represented no political party, only the
general frustrations of the entire African population.

Although they were not linked to Mau Mau, many of them would have accepted
the notion that the constitutional change under which they had been elected was the
result of the revolt. Mboya was later to enumerate the changes brought about as a
result of Mau Mau.[8] The AEMO did not approve of or support Mau Mau, but the
economic and political frustrations behind the revolt were continually pointed out
in the members' speeches.

By refusing to take up ministerial appointments and by being fairly uncompromising in their attack of government policies, the African representatives precipi-
tated a constitutional crisis which was to have tremendous impact on Kenya's
political development. In retrospect, this strategy may have been one of the most
important political decisions made by a group of Africans in Kenya's political development. By refusing ministerial posts, the government could not claim that it
was multiracial nor could it dictate the pace of change. If these elected African
leaders had accepted the appointments and if they had been mild in their comments,
the government could claim that multiracialism was a success and could have
largely determined the length and gradual pace of constitutional change. As things
happened, the constitutional crisis forced an early review of the Lyttelton Constitution. The result was the Lennox-Boyd Constitution of 1958, named after the new
colonial secretary.

The provisions of the new constitution gave Africans six more elected representatives, bringing the total to fourteen. By this provision, African members achieved
"equality in representation with Europeans in the Legislative Council."[9] But the
principle of multiracialism to which the African members were resolutely opposed
was not abandoned. Lennox-Boyd added one more African minister to the Council
of Ministers. The majority of the African members continued to hold out, and because they had more credibility with the African masses than the two who had accepted appointments, the new constitution was doomed to fail. To emphasize their
objection to the new constitution, the AEMO organized a boycott of council proceedings in early 1959. This gesture underscored Africans' objection to the imposed constitutional changes and also their disapproval of multiracialism.

At some other time the government probably would have remained indifferent to
these objections, but in the changed circumstances brought on by the emergency, it
was vital to avoid radicalizing all of the African population. The constant fear of
London and the local government was that too much obduracy and hostility might
give rise to yet another revolt and thereby ruin the chances of a peaceful transfer
of power.

The political success of the AEMO failed to resolve its internal problems. Because these members did not belong to a political party with specific ideals and a
deliberate program, they found it difficult to be subordinate to any one person in

their group. Each one looked at himself as a national leader in his own right. It was inevitable for the AEMO to experience tensions among its members based on rivalry, jealousy, and members' needs to project themselves as strong independent leaders. There were also differences in tactics, with some members eager to pursue multiracial politics. The chief target of rivalry was, of course, Mboya, as Odinga makes abundantly clear in his autobiography.[10] Mboya would have been the target of this rivalry for leadership even if he had not been singled out for praise by the imperial press, as Odinga alleges. His accomplishments in trade unionism and national politics, achieved at an early age, made others uncomfortable around him. Then there were his widely accepted administrative and organizational abilities, which made him "simply head and shoulders above most of his contemporaries."[11] Success brings with it its own follies, and Mboya was no exception. His "arrogance and vanity" and impatience with his colleagues, may have offended their sensibilities and hurt their pride much more deeply than he readily realized at the time.

In 1959, while still boycotting the Legislative Council, African members formed two rival parties; the Kenya National party (KNP) and the Kenya Independence movement (KIM). This broke the delicate balance of unity that had held AEMO together for about two years. For a while, the KNP forged ahead with the idea of a multiracial party, although none of its members accepted ministerial posts. Africans still objected strongly to multiracialism, and indeed only a few months after being founded, the KNP, in Odinga's words, "threw out its Asian officials and announced that its leadership was all-African."[12] The KIM led by Mboya and Odinga appeared in the circumstances of 1959 to be more radical than the KNP, with its consistent emphasis on the importance of African-led politics and eventual self-government.

It would, however, be difficult to ascertain the degree to which these parties commanded national support, for they were never really national parties. They remained short-lived urban organizations with no sizeable organizational or administrative machinery. If specific ethnic groups gave the impression of supporting one of them, this was because the leadership commanded support from specific areas. Neither of these parties built national branches nor were their platforms distributed far and wide throughout the country.

When Iain Macleod, the new colonial secretary, summoned the entire Legislative Council to London for a constitutional conference in January 1960, the need for functional unity was keenly felt by the African members. Lack of unity, they wisely realized, would have greatly handicapped their negotiations for greater concessions from the Colonial Office. The KIM and the KNP, therefore, joined and formed a single delegation headed by Ngala as chairman and Mboya as secretary. This was a crucial conference, for it gave Africans a majority of elected representatives for the first time.[13] What had happened to lead the British government to make these constitutional changes destined to bring African majority rule and independence to Kenya?

One of the major consequences of the emergency was that the British government actively reserved the right, unlike in the past, of dictating the pace of constitutional change in Kenya. This provision was clearly spelled out in the Lyttelton

Constitution, and subsequent colonial secretaries utilized it to dismantle the white settlers' political power in Kenya. Whereas in the past, London rarely overruled the judgment of the "people on the spot," in the circumstances after 1952 the local administration in Nairobi and the settlers found that they were responding defensively to a pace of change dictated in London that was faster and more drastic in consequences than anything hitherto experienced.

Britain, it needs to be repeated here, had been severely exhausted by the Second World War and did not, therefore, have the resources to continue to impose colonialism by the barrel of a gun.[14] But more crucial to this story of decolonization was the unrest and agitation for political freedom by the colonized peoples in the various colonies in Africa. Even the Conservative party in Britain had come to reluctantly acknowledge this fact. Addressing the annual conference of the Conservative party in 1956, Lennox-Boyd, the colonial secretary, said that, "any other policy but that of moving towards self-government and satisfaction of nationalist aspirations in the colonies would be 'fraught with disaster.' "[15] This did not mean, however, that Britain was, in 1956, eager to grant independence to all its African colonies immediately. What had been accepted was the principle of eventual self-government for these colonies in the near, but unspecified, future.

The Labour party in Britain in 1954, while enumerating its various colonial achievements, was equally vague on the timing of dissolution of the empire.[16] James Griffiths was still talking of preparing these territories, whose poverty "the British had not created," for self-government by providing them with conditions (economic and political) to sustain a democratic system of government when eventually independent.[17] These were still general pronouncements, and although the Labour party may on occasion have appeared more receptive to complaints from the colonies, there was no general commitment on its part to dissolve the empire immediately. In any case, after its election defeat in 1951, the Labour party stayed out of government for over ten years, during which time the empire was dismantled under the watchful eye of the Conservative party.[18]

There was a significant, if not dramatic, change in the implementation of colonial policy in late 1959 when Iain Macleod was appointed the new colonial secretary.[19] Although a stranger to the colonial questions, he held the view, shared by Harold Macmillan, that because of Britain's diminished power it was "too dangerous to go too slow" on decolonization.[20] At any rate, "National Service was due to end in 1960, so that even if the will to remain in Africa was there, it was unlikely that there would be sufficient armed force to contain the anticipated unrest."[21] Decolonization caused a lot of stress and soul searching within the Conservative party, looked upon as the natural patron of imperialism. These debates, admirably covered by Dan Horowitz in his article in *African Affairs* (1970), reveal not only the apprehensions of diehard imperialists at the dissolution of the empire but also the skill which Harold Macmillan employed to neutralize criticism and respond to pressures of African mass nationalism.[22]

The Hola camp massacre, which generated heated criticism of government policy in London, proved to be a turning point in Kenya's colonial history. The African representatives on the Legislative council were quick to seize the opportunity offered by the tragedy to intensify their criticisms of the overall emergency policy. In London the government endured bitter criticisms not only from the Labour party but also from some of its own backbenders, notably Enoch Powell.[23] On top of this, the government was shocked by the Devlin Report on the Nyasaland uprising which described the colony as "a police state."[24] It was clear, therefore, that colonialism could not be maintained in its old form in East and Central Africa.

Macleod, in response to African mass nationalism in Kenya, "recognized that independence could not be withheld simply on the grounds that a white settler community had become established there."[25] This settler community had neither the "numerical, economic nor financial strength to live in isolation" or withstand African nationalism unaided by the British government.[26] If in the past successive British governments had been somewhat careful to avoid openly offending the settlers because of possible political repercussions in London, in 1959 this concern could be dispensed with without too much concern. The international circumstances had changed, and there had been the Mau Mau revolt and several scandals associated with the government's response to it. The settlers not only had opened the way for the revolt through their intransigence but also had proved unable to defend themselves. Because they were unable to defend British interests, it was only natural that Britain came to terms with the rising new force: African nationalism. Also, Britain maintained a large military presence in Kenya even after the emergency and could have easily thwarted any settlers' rebellion.

Iain Macleod and Harold Macmillan had not "invented nationalism in Africa"; rather they were merely responding to its force in their policy decisions.[27] Macmillan himself had in the now famous speech in South Africa in 1960 stated that "the wind of change is blowing through the continent, and, whether we like it or not, this growth of national consciousness is a political fact. We must accept it as a fact, and our national policies must take account of it."[28]

Britain's fear, and indeed that of the Western countries at this time, was the ideological orientation of the rising tide of nationalism. The strategy, clearly expressed by Macmillan, was to steer the nationalists away from communism.[29] Protracted agitation and deliberate alienation of "moderate elements" would, it was feared, deliver these nationalists into the hands of communism. Britain and the Western countries saw this as intolerable. Decolonization had to proceed, therefore, in such a manner that power and authority would be handed to the right African personnel, those agreeable to Britain and its interests.

The peaceful transfer of power in Kenya was still hampered, in 1960, by what can be called the Kenyatta factor. There were many officials in the government (both in Nairobi and London) with lingering doubts about his association with Mau Mau.[30] The propaganda had been too convincing, and very few officials were willing to revise their deeply held suspicions and hostility against him and the movement the government said he had masterminded. Settlers naturally resented the idea of setting him free, and his entry into national politics was seen as intolerable. The government had participated actively in the propaganda offensive aimed at diminishing if not extinguishing Kenyatta's influence. His name "had been unmentioned and unmentionable" ever since his conviction at Kapenguria.[31] It was therefore with considerable astonishment and disbelief that the still white-dominated Legislative Council heard Odinga proclaim that Africans still respected Kenyatta as their political leader.[32] It was, given the circumstances of 1958, a very unexpected assertion. Its general implications disturbed not only the whites and the loyalists but also the other African members of the Legislative Council.

African representatives were initially hostile to Odinga's remarks.[33] These members specifically included those from the Kikuyu, Embu, and Meru areas. Other than the obvious fact that these representatives had disowned and dissociated themselves from Mau Mau, they also wanted to project themselves as the new leaders, owing allegiance to no one. In addition, they feared government reaction to their association with Kenyatta, who at this time was considered the most prominent public enemy. Loyalists and those who had participated in some anti-Mau Mau activities feared that the rehabilitation of Kenyatta might make them vulnerable to revenge, for they still believed, as they had been told, that Kenyatta was the father and symbol of the Mau Mau revolt.

In a relatively short time, by 1960, African representatives had reversed themselves and come to accept that the release of Kenyatta from detention was not only desirable but also an inescapable component of the struggle for independence. The change was dictated by the realities on the ground. These politicians discovered that, for Africans, Kenyatta was still the dominant symbol of the struggle for freedom and that it would have been an act of political suicide on their part to remove him from center stage.[34] Instead, they chose to lead the campaign for his release, a campaign which gathered national momentum in 1960. Europeans panicked, and some made arrangements to leave the country.[35] While this uncertainty led to a fall in "share and house prices," there was little the government could do to dissuade Africans from this campaign, save for releasing Kenyatta.

The new governor, acting against the advice of the Colonial Office and after having threatened to resign, made a most unfortunate speech about Kenyatta. He wanted to restore European confidence in Kenya, but in the process he offended the African majority. After outlining the deplorable aspects of Mau Mau as understood by the government, Renison concluded that Kenyatta was not only its leader but also the "African leader to darkness and death."[36] Kenyatta would not be released, for Renison believed (based on the Corfield Report which was later discredited) that Kenyatta was "an implacable opponent of any cooperation with other people, tribes, or races, who live in Kenya."[37]

This speech only fueled the "free Kenyatta" campaign, and even some key British papers started to urge the government to release him. The fear as the *Guardian* discussed it was that "if Kenyatta continues to be outlawed during British rule, it is the Kikuyu loyalists who will be blamed" and that "when an African government is able to release him on its own account, the revenge taken may be much worse."[38] Like in other matters at this time, the view from London prevailed. Kenyatta was released in stages, initially to Lodwar, then to Maralal. At Maralal Kenyatta faced the world press for the first time since his trial at Kapenguria in 1953.

At the press conference in April 1961, Kenyatta denied that he had any enmity toward Europeans in Kenya. He had, he said, "spent many years in England or in

Europe," and still had many friends in many different nations.[39] He also denied that he had communist affiliations or even tendencies. His visit to Russia, which had been the source of great speculation as to his ideological leanings, was "for educational purposes only." Then he stated his verdict on communism: It "had no place in an African society."[40] Other than discounting the relevance of communism in modern African society, Kenyatta also said that he "had never advocated for the eviction of Europeans from the Highlands."[41] He did not foresee nor approve of the compulsory expropriation of European lands. After denying that he had ever been a violent man, he told the press and the people of Kenya that he would continue to disapprove of violence when set free.

For the next four months Kenyatta received an endless stream of visitors at his house in Maralal. Predictably these visitors included some white settlers eager to get some sense of his true intentions toward them. There were also prominent loyalists like Bishop Obadiah Kariuki, who wanted some reassurance of their fate and status in an independent Kenya. Representatives of "world powers, lawyers, photographers, doctors, foreign visitors, friends, relatives, . . . all came to see Kenyatta at Maralal and returned able to reassure their friends that, after all, he was the man to safeguard their interests in an independent Kenya."[42]

The British press was specifically interested in his views on Mau Mau. At Maralal he went out of his way to denounce it. This denunciation was repeated upon his release from detention on 14 August 1961. At his house in Gatundu, newly built for him by the government, Kenyatta reiterated his disapproval of the revolt. "In answer to a direct question, 'Do you oppose it?,' he said, 'I have said all along that I oppose it.' "[43]

Kenyatta came home to a divided nationalist movement. The functional unity forged for the Lancaster House constitutional conference collapsed at its end, when it was realized that independence would be achieved in a shorter time than previously speculated. Macleod had "prefaced the January 1960 conference . . . with the words 'we intend to lead Kenya to full self-government or, if I may use a plainer word, to independence.' "[44] When he brought the conference to a close, after heated and sometimes bitter arguments, and gave Africans a majority in the legislature for the first time, Mboya believed Kenya was now recognized as "an African country." More crucial for African politics was Macleod's authorization of African national political parties. No date for independence was fixed, although it was clear to Africans and white settlers alike that the wind of change was indeed blowing through Kenya.

The lack of unity among African nationalist leaders and their constituency had more to do with the future than the present. The crux of the matter was the share of benefits that would accrue to each ethnic group (and their spokesmen) upon the attainment of independence. Having subsisted on official propaganda and tactics of divide and rule for a considerable period of time, it was inevitable that different ethnic groups should be somewhat suspicious of each other. Besides, there had been no concerted effort to contradict these imperial rumors and distortions. This problem of disunity was further exacerbated by the rivalry and squabbles that African representatives, clearly identified with specific ethnic groups, allowed to develop among themselves in this crucial period. Rumors, with all their inevitable distortions, easily spread, arousing fears and generating anger and suspicions. One must not discount the effect of this disunity and distrust on the emotions of those proclaiming the nationalist political message during this tense and unsettled period.

The KANU (Kenya African National Union), the first national party, was formed at a conference attended by a majority of the African representatives at Kiambu in May 1960. According to Odinga, each member of the Legislative Council was to bring sixteen representatives.[45] Determined to use Kenyatta "as a symbol around which to build a mass movement," the KANU elected him president of the party in absentia; Gichuru was elected acting president, with Odinga as vice-president and Mboya as secretary general.[46] However, it soon became clear that the KANU was not supported by all African elected members.

Those members who held out saw themselves and their ethnic groups as threatened by what they called the dictatorship and dominance of Kikuyu and Luo in the KANU. If this dominance were allowed to go unchecked, these members speculated, then the smaller ethnic communities and groups would have their interests and welfare submerged and subordinated to majority dictatorship in an independent Kenya.[47] It was the fear of what *could* happen, not what was happening, that fueled suspicions.

In a gathering at Ngong, just outside Nairobi, on 25 June 1960, these minority members gave substance to their fears by forming the KADU (Kenya African Democratic Union). It brought together the Kalenjin Political Alliance led by Daniel Arap Moi, the Maasai United Front, the Coast Political organizations under Ronald Ngala; and Muliro's Kenya African People's party.

The KANU saw itself from the start as the heir to the KAU. It therefore had considerable support from the people of Central Province, who had been the backbone of the KAU before its proscription. Through the vigorous efforts of Odinga, the Luo people also, on the whole, supported the KANU. In terms of demography alone, this party had an overwhelming advantage over the KADU, and it is this factor, which in the end, settled the rivalry between them. What was this rivalry, this competition, centered upon? Speaking in London in September 1960, Gichuru said the difference between the KANU and the KADU was one of personalities. According to him, the KADU was formed by those who had not won offices in the KANU.[48] This explanation oversimplifies the underlying causes of the rift between the two parties. Ngala and Moi were elected treasurer and vice treasurer respectively of the KANU, positions they rejected when they helped form the KADU.

Although both the KANU and the KADU worked for African independence, they had profound differences over one issue: land. Throughout colonial Kenya (and some may say even post-colonial Kenya), land remained the chief cause of political agitation or loyalty.[49] It was, after all, the chief means of production, and access to it was crucial not only for economic survival and prosperity but also for power. The KADU's fears were rooted in the belief that the KANU, with its demographic superiority, would descend on lands historically linked to and claimed by the minority ethnic groups and thereby deny them their "natural heritage." To offset this development, the KADU advocated a regional system of government, that is, a modified federation framework. Ngala as leader of the KADU advocated the "decentralisation of power, so that power is shared between [sic] many." This would entail the division of power between "a central government and regional authorities."[50] It so happened that the regions demanded by the KADU were roughly the same as the provinces, which on the whole tended to coincide with residential locations of the different ethnic groups.

The bitter opposition of the KANU to the KADU's regionalism and other constitutional safeguards was rooted in the demands of its key constituent: the Kikuyu. Land had been the chief cause of the Mau Mau revolt, and land still remained the most emotional issue in Central Province. If the KADU's arguments for regionalism became the law, then the Kikuyu would be frozen in their congested Central Province and denied access to the coveted lands in the Rift Valley—the so-called White Highlands.

In the 1961 general elections, conducted under the new Macleod Constitution, both parties sought to increase their national mandate. They were, however, still in their infancy, and neither party had established adequate administrative machinery to coordinate political campaigns and disseminate their political platforms. The establishment of branches throughout the country had not yet been accomplished.[51] The elections therefore benefited only minimally from the newly formed parties. Instead, the dominant role was played by key personalities who were identified with specific districts and ethnic groups.[52] Their interpretation of their party's platform was more crucial to the outcome of the elections than was the general party administrative machinery. In these circumstances verbal radicalism was valued, largely uncoordinated, and evidently not uniform throughout the campaign.

The KANU emerged victorious, largely because it had "the effective support of the Kikuyu, Embu, Meru, Kamba, Luo and Kisii," who represented about 60 percent of the African population.[53] It captured nineteen seats in Parliament, while the KADU trailed with eleven seats. Faithful to its election pledge, the KANU refused to form or enter the government until Kenyatta was set free. After some time of hesitation and caution, the KADU agreed to form a minority government with Michael Blundell's New Kenya party (NKP), an all white party. Thus, the elections had not solved the political problems in Kenya; rather, the majority party was still outside government and its constituents' economic problems threatened to undermine the delicate business of peacefully handing over power to Africans. By 1962 the deadlock had to be broken. There was yet another constitutional conference in London, this time attended by Kenyatta, who had entered the Legislative Council on a seat vacated for him by Kinyanjui Njiri, the son of a prominent chief and loyalist.[54] Of all the issues that concerned this Lancaster House conference, none was so vital and none aroused as much emotion as the question of land.

The KANU's position on land was forcefully put by Gikonyo Kiano, a former university lecturer. According to him, "land was so important to the economy of Kenya that it must ultimately be under the control of the Central government."[55] He dismissed the importance of historical claims to ownership of specific lands. "To dig back in history in order to find which tribes originally occupied this land or that," Kiano argued, "would lead only to unrest. What mattered more were the economics of the situation."[56] Daniel Arap Moi, one of the key leaders of the KADU, responded by saying that "his people of Kalenjin were prepared to fight and die for their land, which, after all, in Kenya, belonged to the people of the various tribes and not to the Kenya government."[57] At issue was the question of ethnicity and property ownership of certain lands. Ole Tipis of the KADU again restated the controversial view that "all land in Kenya was tribal and should remain in the hands of the tribes."[58] Taking advantage of the emotionally charged environment in which these discussions were held, Wafula Wabuge of the KADU asserted that "the people of one tribe would not be prepared to let the people of another tribe settle on their land."[59] According to this scheme, chaos and unrest could only be avoided by restricting people to lands traditionally and historically owned by their ethnic groups. The chief losers, if this formula had been adopted wholesale, would have been the Kikuyu.

Whereas "most of the ethnic groups could and did base their claims to land in the White Highlands on historical rights," the Kikuyu could not.[60] They had no historical claim to these lands. The Kikuyu instead based their claim to these lands on their labor which had long been associated with the White Highlands. The crux of their argument, strongly disputed by the Kalenjin and Maasai, was that their labor had developed the highlands and that therefore they had a right to settle there upon the attainment of independence.

The controversy surrounding land was one issue which loyalists, former detainees, and Mau Mau guerrillas agreed on as central. The loyalists who had benefited from land consolidation and other reforms under the emergency wanted to expand their property holdings into the Rift Valley and to other lands outside Central Province. The landless ahoi, displaced by land consolidation, saw their salvation in the Highlands, as did the squatters and those who owned small pieces of land or had lost land during consolidation. For them, it was imperative that the new independent government guarantee and facilitate their access to lands long-coveted in the Rift Valley. Thus, if there was any basis for Kikuyu support of the KANU, it was on the land question. A strong unitary government that controlled land ownership was seen as more suited to their needs than a federal type of government that restricted their ownership of land outside their already congested province.

The KANU's many difficulties at this time prominently included the discernible discrepancy between its verbal radicalism, especially over land, and its modest, even conservative, party manifesto. This verbal radicalism, especially at the local level, did not reflect the official view of the party. There were those in the party, especially some of the former detainees, ahoi, and former guerrillas, who still longed to drive the settlers from the Highlands and take over their farms. Some of these later formed the Kenya Land and Freedom Army (KLFA) that was relatively active between 1960 and 1962.[61] Exclusively Kikuyu in composition, it sought to recover the Highlands for the Kikuyu.[62] It was the KLFA's objective that aroused controversies in the KANU. The KLFA, seen as an offshoot of Mau Mau, had an agenda that ran counter to the KANU coalition, for it excluded several ethnic groups. How could the Luo, Kisii, Kamba, and other groups enthusiastically support the KANU if they were excluded, through the KLFA's tactics and objectives, from the major prize of independence? This prize was, of course, land in the Highlands.

Moreover, the KLFA and the KANU disagreed over the manner of acquiring land in the Highlands. The KLFA's position was that land should be confiscated by the government and distributed freely to Africans, especially to the Kikuyu. This position represented, in essence, the radical wing of the KANU, whose prominent advocate was Kaggia. A former detainee jailed with Kenyatta, he supported the KLFA platform. The KANU's vigorous verbal campaign for land distribution and settlement had made it a party of choice for the ex-detainees and former guerrillas. But as a party, it did not approve of nor condone seizure of European land or free distribution of land.

The KANU manifesto made an indirect acknowledgment of the role played by Mau Mau in Kenya's struggle for freedom. "We cannot deny" the manifesto stated, "that a great impetus was given to the national movement for independence by events of and after 1952."[63] Its detailed program, while seeking "undiluted democracy," also made it clear that resettlement of landless people would not be "at the cost of the high standard of agriculture already attained,"[64] Resettlement would not be allowed to disturb or ruin white settler agriculture. While the manifesto deplored the living conditions of squatters, it could only issue a vague promise to rectify the problem.

The KANU's official policy was quite consistent with the thinking and ideas that its leadership had held for a long time. As early as 1959, Mboya had argued that political expedience made the exclusive reservation of the Highlands for whites both unwise and indefensible.[65] He advocated a program of land reform that would not be injurious to the "economic interest of the country" but would all the same "require the surrender of part of the land now held by some of the very big land owners."[66] Land so surrendered would be "fairly compensated," and there would be no seizure of lands. This thinking was consistent with that of Kenyatta who, as already seen, opposed seizure of European lands. It is not, therefore, surprising that the KLFA "had no support among African political leadership" in the KANU.[67] This leadership, it needs to be pointed out, included a considerable number of former Mau Mau detainees who now occupied political offices, especially at the local level.[68]

The KADU's program on land was, as expected, more restrained than the KANU's modest and conservative manifesto. Clearly sidestepping the question of Mau Mau, the KADU grudgingly acknowledged that there had to be land reform. But unlike the KANU, the KADU's major thrust was on increasing production "on existing and new settlement schemes."[69] Like the KANU, it forbade and disapproved of "the seizure of farms and farm property without payment of fair compensation."[70] On the question of free distribution of land, the KADU emphasized that "land is free only in a subsistence economy" and so it was irresponsible to expect free land in Kenya.[71] Closer to the controversy over ethnic ownership of land, the KADU's program declared that "regions must have power to reallocate undeveloped land in their area," a strategy that would effectively exclude people from other regions. The party calculated that about "20,000 new farms" were needed to cope with the problems of landlessness. Still, it was the view of the KADU that the needed "settlement schemes can best be located within the traditional spheres of influence of the people concerned."[72]

On other matters of policy, the KANU and the KADU were much closer. Both parties advocated personal freedom (a deliberately vague and unbinding phrase) and also the economic and social development of Africans. Both parties believed in "security of private property," with the KADU advocating "individual land tenure" throughout the country.[73] For the KANU, Kenyatta stated that the party "had accepted the principle of private ownership in land and free enterprise."[74] These parties were eager also to preserve the British judicial system and tradition. Gichuru spoke of the KANU's pledge to maintain this tradition "with each independent test."[75]

The 1962 Lancaster House conference led to a coalition government, in which the KANU entered the government for the first time. Both parties were represented in the government, and Kenyatta together with Mboya became ministers. This conference also produced "one of the most complicated constitutions ever devised" and incorporated the KADU's regionalism.[76] Although provision was made for a central government, it was clear that the devolution of power to the regions greatly limited its authority. This made the business of governing not only clumsy but also expensive, for "the regions were to have their own legislature, administration, financial and executive power, and control over land and police."[77] With some minor adjustments, Kenya gained her independence in 1963 under this complex and somewhat ponderous constitution.

This conference also ratified settlement schemes already in progress that sought to address the twin problems of European ownership of land and African landlessness. As this study has consistently demonstrated, landlessness as a social and economic problem was officially known. What the colonial government had consistently failed to realize was its threat to social order. Landlessness was not only an economic problem but also a political problem that could lead to revolt, as the events of the emergency had amply demonstrated. In the closing days of colonialism, when majority rule was inevitable, the colonial government came up with settlement schemes that also addressed the worries of European settlers. Many settlers were bitter and felt betrayed by Macleod, and they now feared that their lands would be confiscated by an African government. The value of their land had slipped considerably; if forced to sell at the 1961 prices, settlers would have failed to reap substantial profit.

In 1961 the government created the Land Development and Settlement Board (LDSB) dominated by settler interests. Clearly, given the circumstances of this tense and fluid period, the government's chief concern was to "provide a market for and thereby stabilise the price of European owned land."[78] The LDSB was authorized to purchase land from settlers in the White Highlands for distribution to two groups of Africans: the "yeoman" farmers and the peasants. The board in its transactions would purchase the land at 1959 prices, which were, of course, considerably higher than those of 1961.[79] This first phase of the land settlement scheme was not aimed at poor landless peasants. Both the yeoman and peasants who got land under this scheme were, as Leo notes, "either members of the petty bourgeoisie or better off [sic] peasants," for they had to produce some working capital and demonstrate they had considerable experience at farming.[80] The poor landless peasants had neither the requisite experience nor the capital to benefit from this scheme. The government had again miscalculated, for as it turned out most of the yeoman farmers were either prosperous former loyalists or petty bourgeoisie from other ethnic groups.

Peace and tranquility could not be achieved in the reserves, especially in Central Province, unless some major land transfer from Europeans to Africans was seen to be taking place. It should be recalled that in its policy of rehabilitation, the government was keenly aware of the danger posed to its success and survival by landlessness and unemployment in Central Province. It was not surprising that toward the end of 1961 the government had to rethink its strategy. There was, as always, the constant need to provide a market for European farms at fairly high prices, but there was also the fear that gross neglect of the problem of landlessness might lead to civil strife "during the transition to independence."[81] This was a chilling prospect which neither the government nor the emerging African elite wanted to see.

A new expanded settlement scheme was negotiated with the British government to provide funds as a loan for the purchase of "20,000 acres annually over a period of five years" starting in 1962 "for the settlement of 50,000 to 70,000 families."[82] This became the "million-acre scheme" and represented the most controversial aspect of Kenya's post-colonial agricultural policy. For the moment, however, the aim was to decrease racial tension by showing it as a genuine gesture of land transfer to Africans.

This expanded settlement scheme was not allowed to interfere with European farming. Resettlement was to be in the undeveloped areas, areas that although in the White Highlands, were not particularly productive.[83] The LDSB justified the preservation of European farming on the grounds that large scale farming was needed to "supply the towns, and the African market, with bread, meat and dairy products."[84] Were these settlement schemes viable economic propositions? According to the LDSB they were not. Their value was political, and the board felt that it would be a long time, if ever, before they made a substantial contribution to the economy.[85] Of course, this can be dismissed as a mere plea by European farmers eager to emphasize their indispensability to the economy. Yet it is vital to remember that these schemes ran into considerable economic difficulties in the postcolonial era.[86]

In 1963, when the KANU won elections and formed the government, with the KADU in opposition, it inherited a land policy that gave no special preference or treatment to ex-detainees or former guerrillas. The million-acre scheme managed to distribute some land to landless peasants, but they, in turn, incurred a debt that had to be paid back. Kenyatta's government had bought land for them, but they had to buy it from the government through loans and credit. There was no free land. Several social classes benefited from this scheme. Key loyalists in government and agriculture, civil servants from other nonKikuyu ethnic groups, businessmen, and petty bourgeoisie all got some land.[87]

Land settlement schemes also helped to reinforce the colonial government's policy of rehabilitation. Those landless peasants who were allocated land were thoroughly investigated by chiefs, local headmen, the Special Branch, and other intelligence-gathering agencies.[88] No land was allocated to any peasant suspected of subversive activities, which in the circumstances of 1962 referred to those who had participated in the KLFA activities. Land settlement was used to extend government authority and dissuade peasants from joining underground resistance groups. Since this was going to be a five-year program, all those who did not get land in 1962 or 1963 had reason to be hopeful that they would be lucky next time. Meanwhile, they had to be obedient and law-abiding, refraining from any activity which might disqualify them from acquiring land. The situation in the countryside, although not perfectly calm, was stable enough for the colonial and then the African government to isolate the KLFA, denounce it, and round up many of its remaining sympathizers.[89]

The KLFA represented the sentiment, held by some former guerrillas, that Kenyatta and his government had betrayed them. Betrayal in this instance was specific. It referred to Kenyatta's position (and the KANU's and the KADU's) that there would be no free land given to any person, including former guerrillas and detainees. But had Kenyatta changed from being a radical revolutionary to a conservative nationalist? Were the KLFA and other ex-detainees justified in their accusations? Did they really know Kenyatta and his ideological leanings?

All available evidence indicates that Kenyatta's ideological leanings and positions remained constant. He remained a conservative nationalist who "never preached revolution during his long political career."[90] He had been the symbol of the struggle for independence, and many groups had used this symbolism to justify their own unique positions. This had been the case during the oath-taking campaign both before and after the declaration of the emergency. In the forests, both the guerrillas and their numerous layers of leadership recognized his symbolic leadership and never challenged it. In each of these cases, Kenyatta never associated himself with the positions of these movements. He remained aloof, noncommittal, but increasingly he singled out Mau Mau for condemnation and denunciation. Even after his release from detention, he condemned oath-taking and the KLFA activities. In 1962, addressing a special meeting of former detainees and guerrillas, he again denounced Mau Mau, stating that it had been "a disease which had been eradicated and must never be remembered again."[91] As president, he denounced as outlaws the few Mau Mau guerrillas who remained in the forests. Then he dispatched the army to dislodge them.[92]

Kenyatta basically had been a loner who "kept himself free from ideological commitments," except for stating the need for self-government by Africans.[93] He held no radical revolutionary ideals that he proceeded to betray while in power. Indeed, no one could point to such revolutionary positions, utterances, or writings that Kenyatta had previously espoused. The KLFA and ex-detainees did not know Kenyatta personally nor did they have reason to believe that he shared their views. "Looking at Kenyatta," Ngugi has written, "people tended to see what they wanted to see rather than what there was: petty bourgeoisie vacillations and opportunism."[94] Kenyatta's career must by all counts be seen as a triumph of ambiguity.

It is not only the KLFA and some ex-detainees who were forced to revise their positions about Kenyatta. The other group was the European settlers. Even after their interview with him at Maralal and at his home upon release from detention, settlers held suspicions about him. In 1961, six white women wrote to the governor, stating that they could not live under a government led by Kenyatta or in which he played a part.[95] Kenyatta, himself, had been concerned by the hostility expressed by settlers toward him.[96] In August 1963, four months before attaining full independence, Kenyatta addressed about three hundred key settlers in Nakuru, the heart of the Highlands.[97] He assured them that there would be no compulsory acquisition of their lands, nor would their farming activities be interfered with. Their skills were needed, and they were free to stay and contribute to "nation building." Then he urged them "to forgive and forget the past." An almost sudden change occurred in their attitude toward Kenyatta. Whereas in the past he had been the devil, the disruptive influence, now he became the grand old man of Africa, a symbol of stability, one who understood them. After all, hadn't he lived in England for a long time? His association with English people and even his marriage to an English woman, which had been vehemently resented by the settlers, now became positive attributes. These experiences exemplified Kenyatta's openmindedness, vast international experience, and interracial communion. Once again the propaganda machine was activated, only this time it sang songs of praise for Kenyatta. He assured them of the security of their property and their life-style, and they loved him for it. They wanted him to protect them against "outlaws" and other squatters and all those who sought radical changes. And he did.

The goal of both the KANU and the KADU up to 1963 remained the attainment of political independence. In spite of their manifestos, both parties failed to produce any serious analysis of the colonial economic and social system and how this could hinder the development of the Kenyan people after independence. The aim, pursued with singular determination, was to inherit the state. Like their constituents, the political elite in these parties looked to political independence with exaggerated hopes. The colonial state in Kenya, which they were destined to inherit, had evolved over time as a ruthless instrument of oppression and exploitation of Africans. To inherit it, intact, was to continue to advance this pernicious task for which it was so uniquely suited.

There can be little doubt that the brevity of time from the formation of political parties in 1960 to the attainment of independence in 1963 affected the ability of these parties to advance any detailed analysis of national problems and their proposed solutions. These parties simply had no time for study or analysis, let alone research. They were formed at a time when the tempo of activity and change was quite fast and called for improvised strategies and instant pronouncements. These parties had not by 1963 acquired any extensive experience at national politics or even familiarization with the complexities of international economics or politics. Other than Mboya, Kenyatta, Mbiyu Koinange, and Murumbi, none of the politicians had had any significant exposure to international politics. Although the political elite had come to acquire political skill and tenacity, their main objective was to inherit the state rather than to produce any development program or policies that

were radically different from those already in existence. Manifestos produced by
these parties were, therefore, general and slim on analysis.

Ideas that permeated these manifestos were from the leaders and not from the
general population. Rarely were the village and urban populations actively involved
in their formulation, although Africans were constantly addressed at large rallies
during which the party platforms were read and expounded upon. These rallies did
not constitute a dialogue between the leadership and the masses. If the parties had
been well organized at the local grass-roots level with informed activists, then a
meaningful dialogue with the masses would have taken place. As things stood, between 1960 and 1963, no such strategy was meaningfully pursued. Instead, more
emphasis was placed on mass open rallies. The "KANU Manifesto for Independence, Social Democracy and Stability" was, for example, presented at Thika on
20 November 1960 at a rally estimated at 100,000. Predictably it was approved.

The characteristic feature of Kenyan nationalism was conservatism. From the
days of the KCA, the EAA, the KAU and even Mau Mau, Kenyan nationalism was
never socialist, or left-wing, in ideas or inspiration. Its basic demand, advocated
more forthrightly after 1945, was for the right of a people to self-determination.
"Nationalist movements," Minogue writes, "strive for freedom and self-
government."[98] He adds correctly, that "the fate of different classes in the new
nation will vary."[99] And indeed, this was true in Kenya. After 1963, when the political elite had settled in power, there arose frustrations on the part of the general
public, especially those who had not benefited from the "fruits of independence."
It would therefore be accurate to talk of distinct ideological cleavages in the nationalist movement after 1963. Although there were tensions within the KANU
(and even the KADU) as already seen, these were tensions over one issue: land.
Admittedly this was a crucial issue, but its proponents were limited in their objective. The KLFA and even Kaggia were keen to see free land distributed to ex-
detainees and former guerrillas. What was lacking in their program was how this
objective could have been achieved without alienating other ethnic groups which
had their own landless people and who, in any case, also wanted to have access to
the Highlands. The KLFA, obviously indifferent to the intricacies of Lancaster
House talks, pursued a limited objective that did not extend to other sections of
the economy.

No program was articulated up to 1963 with regard to industry, commerce, education, culture, or foreign relations that fundamentally contradicted the largely
conservative platforms of the KADU or even the KANU. Even on the question of
land, the KLFA, which remained a minority voice in Central Province, did not advocate the nationalization of all land nor did it advocate the abolition of individual
ownership of land. Its members (and sympathizers) wanted land of their own. In
post-colonial times no party in Kenya advocated the abolition of individual ownership of land.[100]

Ideological strife within the nationalist movement becomes all the more important when we consider that Oginga Odinga, a veteran nationalist, later broke
away from the KANU to form the KPU (Kenya People's Union) in 1966. The KPU
was a self-declared socialist party.[101] Would it be accurate to say that Odinga's

struggles in the KANU up to 1966 were largely ideological, that he had always been a socialist? Although tempting to do so, it would be wrong to label him a socialist in orientation or commitment prior to 1966. In his autobiography, in which he gives details of his battles in the party, especially with Mboya, he does not claim that he was a socialist prior to 1966.[102] Indeed, the chapter in this autobiography in which he defends the KPU's policies was written after his resignation from government and is therefore different in tone from the rest of the book.[103] His battles with Mboya do not constitute an ideological war between socialism and capitalism but rather a struggle for power within the party and government.[104] "We do not find in the book," Ochieng has written, "clear elucidation of Pan-Africanism, foreign relations, economic and social philosophy, education and culture before 1965."[105] Much of the claim in the British press that he had socialist ideas stemmed from his visits to socialist European countries in the early 1960s and the financial assistance he received from these countries.[106]

The situation altered in texture after 1963. In 1964, Kenya became a republic, and the KADU-inspired constitution of regionalism was abolished. The president's powers were increased tremendously, and he came to rely more on the civil service than on the political party in the running of the country. Through the provincial administration, the president not only enhanced his own authority but also had, at his disposal, instruments of control that were more loyal to him than to a political party.[107] When the KADU was dissolved in 1964 and joined the KANU, Kenyatta's national power was now beyond challenge.

In post-colonial times, the challenge to the state and therefore to Kenyatta came from those sections of the population that felt left out while politicians, civil servants, and company executives enriched themselves by exploiting the power and influence of their offices.[108] And yet it would be difficult to give a single ideological characterization to this opposition. It was disparate and multifaceted with no immediate ideological unity or uniformity. When in 1966, Odinga formed the KPU and articulated a socialist program, it was not immediately apparent that his position was universally accepted.[109] It is interesting to note that following the establishment of the KPU, Kenyatta and his key advisers initiated a massive oath-taking campaign among the Kikuyu. They swore on the Kenya flag (at the president's home) that "the flag of Kenya shall not leave the House of Mumbi," that is, the Kikuyu ethnic group.[110] They swore to safeguard and maintain Kikuyu dominance in politics, economics, commerce, administration, and even land acquisitions. Among those who took the oath were former guerrillas and ex-detainees, the majority of whom had not benefited materially to any considerable degree since Kenya's independence in 1963.

NINE

THE LEGACY OF MAU MAU

A triumphant liberation movement achieves not only political power but also the power to shape its legacy. Through official political and party agencies, a successful movement has the power to influence how it is remembered by the local population. Over time there emerges what can be termed the official version of events, which then constitutes the acceptable legacy of the liberation movement. To be sure, this official version is never completely static, for it is subject to alteration or reemphasis to justify a new official worldview or to accord prestige to a set of new ideas within the governing party.[1] The official view of events is not the only version, even within the country. However, because of the political hegemony of the party which owes its position of power to the liberation movement, other versions do not enjoy as much prestige or acceptance as the official view.

Outside the country, the official view becomes just one of many views of the liberation movement. More often than not, these external views are influenced by ideological leanings. Scholars have their definitions of objectivity and, of course, their own interpretation of data.

For Mau Mau, its failure to achieve a military and political triumph, as a unit, has expectably complicated any discussion about its legacy. Former Mau Mau guerrillas and ex-detainees have been unable to determine the manner in which their movement is to be remembered. They have been quiet (although not always passive) spectators in the shaping of Mau Mau's many legacies. Not represented in the high echelons of power in post-colonial Kenya, the movement's former activists and guerrillas have been powerless in their desire to steer the country in any direction that could come close to celebrating the "glory of the revolt."

A central controversy surrounding Mau Mau is the role it played in the attainment of Kenya's independence. Although lending qualified respect and making vague references to Mau Mau and the sacrifice of the people for independence, the Kenya political elite has studiously avoided awarding the revolt any central role or acknowledging it as the key factor in the struggle for and attainment of independence. It shall be recalled that on independence day in 1963, Kenyatta did not even mention Mau Mau in his formal speech.[2] For Mau Mau activists, there has never been any doubt in their mind that it was their sacrifices that brought independence to Kenya. The truth however is more complicated. William Ochieng has argued that Mau Mau did not play any significant role in the attainment of independence. In his own words, "The issue is not whether Mau Mau brought *Uhuru*, because it did not.''[3] In Ochieng's view, Mau Mau's inability was partly due to the fact that Mau Mau was not led by "university and high school graduates." According to him, "Mau Mau lacked ideology and direction."

What is clearly apparent is that Mau Mau did not shoot its way to the State House, nor were its guerrillas part of the political delegations negotiating for independence in Britain. Yet, as already seen throughout this study, the revolt's aims (especially those related to self-determination and economic reforms) were incorporated in the platforms of the trade unions and the new political parties after 1960. None of the new political elite could credibly disclaim the central role played by Mau Mau in forcing the hand of the British government to institute political and economic reforms. Tom Mboya, as seen in chapter 8, clearly acknowledged this fact. Of course, many of these African politicians denounced Mau Mau's violence. But this is different from denying that this violence which they loathed led to reforms which made constitutional politics and nationalism possible.

A point of dispute is whether or not Kenya effectively attained independence in 1956 as a result of the revolt and that the remaining years up to 1963 had no impact at all on Kenyan nationalism.[4] All available evidence, as seen in chapter 8, shows that the 1956 to 1963 period was no easy ride for nationalism in Kenya. To discount the importance of this period would be wrong, for it would effectively dismiss the central roles played by the trade unions, the newly elected political elite, and the parliamentary battles. Although Mau Mau had made reforms possible, this fact alone, independent of party and parliamentary politics, would not have led to independence in 1963. The Mau Mau revolt did not alone lead Kenya to independence in 1963. This observation does not diminish the contribution of Mau Mau, which made settler colonialism no longer feasible in Kenya and raised the price of colonial control for Britain to an intolerable level.

But was Mau Mau a national movement or merely a Kikuyu affair? Was it a national effort or an ethnic outburst pursued for narrow purposes? National liberation struggles rarely involve every section of the country with equal intensity and commitment. More often than not, the spark of liberation is lit in one part of the country and then spreads to other parts or all of the country.[5] This fact alone does not make the liberation movement any less national than if it had a clear countrywide representation in its ranks. It is national because its aims are national. It is patriotic because its aims and efforts are patriotic. The composition of the liberation movement, although important, should be seen as just one of the factors to be considered in analyzing its political and economic direction.

The majority of Mau Mau guerrillas were of the Kikuyu ethnic group, with the rest from the Embu, Meru, and Kamba groups. The revolt did not extend beyond Central Province, and if there were any Luo or Abaluyia participants, they were few.[6] Outside Central Province, members of other ethnic groups who chose to participate did so as isolated individuals and not as part of an all-out effort on the part of Mau Mau to recruit members outside the Kikuyu cauldron. No such effort was undertaken nor was any active material support solicited outside Central Province. It would have been impossible to undertake external contacts without proper coordination and organization, which as seen in chapter 6 was largely absent in the re-volt's structure.

What makes Mau Mau a national movement is not its composition but its polit-ical aim. Like the KAU before it, and then the KANU and the KADU after it, Mau Mau remained committed to the idea of political freedom. This was the one issue over which there was general agreement in the forests. Freedom was pursued in general terms; no specific details issued from the forest discussions. Still, Mau Mau was determined to eliminate European domination in Kenya and to attain an Afri-can government. This was, without doubt, a national political aim, for the Kikuyu could not have reasonably expected to attain political freedom independent of other ethnic groups. The drive for freedom was therefore seen in national terms. "Mau Mau," Robert Buijtenhuijs has written, "was . . . a case of 'tribalism serving the nation.' "[7]

After independence it became apparent that many of the former guerrillas and detainees failed to assume the key posts of power and influence in the government and the private sector. "Those who fought," Solomon Memia would later lament, "were never given a chance to participate in government . . . under the pretext that they had no education."[8] Young men, most probably sons of former loyalists, who had gone to school during the time of troubles ended up in power, reaping the "fruits of independence." This development, according to many former guerrillas, constituted a betrayal of the movement and its courageous participants. Indeed, it is true that the "Kenya government lacks and has always lacked an official policy to rehabilitate and reward freedom fighters."[9] This does not mean that former guer-rillas and detainees have not benefited at all from the fruits of independence. Even while criticizing the Kenya government for lack of official policy on this matter, Buijtenhuijs has acknowledged that some of the former guerrillas have benefited from what he called the "Kikuyu boom."[10] The "general prosperity of the Kikuyu" ethnic group since independence, Buijtenhuijs argues, has resulted in the ex-freedom fighters' picking up "some crumbs that have fallen from the loaded Kikuyu table."[11] In her studies, Tabitha Kanogo has concluded that "while offi-cially the government has no policy on the welfare of ex-squatters and freedom fighters, a lot has been done for several of them."[12] Whatever may have been done for them, they were never accorded any special status.

The government from 1963 on steered clear of Mau Mau as a group. Paul Ngei, a former detainee with Kenyatta, introduced a motion in Kenya's Parliament in 1963, urging the "government to formulate a programme of training and assistance for ex-detainees and ex-prisoners to fit them for useful occupations in the service of the country."[13] After much heated debate, the motion was amended. It now urged the "government to investigate and take appropriate action as a matter of national urgency the cases of children, widows or persons who have been left destitute as a result of detention or imprisonment during the years of the State of Emergency."[14] This resolution, apart from being vague in scope, was also nonbinding to the gov-ernment. The following year, Mr. Ngala-Abok, raised this matter again in Parlia-ment. He asked the minister of home affairs "whether the government has any plans to establish an organization, both at the central [and] regional levels, which would care for all Emergency victims throughout the country."[15] In his answer, the minister informed Parliament that it was "undesirable to establish a separate organization to deal with Emergency victims only."[16] Emergency victims were, according to the minister, part of "the problem of the needy in general" which the government was tackling.

If the ex-detainees and former guerrillas have reaped some of the fruits of independence, either from the "Kikuyu boom" or from official programs, these have been small-scale benefits compared to those enjoyed by the political and commercial elite. Clearly, the former Mau Mau activists feel that their dreams and hopes have not been realized, that they have not benefited individually as much as they hoped or felt entitled to, given their view that the country owes its independence directly to their efforts. Betrayal of Mau Mau and its dreams has therefore a specific and more limited meaning. Mau Mau can be viewed as a success by these former guerrillas only if their dreams of property acquisitions and attainment of high political offices are realized. On one level, this is an understandable wish; yet on another it is very troubling. The implications of this wish on national politics would be disastrous. If implemented and if all those who participated in Mau Mau were given all or the major part of the national wealth, it would deny Mau Mau its claim to having been a national movement. It would immediately mean that former guerrillas look at Mau Mau as their own "private revolution."[17]

The controversy surrounding Mau Mau in post-colonial Kenya has over a time come to assume ideological distinctions between the Left and the Right. Both the Left and the Right have sought to utilize the revolt to lend legitimacy to their ideological positions. In this regard, it can be said that both the Left and the Right have been involved for their own divergent purposes in the reinvention of Mau Mau.

Any identification with Mau Mau by the Kikuyu political and commercial elite is for utilitarian purposes in the struggle for dominance in Kenya and not because of the revolt's past practices. It is now an obvious fact that "the Kikuyu have since independence dominated the political and economic affairs of the country."[18] The section of the Kikuyu that has been dominant has not included former guerrillas nor those clearly identified with the struggles and sacrifices of the emergency. In 1963, when Kenyatta feared the revolt of former loyalists and settlers, he relegated Mau Mau to silent obscurity. However, after a smooth transition to independence had been achieved, there arose the problem of competition between the Kikuyu and other ethnic groups. To justify their dominance, the Kikuyu governing elite, many of whom had no linkage to Mau Mau, used the memory of the revolt to enhance and maintain their status.[19] They saw themselves as members of an ethnic group that played the decisive role in the struggle for independence and therefore deserved "a bigger share of the national cake."[20]

The Right, therefore, has reinvented Mau Mau both to maintain the Kikuyu's compliance and also to justify its dominance on the national stage. Since the Kikuyu elite is involved in its own struggle on the national level, it needs a weapon of prestige to justify its dominance. That weapon is Mau Mau. It need hardly be emphasized that no registry of former key loyalists has been kept nor has there been any backlash against loyalists. As a result, any Kikuyu elite can, on a general level, identify himself with Mau Mau to justify his or her claim to dominance. This general and strategic identification with the revolt does not mean that the elite has embraced former guerrillas and their movement.

Perhaps more critical for the survival of the Kikuyu political and commercial elite has been the use of Mau Mau to offset class feuds and antagonisms within the Kikuyu ethnic group. It was observed in chapter 8 that when Oginga Odinga formed the KPU and pointed the way to a possible socialist path in Kenya, Kenyatta and his advisers were quick to arrange for massive oath-taking ceremonies to hold their ethnic group together. The very survival of the Kikuyu people and their lifestyle and property were at stake, so the oath-taking strategists claimed. In this type of hysterical and melodramatic activity, more emphasis was placed on emotions and fear than on rational discourse. Many of those who took the oaths in independent Kenya were poor Kikuyu peasants and former guerrillas who had no sizeable property-holdings that were threatened from outside by "other tribes." The memory of Mau Mau was nonetheless utilized to justify Kikuyu domination and also to forestall the emergence of class antagonisms within the ethnic group. The identification of the people has therefore been more along ethnic than class lines.

Ethnic identification in political and ideological terms has served not only the Kikuyu elite but also members of the ruling elite from other ethnic groups. They have found it easy to marshal ethnic loyalty in their struggle for power at the national level by pointing out the unrelenting drive for domination by the Kikuyu tribe. It could be said that the strategy by the Kikuyu elite to thwart class antagonism within its own ethnic group has been adopted in varying degrees by the elite from other ethnic groups.

The practice of a conservative elite utilizing the memory of a revolt to justify its own position is not limited to Kenya. In Mexico the ruling elite has consistently claimed to be heirs of the Mexican revolution of the early 1900s.[21] It has nonetheless been observed that "many Mexicans still suffer wretched poverty and political repression," and so it is difficult to talk of a revolution having occurred.[22] Especially on the question of land reform, many peasants feel the same economic hardships that led to the rise of Zapata and his army.[23] This has not prevented the Mexican government from glorifying the revolution and promoting Zapata as a national hero. There are, hence, instances in which a revolution can be incorporated in the ideology of the conservative elite to lend national and even international respectability to its practices.

The Left in Kenya has also sought to utilize Mau Mau to lend respectability to its ideological positions. Since the banning of the KPU in 1969, there has been no formal organization or party to articulate the political views of the Left. The KPU did not enjoy the support of all members of the Left when it existed. As a political group, the Left in Kenya has remained disparate, scattered, and largely unorganized. As might be expected, the Left's leading figures are intellectuals associated with universities or schools.

Kenya's leading novelist, Ngugi wa Thiong'o, has clearly been identified with the radical interpretation of Mau Mau. Most of his writing has over the years been largely inspired by this movement. According to him, Mau Mau represented not only a fight against colonialism but also against imperialism. Kimathi, one of Mau Mau's major leaders, attempted to forge, so Ngugi contends, "a grand political alliance of Kenyan people to oust the imperialist enemy."[24] In his play *The Trial of Dedan Kimathi* (co-authored with Micere Mugo), Ngugi "seeks to interpret the movement as having been essentially an anti-imperialist movement with clear goals for a socialist Kenya."[25] This association of Mau Mau with a socialist agenda has drawn sharp criticism from some historians and literary artists, even those who would normally be sympathetic to leftist views. E. S. Athieno-Odhiambo, in his review of the play, states that the playwrights have "assumed a high level of class consciousness on part of those who were fighting in the forests as the Mau Mau."[26] He is convinced that this consciousness was not only absent but also not possible given the composition and leadership of the revolt.

The play is not based on any historical evidence nor is it a factual recreation of past events. It is rather "an imaginative recreation and interpretation of the collective will of the Kenyan peasants and workers in their refusal to break under sixty years of colonial torture and ruthless oppression by the British ruling classes and their continued determination to resist exploitation, oppression and new forms of enslavement."[27] Mau Mau is reinvented by the Left in this instance and given new ideological attributes for the purposes of criticizing the political economy of post-colonial Kenyan society.[28] These new ideological attributes make Mau Mau a socialist liberation movement that united Kenyan peasants and workers against imperialism. As this study has demonstrated, no such unity of workers and peasants was forged nor were all peasants even within Central Province involved in the revolt. "Mau Mau movement," writes Al-Amin Mazrui, "remained uninformed about the question of class alliances."[29] In this regard, it may be useful to recall that none of the Mau Mau guerrillas claimed their movement was socialist. Kimathi himself did not make this claim.

Maina wa Kinyatti, a key figure in the radical interpretation of Mau Mau, had once claimed that the revolt marked "a vigorous nationalist upsurge throughout the country in which the workers and peasants became an independent leading political force" and led to the "death of KAU."[30] At a later stage, he altered his position somewhat. "There was no ideological struggle within the Mau Mau movement," he said, "to transform nationalist consciousness into class consciousness, nor was there a serious systematic analysis of imperialism, the class struggle, and the relation of socialism to the Kenyan revolutionary process."[31]

The Left has nonetheless selectively incorporated Mau Mau in its ideological position. There are understandable reasons for this. In the first place, the disparity between the rich and the poor has continued to widen in Kenya, creating both passive and overt discontent on the part of the hungry and dispossessed sections of the population. It so happens that some of the residents of the sprawling shanty towns common in the major urban areas, especially in Nairobi, are either former guerrillas, their widows, children, or those displaced by the emergency. They therefore provide a clear emotive case of a people who sacrificed and have been forgotten. If the Left wants to build its case around Mau Mau, it is not because it approves of all its past practices but rather because of the emotive power of its symbolism. As a result, Mau Mau assumes more definite ideological positions on the questions of exploitation, liberation, national sovereignty, and social justice. Mau Mau guerrillas, Ngugi has insisted, struggled "for land; independence; freedom from hunger; freedom from foreign control; freedom from external and internal social oppression."[32] The Left in this instance has positioned itself as heirs of the Mau Mau spirit.

On the question of class analysis of society, the Left, in using the symbolism of the revolt, seeks to demonstrate that those in power and authority have betrayed the "true intentions" of Mau Mau and that concentration of wealth in the hands of a few is a betrayal of the egalitarian and patriotic spirit of the revolt.[33] In both cases, the Left is battling the Right for legitimacy, claiming to be closer to Mau Mau's dreams than the governing elite. It is a strategy the ruling elite has continually sought to subvert, being conscious of its potential attractiveness. In this regard Mau Mau guerrillas have not been allowed or encouraged to organize themselves as a separate body on a national level nor has any opposition party been allowed to act as their voice.

Among the former guerrillas and detainees themselves, there have been obstacles to the forging of a uniform legacy of their revolt. Splintered leadership has been a major obstacle. As it was in the forest, the guerrillas have not been able to resolve this problem. As stated, the government has discouraged the formation of a national ex-Mau Mau organization. This has made it impossible for these guerrillas to reflect as a group on the meaning and significance of their revolt.[34] In postcolonial times, they have also been involved in the practices and contradictions of party, sectional, and ethnic politics. They have participated as individuals and not as a group with divergent aims from the rest of the community or society. It was observed that at the height of the KPU's struggle with the KANU, former guerrillas were split in their response to the events. Bildad Kaggia had positioned himself as the parliamentary advocate of the interests of former guerrillas, especially on the question of land. It was an issue over which he was later fired by Kenyatta from his minor ministerial post. He later joined the KPU as deputy leader under Oginga Odinga when this new party sought to identify itself more fully with former guerrillas and their economic grievances. Yet Kaggia and the KPU did not enjoy the overwhelming support of former guerrillas and detainees. The KANU under Kenyatta was able to enlist the support of key former Mau Mau leaders like General Kimbo, General Mbaria Kaniu, and Field Marshal Mwariama.[35] When Kaggia ran for election in Murang'a on the KPU platform, which was clearly more sympathetic to the plight of former Mau Mau activists than the KANU platform, he was defeated by a KANU candidate.[36] Ethnic loyalty was invoked, and Kaggia was seen as having "betrayed his tribe" by aligning with Odinga, a member of the Luo ethnic group.[37]

The rehabilitation process has also been a great obstacle in the thinking of former detainees about the legacy of the revolt. The memory of former detainees who denounced Mau Mau differs from those few former guerrillas who escaped the pipeline. There is an added problem of determining who among the former activists, guerrillas, and detainees remained faithful to the movement. This is important, for surely the honor of having been a Mau Mau cannot be extended to those who later betrayed their comrades and the revolt.

In 1986 at Nyeri a large gathering of former guerrillas and detainees met for the first time since 1963.[38] They met to express their loyalty to the KANU government led by Moi and also to "find out ways to gather and publish material on the Mau Mau and to seek how freedom fighters could help in nation building."[39] The meeting's participants maintained that Mau Mau had brought independence to Kenya and disagreed vehemently with university scholars who argued otherwise.[40] They also demanded official recognition of their efforts. But even at this meeting, it was apparent that not every major former Mau Mau leader was present.[41] The question of identity was also raised. General Ndungu wa Gicheru told those gathered that "if in the course of being a freedom fighter you slipped and joined the loyalists, don't hide the fact. If you were a collaborator and then joined the freedom movement, tell it all. There are some people who claim that they were heroes in the war when they did nothing."[42] There can be little doubt that this question of identity is likely to be a source of some significant friction within the ranks of the revolt for some time to come, especially if economic and social benefits were to be attached to the honor.

Within Central Province itself, there is no uniform memory of Mau Mau. This is due not only to the fact that some districts and villages were more involved than others but also because of the split between loyalists and guerrillas during the emergency. It is not surprising that the memory of the revolt, especially with regard to its details, varies a great deal and that people have more information about their own area's involvement as opposed to the general character of the revolt.[43] This "split" memory and myth has been compounded by the realities of post-colonial politics and economics that have led to the reevaluation of individual contributions to the freedom movement. As already indicated, there has been a general tendency among Mau Mau guerrillas and detainees to revise their positions to suit the prevailing political climate or even to fit into some of the ideological debates surrounding the revolt. It was noticed, for example, that after the February 1986 Mau Mau meeting some of the former key guerrilla leaders visited the local KANU office and pledged their support to the party and government. They further stated that "they were strongly opposed to the grouping of Kenyans into pre-independent loyalists and nationalists."[44]

No discussion of the legacy of Mau Mau can be complete without dealing, however briefly, with the role of women in the revolt. Recent scholarship has correctly drawn our attention to this fact. These scholars seek to correct what they see as a deliberate effort to omit the valuable and indispensable contributions of women to the Mau Mau revolt. Cora Ann Presley suggests that this omission may be the result of sources of data, which "have been almost exclusively male, whether they were Europeans or Africans." Such sources of data have, according to Presley, "created the false paradigm that politics was mainly a male concern."[45] Jean O'Barr, on the other hand, feels that the problem goes beyond data. The overwhelming majority of authors and scholars who have written about Mau Mau have been men, and there-fore, among other things, "they fail to account for the contributions women made to the revolt."[46]

What then was the contribution of women to the revolt? Cora Ann Presley states correctly that women's roles "were as multi-faceted as the revolt itself." These roles included "organization and maintenance of the supply lines which directed food, supplies, medicine, guns and information to the forest forces."[47] Those women who went to the forest were "responsible for cooking, water hauling, knit-ting sweaters, etc."[48]

The most detailed account of women's role in Mau Mau is given by Margaret Wangui Gachihi in her M.A. thesis.[49] Gachihi argues that without the active par-ticipation of women, Mau Mau "would not have been as effective, or survived, as long as it did."[50] This active participation was clearly in the courier service. Women formed the valuable link between the forest fighters and the passive wing in the reserves.[51] Those women who went to the forests tended on the whole to be engaged in noncombat roles, acting as "transport, signals, medical corps, and ord-nance to their male counterparts."[52] This leads Gachihi to conclude that "the great-est contribution of women to the Mau Mau was outside the domain of actual combat."[53] Nonetheless, she emphasizes that a few women took part in actual com-bat as part of the forest fighters.

These studies, as valuable and as pioneering as they are, leave several questions unanswered. There is a compelling need for precision in explanations and clarifi-cations. These studies on the whole deal with the question of women on a general basis. There is no clarification with regard to which class of Kikuyu, Embu, and Meru women actively participated in the revolt. To be sure, an attempt is made to indicate that "involvement in Mau Mau cut across 'class' lines."[54] Yet because this point is not pursued to any appreciable degree in these recent studies, it remains a general remark that does not clarify the question of which women participated at what stages in the revolt. It is legitimate to inquire whether women from the squat-ters evicted from the Rift Valley participated more actively than those from the re-serves, or whether any district in Central Province had more women participants than others. On the question of women involvement "cutting across 'class' lines," there is a need to indicate how pervasive this phenomenon was.

A point of great importance here is to determine whether participation by women was an effort on their part to pursue sectional, or more specific, interests that dif-fered from those that had ignited the revolt. In her study, Gachihi came to the re-vealing conclusion that "when one talks of recruitment of the Kikuyu women into Mau Mau, one is not talking as though this was a separate exercise from the re-cruitment of other members into the movement."[55] Colonial pressures of land alienation, overpopulation, and taxation seem to have affected the general African population with unrelenting intensity. The economic welfare of the family and free-dom of the community were threatened by the ever-increasing demands of settler colonialism. To this end, Mau Mau's demand for freedom and the return of stolen lands, "was in no way an exclusive preoccupation of any one special group and not, particularly, a sex group."[56] There does not appear to have existed specific appeals in Mau Mau about problems of gender and sexual division of labor. It is worth noting that tasks assigned to women in Mau Mau tended on the whole to conform to "traditional tasks performed by women in the home." These tasks included cooking, fetching water, and taking care of the sick. Although there were women leaders of exemplary status throughout the revolt, it would be inaccurate to suggest that women on the whole assumed positions of leadership. Leadership in Mau Mau, and especially in the forest, "was overwhelmingly a male domain."[57]

How about the problems of empowerment of women? "Did the nationalist movement empower Kenyan women? Or did it reinforce old assumptions about women, and not contribute to their participation in contemporary life?"[58] There can be no adequate answer to these questions without first considering Mau Mau's political ideologies (as discussed in chapter 6). Mau Mau as a revolutionary movement did not reach the stage where questions of gender, sexism, sexual division of labor, and property ownership were considered crucial to the movement's legitimacy, expansion, and survival. In other peasant-based revolutionary movements in modern Africa, it is clear that answers to these questions were considered within the context of the overall ideology that guided these movements. Stephanie Urdang's study on Guinea-Bissau shows that its revolutionary party (PAIGC) sought to integrate "the emancipation of women into the total revolution." This strategy and assessment grew out of the realization "that women suffer a dual oppression, expressed in Guinea-Bissau as the need for women to 'fight two colonialisms—the one of the Portuguese and the other of men.' "[59] In Angola women made considerable contributions to the wars of liberation and remain deservedly proud of this fact. The fight against colonialism is seen by Angolan women as "the first steps toward their own emancipation."[60]

It is worth nothing that even in countries like Guinea-Bissau, Angola, or Mozambique, where "talk of and on the woman is clearer than elsewhere,"[61] there remain immense problems over the question of women's empowerment in the postcolonial era. Some of these problems are the result of structural obstacles, while others can be traced to what many women organizations in these countries call "people's consciousness," a reluctance on the part of the male elite and nonelite alike to abandon customs, values, and practices which assure them of power and authority over women. "The principle of equality for men and women in society," the Organization of Angolan Women has observed, "is not sufficient to ensure that women are in fact an active element in their country's development or that they participate equally in decision making."[62] The principle of equality and nonsexism can be a reality only in those instances in which "profound changes in social, political and economic structures" have occurred. Urdang's conclusions on Guinea-Bissau would seem to reinforce the position taken by the Organization of Angolan Women. She insists that "true women's emancipation will not come in Guinea-Bissau if the revolution does not get past the super structure."[63] With regard to Mau Mau, there is a clear need for a comparative analysis between it and other African peasant-based revolutionary movements on this vital question of women's empowerment. Available evidence strongly suggests that it is difficult to achieve women's empowerment independent of fundamental and far-reaching societal changes that emphasize egalitarianism and nonsexism.

Above all is the question of what the views of Kenyan women are toward Mau Mau. It cannot be assumed that there exists one uniform view by women in Kenya toward Mau Mau. What has determined these varied views? Can these varied views be traced to different roles played by these women in the revolt or even to their class position during the emergency? Jean O'Barr has concluded with regret that "involvement in Mau Mau did not alter deeply-held beliefs about women's place in the family and how the mother role defines power and position in society at large."[64] Recent events in Kenya would seem to support this position. In July 1991 about nineteen girls were killed and several raped by boys at St. Kizito Mixed Secondary School in Meru district. This event and the horror surrounding it confirmed to many Kenyan women what they had always believed: "Violence is only one of the areas in which Kenyan women are victims of sexism and other discriminatory practices."[65] The lot of the Kenyan woman "is not a happy one"; it continues to be characterized by poverty and powerlessness. Hilary Ng'weno of Kenya's *Weekly Review* has written that the tragedy at St. Kizito School "underscored the abominable male chauvinism that dominates Kenyan social life." He added that "contrary to the high sounding rhetoric that spews out of pulpits and political platforms, the lot of our women and girls is lamentable. We treat them as second-class beings, good only for sexual gratification and burdensome chores."[66] A question must be raised, therefore, about the reasons for this state of affairs in which women continue to be exploited, harmed, and dominated, even though some of them "proved themselves" in Mau Mau and therefore made substantial contributions to the struggle for independence. In any discussion on these issues, it is vital to determine the views of women participants in Mau Mau toward the post-colonial Kenyan society. The participation of women in Mau Mau clearly demands further study.

In letters written to the press by various members of the public after the 1986 Mau Mau meeting, we are able to gain a glimpse into the general public's views on the legacy of the revolt. To be sure, these letters do not tell the whole story, for they represent only limited views of the literate male section of the urban population. The views of ordinary peasants are not represented nor are the views of women, the unemployed or the shanty dweller. But these letters do represent the views of those who, although literate, are not specialists in the field.

In his letter, Elijah Soi asserted, without illustration, that university lecturers and professors were deliberately distorting facts about Mau Mau in order to ridicule it as a mere aimless peasant revolt.[67] While acknowledging that Mau Mau played a crucial role in the attainment of independence, Nelson Obota, in his letter, thought that contributions by Lancaster House delegates should not be forgotten.[68] On the question of who should write Mau Mau's "real history," two letters expressed contradictory views. Butek arap Ndata thought that "anything pertaining to the struggle, . . . history or films on Mau Mau influence, should be entrusted to KANU."[69] M. K. Njeru, on the other hand, thought that this task should be left to "historians to do a thorough research and write refined papers," which could then be made available to Mau Mau participants "for comment."[70] But how about the role of Mau Mau in post-colonial society? Harmon Githinji said he did not "want Mau Mau turned into a political movement in modern Kenya." He was completely against the idea of "accusing other people of past sins" and instead wanted Kenyans to follow Kenyatta's lead to "forgive and forget" the past.[71]

These varied public opinions reflect the larger controversies about Mau Mau within academic and political circles. They also point out the utter necessity of "opening up" the revolt for scrutiny and analysis. Up to now there has been a marked sensitivity about studying this peasant revolt. The resultant scarcity of information has led many people from inside and outside Kenya to resort to generalizations and speculations. This is dangerous, for idle generalizations and speculations are not a province of history. History must immerse itself in facts, and however painful, their presence must be acknowledged. As it relates to Mau Mau, this is crucial, for the majority of Kenyans "were still suckling or were not yet born when the war of independence was taking place."[72] They therefore do not have firsthand knowledge of the revolt and have had to rely for their information on rumors, abbreviated "safe" information in textbooks, and on selective details chosen by ideological combatants to advance their positions. Condemnation without information is as dangerous as glorification without facts, for both positions rely not on empirical evidence but on emotion. This study has shown that there are no shortcuts to the understanding of Mau Mau. Any effort to comprehend this revolt must embrace its general characteristics and also its internal contradictions, setbacks, and triumphs.

ABBREVIATIONS

HMSO	Her Majesty's Stationery Office
IWM	Imperial War Museum
KNA	Kenya National Archives
PRO	Public Record Office
RHL	Rhodes House Library
RIIA	Royal Institute of International Affairs

NOTES

Preface

1. Amilcar Cabral, *Unity and Struggle* (New York: Monthly Review Press, 1979), p. 136.
2. Wunyabari O. P. W. Maloba, "The Mau Mau Struggle in Kenya: An Historical Analysis of the Evolution and Impact of a Peasant Revolt" (Ph.D. thesis, Stanford University, 1988).

Introduction

1. Basil Davidson, *Africa in Modern History* (Middlesex, England: Penguin Books, 1978), p. 263.
2. Ronald Webber, *The Peasants' Revolt* (Lavenham: Terence Dalton, 1980), p. ix.
3. Paul Avrich, *Russian Rebels, (1600–1800)* (New York: Schocken Books, 1972), p. 6.
4. Vo Nguyen Giap, *The Military Art of a People's War* (New York: Monthly Review Press, 1970), p. 98.
5. Guy Fourquin, *The Anatomy of Popular Rebellion in the Middle Ages* (Amsterdam: North Holland, 1978), p. 132. Of the characteristics of a peasant rebellion, Fourquin thinks that "the explosion is sudden, unexpected, destructive and almost always short lived" (p. 132).
6. Ibid., p. 136.
7. Avrich, p. 6.
8. Ernesto Che Guevara, *Guerilla Warfare* (Lincoln: University of Nebraska Press, 1985), p. 85: "Generally guerilla warfare starts from a well considered act of will: some chief with prestige starts an uprising for the salvation of his people, beginning his work in difficult conditions in a foreign country."
9. Fourquin, p. 133.
10. Pierre Goubert, *The French Peasantry in the Seventeenth Century* (Cambridge: Cambridge University Press, 1986), pp. 206–207.
11. Roland Mousnier, *Peasant Uprisings in 17th Century France, Russia, and China* (New York: Harper & Row, 1970), p. 341.
12. Ibid, p. 342.
13. Eric Hobsbawm, *Primitive Rebels* (New York: W. W. Norton, 1959), p. 16.
14. Eric Hobsbawm, *Bandits* (New York: Delacorte Press, 1969), p. 55.
15. Kenneth W. Grundy, *Guerilla Struggle in Africa* (New York: Grossman Publishers, 1971), p. 47.
16. A classic illustration of this point is the politicization effort by FRELIMO in Mozambique. Although most of the peasants were illiterate, FRELIMO found means and ways of reaching them with its revolutionary message. For details see Barbara Cornwall, *The Bush Rebels* (New York: Holt, Rinehart & Winston, 1972), pp. 31–39.
17. Basil Davidson, "African Peasants and Revolution," *Journal of Peasant Studies* 1, no. 3 (1974), p. 279.
18. The rural and urban uprisings in Angola in 1961 were indeed spontaneous. In Luanda, there was a spontaneous uprising by Africans intent on freeing political prisoners before they could be sent into exile or executed. In the rural areas, there was an uprising by African agricultural laborers. For details see Basil Davidson, *In the Eye of the Storm* (New York:

Doubleday, 1972); and John A. Marcum, *The Angolan Revolution Vol. 11* (Cambridge, Mass.: M.I.T. Press, 1978). After 1961, the MPLA sought to organize a people's war against the Portuguese by relying on the power of its message for a new future in Angola.

19. Mao Tse-tung, *On Guerilla Warfare* (New York: Frederick A. Praeger, 1961), p. 43.

20. Samuel Popkin, *The Rational Peasant* (Berkeley/Los Angeles: Univeristy of California Press, 1979), p. 6. For details about the moral economy, see James C. Scott, *The Moral Economy of the Peasant* (New Haven: Yale University Press, 1976).

21. Ibid., p. 252.

22. Gerard Chaliand, *The Peasants of North Vietnam* (Baltimore, Md.: Penguin Books, 1969). See the preface by Phillippe Devillers, p. 7.

23. Allen Isaacman, "Peasants and Rural Social Protest in Africa," *African Studies Review* 33, no. 2 (September 1990).

24. Ibid., p. 3.

25. Eric Wolf, *Peasant Wars of the Twentieth Century* (New York: Harper & Row, 1969), p. xii.

26. Carl G. Rosberg and John Nottingham, *The Myth of Mau Mau: Nationalism in Kenya* (New York: Hoover/Praeger, 1966), p. 261.

27. M. Clough and K. Jackson, *A Bibliography on Mau Mau* (Stanford University, 1975), p. 6.

28. Rosberg and Nottingham, p. 276.

29. Luise White, "Separating the Men from the Boys: Constructions of Gender, Sexuality, and Terrorism in Central Kenya, 1939–1959," *International Journal of African Historical Studies* 23, no. 1 (1990).

30. Isaacman, p. 53.

31. White, "Separating the Men," p. 9.

32. Ibid., p. 4.

33. Ibid., p. 10.

34. Ibid., p. 13.

35. For details about prison conditions and labor performed by inmates in the US, see Leonard Orland, *Prisons: Houses of Darkness* (New York: Free Press, 1975) and Ben H. Bagdikian, *The Shame of the Prisons* (New York: Pocket Books, 1972).

36. John Lonsdale, "Mau Maus of the Mind: Making Mau Mau and Remaking Kenya," *Journal of African History* 31 (1990).

37. Ibid., p. 417.

38. Ibid., p. 397.

39. Ibid., p. 413.

40. *East African Standard* (11 September 1953), p. 68.

41. *East African Standard* (12 October 1955), p. 145.

42. B278 and B279 (KNA), *The Church and Mau Mau* (Official Church of Scotland Report and Analysis, 1953), p. 7.

43. Ibid., p. 10.

44. Accession Number 10224/4; interview with Sir Anthony Swann (IWM), pp. 42–43.

45. Frank Furedi, "The Social Composition of the Mau Mau Movement in the White Highlands," *Journal of Peasant Studies* 1, no. 4 (1974).

46. Ibid., p. 504.

47. Bildad Kaggia, *Roots of Freedom* (Nairobi: East African Publishing House, 1975).

48. Basil Davidson, *The Liberation of Guinea* (Baltimore, Md.: Penguin Books, 1969), p. 69.

49. Bethwell A. Ogot, "Introduction," *Kenya Historical Review* 5, no. 2 (1977), p. 169.

50. Recent studies by anthropologists seem to indicate that kinship alone cannot be relied upon to ensure loyalty among kinspeople. "Social anthropologists have observed a gulf," Keesing writes, "between the way peoples say kin should act toward one another—ideal standards or norms—and what they actually do. Close relatives, or fellow clansmen, should support one another, cooperate, avoid quarrels, and so on; yet the anthropologist often

observes enmity, not amity, subversion not support, and feuding not solidarity.'' Roger M. Keesing, *Kin Groups and Social Structure* (New York: Holt, Rinehart and Winston, 1975), p. 122.

51. Robert H. Lauer, *Social Movements and Social Change* (Carbondale: Southern Illinois University Press, 1976), p. XIX. Also see J. A. Banks, *The Sociology of Social Movements* (Macmillan, 1972).

52. Lauer, p. XIX.

53. Frank Furedi, *The Mau Mau War in Perspective* (London: James Currey; Nairobi: Heinemann Kenya; Athens: Ohio University Press, 1989), pp. 9, 18, 19.

54. Ibid., p. 140.

55. President Moi later ordered ''an immediate stop to the Mau Mau debate.'' He observed that ''some people were using the Mau Mau issue to create disunity.'' *The Standard* (Nairobi, 22 March 1986), p. 1.

56. This seems to be a common, though serious, problem for researchers on this issue. Margaret Wangui Gachihi in her Master's degree thesis ''The Role of Kikuyu Women in the Mau Mau'' found that ''it was quite difficult to get an informant to relate the actual events of the ceremonies as they were actually performed.'' So she resorted to colonial documents ''as related by 'those who had had a change of heart.' '' Margaret Wangui Gachihi, ''The Role of Kikuyu Women in the Mau Mau'' (M.A. thesis, University of Nairobi, 1986), p. 30.

1. The Economics of Desperation

1. M. P. K. Sorrenson, *Land Reform in the Kikuyu Country* (Nairobi: Oxford University Press, 1967), p. 5.

2. G. Muriuki, *A History of the Kikuyu, 1500–1900* (Nairobi: Oxford University Press, 1974), p. 75.

3. L. S. B. Leakey, *The Southern Kikuyu before 1903*, vol. 1 (London: Academic Press, 1977), p. 116.

4. Ibid., p. 117.

5. For details see M. P. K. Sorrenson, *Origins of European Settlement in Kenya* (Nairobi: Oxford University Press, 1968).

6. Ibid., p. 36.

7. ''These conditions included the demand for a Jewish governor, and the power to legislate for 'internal administration,' to levy taxes, to control immigration and to appoint judges. Finally, Jewish religion and social customs were to be respected.'' Ibid., p. 38.

8. Ibid., p. 27.

9. Sir Charles Eliot, *The East Africa Protectorate* (New York: Barnes & Noble, 1966), p. 92.

10. Sorrenson, *Origins of European Settlement*, p. 1.

11. E. S. Atieno-Odhiambo, ''The Colonial Government, the Settlers and the Trust Principle in Kenya, 1939,'' *Trans-African Journal of History* 2, no. 2 (1972), p. 97.

12. The Crown Lands Ordinance, 1915 (Ordinance no. 30), in G. H. Mungeam, ed., *Kenya Select Historical Documents 1884–1923* (Nairobi: East African Publishing House, 1978), p. 346.

13. M. P. K. Sorrenson, *Origins of European Settlement*, p. 234.

14. R. M. A. Van Zwanenberg, *Colonial Capitalism and Labour in Kenya* (Nairobi: East Africa Literature Bureau, 1978), p. 1. It had taken the government over thirty years to establish white farmers in Kenya, and it was not now willing to forsake them when faced with the economic catastrophe brought on by the depression. Van Zwanenberg suggests that the commitment was in part the result of racial solidarity (p. 27).

15. M. P. K. Sorrenson, *Land Reform*, p. 21.

16. Robert L. Tignor, *The Colonial Transformation of Kenya* (Princeton, N.J.: Princeton University Press, 1976), p. 45.

17. G. Muriuki, "Background to Politics and Nationalism in Central Kenya," *Politics and Nationalism in Colonial Kenya*, ed. B. A. Ogot (Nairobi: East African Publishing House, 1972), p. 13.

18. Report of the Kenya Land Commission, cmd. 4556 (1934), p. 144, cited in M. P. K. Sorrenson, *Land Reform*, p. 80.

19. The East African Statistical Department, "Geographical and Tribal Studies, 1950." Cited in M. P. K. Sorrenson, *Land Reform*, p. 80.

20. *Annual Report of the Colony and Protectorate of Kenya, 1946* (HMSO, 1948), p. 7.

21. D. W. Throup, "The Governorship of Sir Philip Mitchell in Kenya, 1944–1952." (Ph.D. thesis, Cambridge: Cambridge University, 1983), p. 93.

22. See Frank Furedi, "The Social Composition of the Mau Mau Movement in the White Highlands," *Journal of Peasant Studies* 1, no. 4 (1974). "According to estimates in 1948, 40 per cent of the population in Kiambu district was without land and by 1953, 50 per cent of the population of the Kikuyu reserves were landless," p. 488.

23. *Post War Five Year Development Plan; Central Province* (DC/NY1/3/3. KNA), p. 213.

24. Sir Philip Mitchell, *The Agrarian Problems in Kenya* (Nairobi: Government Printer, 1947), p. 11.

25. *Nyeri Handing-Over Reports, 1950* (DC/NY1/2/1. KNA), p. 4.

26. *Kenya Land Commission Report: Summary of Conclusions Reached by His Majesty's Government, cmd. 4850, 1934.* (Migrated Archives Project, EAO 73/81 (27) KNA), p. 4.

27. S. H. Fazan, "An Economic Survey of the Kikuyu Proper 1931–1963" (DC/KBU/6/3. KNA), p. 70.

28. DC/NY1/3/3, *Post War Plan*, p. 4.

29. Ibid., p. 22.

30. For a detailed analysis of the governorship of Sir Philip Mitchell in Kenya, see D. W. Throup, "Governorship of Sir Philip Mitchell."

31. Sir Philip Mitchell, "Kenya No. 44" (Migrated Archives Project, EAO/73/81 (38) KNA), p. 1.

32. Sir Philip Mitchell, *The Agrarian Problems in Kenya* (Nairobi: Government Printer, 1947), p. 1.

33. Ibid., p. 2.

34. Ibid., p. 3.

35. Ibid., p. 3.

36. M. P. K. Sorrenson, *Land Reform*, p. 55.

37. D. W. Throup, "Governorship of Sir Philip Mitchell," p. 47.

38. Ibid., p. 6.

39. DC/NY1/2/1, *Post War Plan*, p. 3.

40. M. P. K. Sorrenson, *Land Reform*, p. 85.

41. Frank Furedi, "The African Crowd in Nairobi," *Journal of African History* 14, no. 2 (1973), p. 277.

42. D. W. Throup, "Governorship of Sir Philip Mitchell," p. 276.

43. "Probably the biggest factor that has caused African discontent in urban areas is the lack of accommodation." *Annual Report of Colony and Protectorate of Kenya, 1947* (HMSO, 1949), p. 17.

44. *East Africa Royal Commission, 1953–1955 Report* (HMSO, 1955), p. 210. On urban living conditions by Africans the Royal Commission observed, "Only a minority of Africans bring their families to the towns. The remainder either leave their families on their holdings in their tribal areas or are unmarried. The evils associated with the absence of family life— drunkenness, prostitution, and venereal disease are rife in the towns with large African populations. A large proportion of the women who come to the towns to escape from customary marriages earn their living by prostitution or enter into irregular unions" (p. 208).

45. *Report of the Committee on African Wages (The Carpenter Report)* (Nairobi: Government Printer, 1954).

46. Ibid., p. 139.
47. Ibid., p. 95.
48. *Annual Report of the Colony and Protectorate of Kenya, 1947* (HMSO, 1949), p. 14.
49. *The Carpenter Report*, p. 140.
50. *Annual Report of the Colony and Protectorate of Kenya, 1948* (HMSO, 1950), p. 15.
51. *The Carpenter Report*, p. 140.
52. M. P. K. Sorrenson, *Land Reform*, p. 86.
53. D. W. Throup, "Governorship of Sir Philip Mitchell," p. 263.

2. Frustrations of Nationalism

1. Carl G. Rosberg and John Nottingham, *The Myth of Mau Mau: Nationalism in Kenya* (New York: Hoover/Praeger, 1966), p. 45.
2. Harry Thuku, *An Autobiography* (Nairobi: Oxford University Press, 1970), p. 23.
3. "Inquest Verdict on Nairobi Native Riot," *The Leader of British East Africa* (1 April 1922) and "The Shooting Finding" *Daily Leader* (29 March 1922), cited in G. H. Mungeam, ed., *Kenya: Select Historical Documents 1884–1923* (Nairobi: East African Publishing House, 1978), pp. 523, 526.
4. Makhan Singh, "The East African Association, 1921–1925," *HADITH, 3*, ed. B. A. Ogot (Nairobi: East African Publishing House, 1971), pp. 131–32.
5. See, for example, his letter to the Tuskegee Institute, cited in Mungeam, p. 405.
6. John Spencer, "The Kikuyu Central Association and the Genesis of Kenya African Union," *Kenya Historical Review*, 2, no. 1 (1974), p. 74. Thuku contends he never received any such large sums of money from the KCA. According to him, he knew "that people had been collecting money for themselves in my name. They would tell the KCA supporters that a collection was being made to buy Harry Thuku something, and I would never receive it. In fact—the only money I received the whole of my nine years was the Shs. 30 from Luka Muciri." Thuku, p. 49.
7. Robert L. Tignor, *The Colonial Transformation of Kenya* (Princeton, N.J.: Princeton University Press, 1976), p. 239.
8. John Spencer, *The Kenya African Union* (London: KPI, 1985), p. 96.
9. "In 1933 it had 50 members. In 1936 it claimed a membership of 300. By 1938 it had 800 members." *Historical Dictionary of Kenya*, ed. B. A. Ogot (London: Scarecrow Press, 1981), p. 138.
10. Rosberg and Nottingham, p. 186.
11. Spencer, *Kenya African Union*, p. 84.
12. Spencer, "The Kikuyu Central Association" p. 74. There is every indication that Harry Thuku was extremely upset for having been denied the chance of going to England in 1931, when Kenyatta ultimately went. He felt he was more entitled to it than Kenyatta.
13. Harry Thuku, pp. 43–46.
14. Ibid., p. 60.
15. Ibid., p. 60.
16. Statement by Ng'otho Goro in *Kenyatta* (KNA). Film.
17. Ibid. Originally Kang'ethe had been chosen but declined, for he did not have the language and sophistication in which to conduct negotiations. Interestingly, Kenyatta's friends in London thought his "English was far from perfect, and in 1931 his Quaker friends arranged for him to go as a student to Woodbrooke College in Selly Oak." Guy Arnold, *Kenyatta and the Politics of Kenya* (London: J. M. Dent, 1974), p. 27.
18. Steven H. Jones, "Jomo Kenyatta: Anthropologist and Cultural Nationalist—And Political Chameleon." (Unpublished Paper, Department of History, Kenyatta University, June 1986), p. 3.
19. Arnold, p. 98.

20. Ibid., p. 32.

21. Ibid., p. 31.

22. Ibid., p. 106.

23. Spencer, *Kenya African Union*, p. 146.

24. M. P. K. Sorrenson, *Origins of European Settlement in Kenya* (Nairobi: Oxford University Press, 1968), p. 242.

25. Ibid., p. 243.

26. E. A. Brett, *Colonialism and Underdevelopment in East Africa* (New York: NOK Publishers, 1973), p. 40.

27. Lord Lugard, *The Dual Mandate for British Tropical Africa* (Hamden, Conn.: Archon Books, 1965), p. 69–72.

28. Elizabeth Hopkins, "Racial Minorities in British East Africa," *The Transformation of East Africa*, ed. Stanley Diamond and Fred G. Burke (New York: Basic Books, 1966), p. 94.

29. Richard Frost, *Race against Time* (London: Rex Hollings, 1978), p. 83.

30. Ibid., pp. 92–93.

31. Rosberg and Nottingham, p. 228.

32. Bruce J. Berman, "Administration and Politics in Colonial Kenya," (Ph.D. thesis, Yale University, 1974), p. 397. Also see his recent book *Control and Crisis in Colonial Kenya* (London: James Currey; Nairobi: Heinemann; Athens: Ohio University Press, 1990).

33. Joseph Murumbi's remarks in *MAU MAU* (KNA). Film.

34. M. P. K. Sorrenson, *Land Reform in the Kikuyu Country* (Nairobi: Oxford University Press, 1967), pp. 89–90.

35. *East African Standard*, February 9, 1951.

36. O. J. E. Shiroya, "The Impact of World War II on Kenya: The Role of Ex-Servicemen in Kenya Nationalism." (Ph.D. thesis, Michigan State University, 1968), abstract. In a further elaboration on the contribution of ex-Askaris on Kenyan political events, Shiroya states, "Because ex-Askaris organizations, as such, did not exist, because they were rigidly controlled by the government between 1946 and 1961, their direct impact on Kenyan political events and nationalism seems to have been rather slight" (p. 201).

37. Frank Furedi, "The African Crowd in Nairobi: Popular Movements and Elite Politics," *Journal of African History* 14, no. 2 (1973), p. 282.

38. Ibid., p. 285.

39. Ibid., p. 284.

40. Bildad Kaggia, *Roots of Freedom* (Nairobi: East African Publishing House, 1975), p. 9.

41. Ibid., p. 66.

42. Rosberg and Nottingham, p. 267.

43. Ibid., p. 271.

44. Ibid., p. 259.

45. Solomon Memia's remarks in *MAU MAU* (KNA). Film.

46. Frank Furedi, "The Social Composition of the Mau Mau Movement in the White Highlands," *Journal of Peasant Studies*, 1, no. 4, (1974). See also M. Tamarkin, "Mau Mau in Nakuru," *Journal of African History*, 17, no. 1 (1976).

47. Kaggia, p. 107.

48. Addenda to a memorandum on Mau Mau intimidation prepared by the CID for the Member of Law and Order, 30 April 1952 (CO822/438, PRO, London).

49. Kaggia, p. 113.

50. Ibid., p. 108.

51. Ibid., p. 109.

52. D. W. Throup, "The Governorship of Sir Philip Mitchell," p. 263.

53. Kaggia, p. 108.

54. Brian Lapping, *End of Empire* (New York: St. Martin's Press, 1985), p. 409.

3. 1952

1. Bildad Kaggia, *Roots of Freedom* (Nairobi: East African Publishing House, 1975), p. 108.

2. Key details of this oath are given in Donald L. Barnett and Karari Njama, *Mau Mau from Within* (New York: Monthly Review Press, 1966), pp. 58–59.

3. Brian Lapping, *End of Empire* (New York: St. Martin's Press, 1985), pp. 409–410.

4. Ibid., p. 410.

5. Waruhiu Itote, *Mau Mau General* (Nairobi: East African Publishing House, 1967), pp. 43–44.

6. Barnett and Njama, p. 66.

7. Ibid., p. 65.

8. Ibid., p. 64. See also The Johnson Papers (MSS. Afr. S. 1484. RHL, Oxford University) for other details provided by detainees.

9. Kaggia, p. 110.

10. MS. Afr. S. 1534 (RHL, Oxford University, no. 3468, Athi River Camp), p. 9.

11. Ibid., p. 10.

12. Barnett and Njama, p. 66.

13. Kaggia, p. 109.

14. Barnett and Njama, p. 67.

15. M. Tamarkin, "Mau Mau in Nakuru," *Journal of African History,* 17, no. 1, (1976).

16. Ibid., p. 125.

17. Ibid., p. 127.

18. Ibid., p. 126.

19. Barnett and Njama, pp. 67–69. The authors provide one of the most detailed accounts of this Batuni oath. It was long and elaborate. In part the warriors swore to "kill the enemy . . . even if that enemy be my father or mother, my brother or sister" (p. 68).

20. M. Tamarkin, p. 130.

21. Waruhiu Itote, p. 47.

22. Barnett and Njama, p. 69.

23. Cited in Robert Buijtenhuijs, *Essays on Mau Mau* (Leiden/The Netherlands: African Studies Centre, 1982), p. 38.

24. Waruhiu Itote, p. 48.

25. Ibid., p. 53.

26. *Catalogue of Assaults on Government Servants in 1952* (CO822/437, PRO, London), p. 40. "*January; Nyeri:* 10 huts belonging to either Headmen, police informers, pro-Beecher teachers burnt down. *February;* 4 huts belonging to a Headman, an ex-chief, a chief's messenger and also a locational councillor burnt down. *Fort Hall:* Headman's hut burnt down. Attack on Chief's Office. *April; Kiambu:* Chief's office attacked and a messenger seriously beaten up. Tax clerk attacked. *June; Kiambu:* 2 police informers shot and bodies found in river. *July; Fort Hall:* Chief's Messenger murdered and body found in river. *Kiambu:* Headman attacked and wounded. *August; Fort Hall:* Headman badly beaten and his hut burnt down. *Kiambu:* 2 police informers murdered. *Laikipia:* 2 or more Crown witnesses murdered" (p. 43).

27. John Spencer, "KAU and Mau Mau: Some Connections," *Kenya Historical Review,* 5, no. 2 (1977), p. 218.

28. Kenyatta initially had denounced Mau Mau in 1951 at the instigation of Sir Charles Mortimer, chairman of the newly formed multiracial Kenya Citizens Association. See Guy Arnold, *Kenyatta and the Politics of Kenya* (London: J. M. Dent, 1974), p. 106.

29. Kaggia, p. 113.

30. Jeremy Murray-Brown, *Kenyatta* (London: George Allen & Unwin, 1972), p. 244.

31. Ibid., p. 244.

32. Ibid., p. 249.

33. Lapping, p. 411. See also Kaggia, p. 114: "The Mau Mau Central Committee asked Kenyatta to see them [and] for the first time Kenyatta met the Mau Mau Central Committee. He was surprised to see Kubai and myself there. And he noticed to his further surprise that other leaders, whom he did not know, were running the meeting."

34. Fenner Brockway, *African Journeys* (London: Victor Gollancz, 1955), p. 90.

35. CO822/436. (PRO, London).

36. Ibid.

37. Ibid.

38. Ibid.

39. *African Affairs Department Annual Report, 1948* (Government Printer, Nairobi, 1950).

40. *African Affairs Department Annual Report, 1949* (Government Printer, Nairobi, 1951), p. 2.

41. *African Affairs Department Annual Report, 1950* (Government Printer, Nairobi, 1951), p. 2. See also Kiambu District Annual Report, 1950 (DC/KBU/1/41, KNA), pp. 6, 6A.

42. Carr, H. A. Magistrate's Case File on Mau Mau Criminal Case No. 1065. (MSS. Afr. S. 1352, RHL, Oxford University).

43. *African Affairs Department Annual Report, 1951* (Central Province) (Government Printer, Nairobi, 1951), p. 33.

44. Ibid., p. 33.

45. See remarks by Sir Evelyn Baring, (MSS Afr. S. 1574, RHL, Oxford University), p. 7.

46. Sir Philip Mitchell, *African After Thoughts* (London: Hutchinson, 1954), p. 253. It is important to note that Mitchell refused to accept responsibility for the outbreak of the Mau Mau revolt. He remained defiant and unrepentant stating, "I have no intention whatsoever of offering any explanation or defence of myself or my government for what we did or did not do; if it gives any one any satisfaction to believe that what has happened since I retired is all my fault, he is welcome to do so" (p. 252).

47. Hughes Papers (WM/A 3265, KN MSS. 16, KNA), Nyeri District 1949–1952; Intelligence Organisation, 1949–1952, p. 4.

48. Ibid., p. 4.

49. Sir Philip Mitchell, p. 255.

50. Ibid., p. 261.

51. Bruce J. Berman, "Administration and Politics in Colonial Kenya" (Ph.D. thesis, Yale University, 1974), p. 402.

52. Peter Evans, *Law and Disorder* (Secker and Warburg, 1956), p. 24. See also *African Affairs Department Annual Report, 1952* (Government Printer, Nairobi, 1954), p. 22. This report states in part that "to counteract the administration of the *Mau Mau* oath, various steps were taken. In Kiambu, Fort Hall, and Nyeri, African elders, accompanied by Chiefs, administered an oath on the *Githathi* stone, prohibiting people from participating in Mau Mau activities and, for those who had already partaken of the Mau Mau oath, a cleansing ceremony was introduced." Even though these oaths proved ineffective in stemming the tide of militancy, the government did not give up easily. In one case "a Mkamba wizard toured the farms in Thika District and administered cleansing and nonparticipation oaths" (p. 22).

53. *African Affairs Department Annual Report, 1952*, p. 24. In a letter to the Colonial Office on 14 May 1952, the Secretariat in Nairobi explained that "We may have to fight this African excursion into magic with similar weapons if those indeed are the only ones that the African understands. . . . " But still maintaining imperial distance, the Secretariat was keen to point out that "anything that we do of this nature, however, has got to come from the Africans themselves!" (CO822/435, PRO, London).

54. See, for example, the letter from C. J. Wilson of Hartree, Kikuyu, Kenya to the governor of Kenya on 31 July 1952 concerning the huge KAU meeting held at Nyeri on 26 July 1952 (CO822/435, PRO, London).

55. Berman, p. 403.

56. *Hughes Papers*, p. 10.

57. *News Chronicle*, 21 August 1952 (CO822/436, PRO, London).

58. Murray-Brown, p. 237.

59. CO822/443 (PRO, London).

60. Ibid.

61. Charles Douglas-Home, *Evelyn Baring: The Last Pro-Consul* (London: Collins, 1978), p. 230.

62. CO822/444 (PRO, London).

63. CO822/450 (PRO, London).

64. Kaggia, p. 117. John Spencer has observed that "none of the KAU or Mau Mau leaders wanted the Government to declare an emergency, for the dwindling few in KAU who believed in constitutional advance, the Emergency and the jailing of the party leaders ended the chances for reasonably negotiated African advancement. For the leaders of the militants, such as Kubai, the Emergency came far too soon" (Spencer, pp. 215–16).

65. Defence, Deposit 13, Piece 10 (KNA), p. 117/2.

4. British Military Strategy

1. John Pimlott, "The British Army," *Armed Forces and Modern Counter-Insurgency*, ed. Ian Beckett and John Pimlott (New York: St. Martin's Press, 1985), p. 16.

2. Ibid., p. 16.

3. Anthony Clayton, *Counter-Insurgency in Kenya* (Nairobi: Transafrica Publishers, 1976), p. 1.

4. *History of the Loyalists* (Nairobi: Government Printer, 1961), p. 25.

5. Clayton, p. 8.

6. Charles Douglas-Home, *Evelyn Baring: The Last Pro-Consul* (London: Collins, 1978), p. 250.

7. Ibid., p. 243.

8. *City Council of Nairobi Annual Report, 1953* (KNA), p. 3.

9. Ibid., p. 6.

10. Ibid., p. 26.

11. Clayton, p. 6. Erskine arrived in Kenya in June 1953.

12. Clayton, p. 11. See also Sir Michael Blundell, *So Rough a Wind* (London: Weidenfeld & Nicolson, 1964), p. 166. For a discussion on the disagreement between Erskine and Baring see Fred Madjalany, *State of Emergency* (Boston: Houghton Mifflin, 1963), p. 230.

13. CO822/441, appendix A (PRO, London), p. 1.

14. Clayton, p. 8.

15. Ibid., p. 33.

16. CO822/440 (PRO, London), p. 259.

17. By April 1953 the government produced a secret document citing details about the organization of Mau Mau. See MSS. Afr. S. 1676 (RHL, Oxford University).

18. Madjalany, p. 194.

19. Johnson Papers (MSS. Afr. S. 1949, RHL, Oxford University), p. 1. The government thought the information given by General China was "undoubtedly true. Part is supported by documentary evidence by way of papers and books found on China and in the area where he was engaged. Other matters he mentions are already known having been the subject of reports by independent agents prior to his capture" (p. 2).

20. Ibid., p. 3.

21. Ibid., p. 5.

22. Ibid., p. 7.

23. Ibid., p. 25.

24. Ibid., p. 30.

25. Madjalany, p. 195.

26. Ibid., p. 196.

27. Waruhiu Itote, *Mau Mau General* (Nairobi: East African Publishing House, 1967), p. 190.

28. Madjalany, p. 201. Itote, p. 164, dismisses the importance of the books found on him during his capture by stating that "they contained nothing of any importance except the names of my companies and their commanders." The government, on the other hand, found these books full of useful information, which was used among other things to identify members of the "passive wing" closely connected with General China.

29. *New Commonwealth* (29 April 1954), p. 459. See also Donald Barnett and Karari Njama, *Mau Mau from Within* (New York: Monthly Review Press, 1966), p. 331.

30. Madjalany, p. 204.

31. *City Council of Nairobi Annual Report 1954* (KNA), p. 4.

32. Madjalany, p. 207.

33. Blundell, p. 166. About 16,538 ended up in detention camps; see Lord Carver, *War Since 1945* (New York: G. P. Putnam's, 1980), p. 40.

34. Defence, Deposit 6, Serial 19 (KNA), p. 7A.

35. Ibid.

36. Defence, Deposit 6, Serial 19 (KNA), p. 7A.

37. Ibid., p. 119.

38. Defence, Deposit 6, Piece No. 16 (KNA), p. 10/1.

39. Clayton, p. 26.

40. *Kiambu District Annual Report 1954* (DC/KBU/1/45, KNA), p. 4.

41. Hughes Papers (WM/A 3265, KN. MSS 16, KNA), p. 1.

42. Ibid., p. 1.

43. Col. G. A. Rimbault, "Kenya and the Mau Mau," *The Lancashire Land*, vol. 5, new series, no. 3 (1954), p. 113.

44. Robert B. Asprey, *War in the Shadows: The Guerilla in History* (New York: Doubleday, 1975), p. 971.

45. CO822/436 (PRO, London).

46. Anthony Lavers, *The Kikuyu Who Fight Mau Mau* (Nairobi: The Eagle Press, 1955), p. 8.

47. Ibid., p. 2.

48. B. A. Ogot, "Revolt of the Elders," *Politics and Nationalism in Colonial Kenya*, ed. B. A. Ogot (Nairobi: East African Publishing House, 1972), p. 142.

49. M. P. K. Sorrenson, *Land Reform in the Kikuyu Country* (Nairobi: Oxford University Press, 1967), p. 107.

50. Ibid., p. 107.

51. Clayton, p. 29.

52. CO822/440 (PRO, London), p. 155A.

53. Lavers, p. 18.

54. CO822/440, (PRO), p. 259.

55. Lord Carver, *War Since 1945* (New York: G. P. Putnam's 1986), p. 37.

56. David Galula, *Counter-Insurgency Warfare* (New York: Frederick A. Praeger, 1964), p. 75.

57. Ibid., p. 75.

58. Julian Paget, *Counter-Insurgency Operations* (New York: Walker, 1967), p. 91.

59. For details of the Algerian war of independence few books are as informative as Alistair Horne, *A Savage War of Peace* (Middlesex, England: Penguin Books, 1979).

60. Alf Andrew Heggoy, *Insurgency and Counter-Insurgency in Algeria* (Bloomington: Indiana University Press, 1972), p. 261.

61. Paget, p. 92.
62. Clayton, p. 29.
63. Blundell, p. 170.
64. WC/OM/1/75–1/95 (KNA), p. 1.
65. M. Evans, *Fighting against Chimurenga, 1972–1979* (Harare: The Historical Association of Zimbabwe, 1981), p. 12.
66. Donald L. Barnett and Karari Njama, *Mau Mau from Within* (New York: Monthly Review Press, 1966), p. 332.
67. *Kiambu District Annual Report, 1955* (DC/KBU/1/45, KNA), p. 4.
68. Barnett and Njama, p. 332.
69. WC/CM/1/1/6 (KNA), Flag *B*.
70. ARC/MAA/2/5/183 (KNA), p. 176.
71. Ibid., p. 120.
72. WC/OM/1/75–1/95 (KNA), appendix.
73. Ibid. "Special favours should be shown to Loyalists and restrictions relaxed in areas where the population co-operates" (p. 1).
74. Hughes Papers, (KNA), p. 1.
75. Ibid., Administrative Directive No. 5., p. 1.
76. Margery Perham, "Struggle Against Mau Mau," *The Times*, 22 April 1953.
77. CO822/474 (PRO, London), p. 42.
78. Ibid.
79. PGB/134/80 (Migrated Archives Project, KNA), p. 1.
80. Ibid.
81. B278 and B279, Church of Scotland Mission (KNA).
82. Perham, 22 April 1953.
83. WC/OM/1/75–1/95, (KNA), p. 1.
84. Douglas-Home, p. 250.
85. Papers of Sir Arthur Young (MSS. Brit. Emp. S. 486, RHL, Oxford University), box 5, file 1.
86. Ibid., narrative, 1954. Before Young resigned on 4 November 1954, the governor wrote to him on the status of police in Kenya. He said, "The whole subject received long and anxious consideration by the Council of Ministers . . . and a considerable majority of the Council of Ministers advised me, and I accepted, that the U.K. Common Constable concept with the Police exercising an authority independent of Government could not, and should not, be applied to Kenya."
87. Ibid., Box 5, File 1, p. 23.
88. Elizabeth Hopkins, "Racial Minorities in British East Africa," *The Transformation of East Africa*, ed. Stanley Diamond and Fred G. Burke (New York: Basic Books, 1966), p. 115.
89. CO822/495 (PRO, London), p. 2.
90. Ibid., p. 1. In response to a confidential inquiry from the Colonial Office on "the shooting dead of Africans after being called upon to stop by authorised officers," the Secretariat in Nairobi noted that it was "impossible to instruct fully the lower ranks of the security forces in all the subtleties of the law in this respect, neither would it be reasonable in the light of strict limitations of the ordinary law" (CO822/474, PRO), pp. 75, 62.
91. Douglas-Home, p. 250.
92. Clayton, p. 37.
93. Rimbault, p. 112.
94. Papers of Sir Arthur Young, (RHL), box 5, file 1, p. 6. An example of this "lack of consideration for the African" is the case of Captain Griffiths. He ordered a hole to be carved in a prisoner's ear and others to be shot dead. In his defense, he said that "leading a native prisoner by the ear is quite proper and does not cause pain." *Time* (22 March 1954), p. 37.
95. Hopkins, p. 115.

96. G. Carlson, "Ape-Like Bestial Brutes?" *Socialist Review*, 3, no. 7, p. 4.

97. MAC/KEN/34/9 (KNA).

98. Papers of Sir Arthur Young, Narrative, 1954 (RHL), p. 20.

99. E. Carey Francis, "The Emergency in Kenya as Seen by a School Master in the Kikuyu Area" (RIIA, London, 3 March 1955), p. 5.

100. David F. Gordon, *Decolonization and the State in Kenya* (Boulder: Westview Press, 1986), p. 119.

101. C. M. Nwankwo, "Women, Violence and the Quest for Social Justice in the Works of Ngugi wa Thiong'o" (Ph.D. thesis, University of Texas, Austin, 1982), p. 159. For a critical analysis of Ngugi wa Thiong'o's books, especially as they relate to Mau Mau, see *Critical Perspectives on Ngugi wa Thiong'o*, ed. G. D. Killam (Washington, DC: Three Continents Press, 1984).

102. William W. Baldwin, *Mau Mau Movement* (New York: E. P. Dutton, 1957), pp. 92–93.

103. Clayton, p. 47. Francis, p. 7, also mentioned reports which argued that Home Guards would "lose morale if they were blamed for their illegal actions."

104. Blundell, p. 190.

105. H. K. Wachanga, *The Swords of Kirinyaga* (Nairobi: Kenya Literature Bureau, 1975), p. 96.

106. Barnett and Njama, p. 455.

107. Blundell, p. 192.

108. For details see Frank Kitson, *Gangs and Counter-Gangs* (London: Barrie and Rockliff, 1960).

109. *History of the Loyalists*, p. 70.

110. Madjalany, p. 212.

111. *Corfield Report* (HMSO, 1960).

112. Lieutenant General Sir Gerald Lathbury, "The Security Forces in the Kenya Emergency," *The Oxfordshire and Buckinghamshire Light Infantry Chronicle* 59 (1957), p. 85.

113. Ian Henderson, *Man Hunt in Kenya* (New York: Doubleday, 1958). Author makes no mention of how "pseudo-gangs" were "converted." Instead emphasis is on Henderson's knowledge of the Kikuyu. "His deep knowledge of the Kikuyu people, their language and their customs enabled him to reach into their minds and influence their thoughts in the way he did" (from the Foreword).

114. Frank Kitson, "Counter Insurrection in Kenya," *Guerilla Strategies*, ed. Gerard Chaliand (Berkeley: University of California Press, 1982), p. 171.

115. Ibid., pp. 171–72.

116. Frank Kitson, *Gangs and Counter-Gangs*, pp. 72–73.

117. Barnett and Njama, p. 456.

118. Henderson, p. 15.

119. *East African Standard* (24 February 1956), p. 22.

120. Henderson, p. 16.

121. *Corfield Report*, p. 316.

5. Propaganda and the Oaths

1. Bildad Kaggia, *Roots of Freedom* (Nairobi: East African Publishing House, 1975), p. 131.

2. Charles Douglas-Home, *Evelyn Baring* (London: Collins, 1978), p. 246.

3. C. Ojwando Abuor, *White Highlands No More* (Nairobi: Pan African Researchers, 1970), p. 383.

4. Jeremy Murray-Brown, *Kenyatta* (London: George Allen & Unwin, 1972), p. 263.

5. Douglas-Home, p. 247.

6. Ibid., p. 246.

7. Guy Arnold, *Kenyatta and the Politics of Kenya* (London: J. M. Dent, 1974), p. 146.

8. Ibid., p. 129. In his book *Law and Disorder* (1956), Peter Evans states that "a few weeks before 20th October . . . a 'Get Jomo' bureau was specially formed in the Secretariat in Nairobi," p. 147. In spite of this and other surveillance by the administration and police, no evidence was found to link Kenyatta to Mau Mau.

9. Peter Evans, *Law and Disorder* (London: Secker and Warburg, 1956), p. 54.

10. Arnold, p. 125.

11. Montagu Slater, *The Trial of Jomo Kenyatta* (London: Mercury Books, 1965), p. 7.

12. Carl Rosberg and John Nottingham, *The Myth of Mau Mau* (New York: Hoover/Praeger, 1966), p. 283.

13. Slater, p. 234.

14. Murray-Brown, pp. 271–72.

15. Fenner Brockway, *African Journeys* (London: Victor Gollanz, 1955), p. 169.

16. Ibid., p. 169.

17. Evans, p. 174.

18. *History of the Loyalists* (Nairobi: Government Printer, 1961), p. 31.

19. Donald L. Barnett and Karari Njama, *Mau Mau from Within* (New York: Monthly Review Press, 1966), p. 137.

20. M. P. K. Sorrenson, *Land Reform in the Kikuyu Country* (Nairobi: Oxford University Press, 1967), p. 100.

21. *History of the Loyalists*, p. 31.

22. Blundell, *So Rough a Wind* (London: Weidenfeld & Nicolson, 1964), p. 140.

23. Sorrenson, *Land Reform*, p. 100.

24. *Report of Parliamentary Delegation to Kenya* (HMSO, 1954), p. 4.

25. Ibid., p. 4.

26. *The Times* (London), 7 November 1952.

27. Papers of Rev. Canon Peter Bostock (PGB/134/80, KNA).

28. Barnett and Njama, p. 123.

29. Ibid., p. 57.

30. J. M. Kariuki, *Mau Mau Detainee* (London: Oxford University Press, 1963), p. 25.

31. Barnett and Njama, p. 58.

32. Ibid., p. 118.

33. Kariuki, op. cit., p. 27.

34. Barnett and Njama, p. 58.

35. Ibid., p. 320.

36. Ibid., p. 13.

37. Kariuki, p. 29.

38. Ibid., p. 28. See also Barnett and Njama, p. 132.

39. "Even some of those administering the first oath had not yet taken the *Batuni*." Kariuki, p. 31.

40. *Kiambu Annual Report 1952* (DC/KBU/1/43, KNA), p. 1.

41. Fred Madjalany, *State of Emergency* (Boston: Houghton Mifflin Company, 1963), p. 79.

42. M. Tamarkin, "Mau Mau in Nakuru," *Journal of African History* 17, no. 1 (1976).

43. MSS. Afr. S. 424 (RHL, Oxford University), ff. 341.

44. H. K. Wachanga, *The Swords of Kirinyaga* (Nairobi: Kenya Literature Bureau, 1975).

45. Ibid., preface.

46. Kariuki, p. 33.

47. Mutonyi's remarks cited in Robert Buijtenhuijs, *Essays on Mau Mau* (Leiden: The Netherlands, 1982), p. 98.

48. Barnett and Njama, p. 126.

49. Ibid., p. 126.

50. Buijtenhuijs, p. 110.
51. Brian Lapping, *End of Empire (Kenya)*, Granada Film/Television, London, 1985. Videotape.
52. PGB/134/80 (KNA), p. 1.
53. PGB/134/80 (KNA). Papers of Rev. Canon Peter Bostock.
54. The Papers of Sir Frank Loyd & Co. (RHL, Oxford University), p. 9.
55. PGB/134/80 (KNA).
56. Ibid.
57. MSS. Afr. S. 424 (RHL). According to the information in this collection, most of these oaths involved extensive use of women for intercourse during the oath-taking ceremony. For example, during the fifth-level oath, "a naked woman is present at the meeting. As the initiate approaches, the woman lies on her back and the initiate inserts his penis seven times. The man then jumps over the prostrate body of the woman. During this oath, the oather [sic] stands by to make sure no time is wasted. Ejaculation is not encouraged."
58. Kariuki, p. 31.
59. Ibid., p. 33.
60. *Time* (10 November 1952), pp. 30, 31.
61. *Time* (3 November 1952), p. 36.
62. *Time* (3 November 1952), p. 34.
63. *Time* (30 March 1953), p. 31.
64. Elizabeth Hopkins, "Racial Minorities in British East Africa," *The Transformation of East Africa*, ed. Stanley Diamond and Fred G. Burke. (New York: Basic Books, 1966), p. 114.
65. *Life* (16 February 1953), p. 120.
66. Papers of Sir Arthur Young (RHL, Oxford University), box 5, file 1, p. 11.
67. *Time* (10 November 1952), p. 40.
68. Papers of Sir William R. N. Hinde (RHL, Oxford University), file 10, p. 10.
69. Ibid., p. 12.
70. Terence H. Qualter, *Opinion Control in the Democracies* (London: Macmillan, 1985), p. 123.
71. Papers of Sir William R. N. Hinde (RHL), file 9. See also *The Mau Mau in Kenya* (London: Hutchinson, 1954).
72. Ibid.
73. Thomas Grandin, "The Political Use of the Radio," *Geneva Studies* 10, no. 3 (August 1939), p. 7.
74. Papers of Sir William R. N. Hinde (RHL), War Council minutes 1436: Psychological Warfare.
75. WC/CM/1/1/16 War Council Papers (KNA) 14 July 1954.
76. Ibid.
77. Ibid.
78. Ibid.
79. Ibid.
80. Sam Keen, *Faces of the Enemy* (San Francisco: Harper & Row Publishers, 1986), p. 12.
81. Ibid., p. 25.
82. Lapping, *End of Empire*, Granada Film/Television, 1985. Videotape.
83. Frank Kitson, *Gangs and Counter-Gangs* (London: Barrie & Rockliff, 1960), p. 2.
84. Ibid., p. 2.
85. Keen, p. 27.
86. William W. Baldwin, *Mau Mau Manhunt* (New York: E. P. Dutton, 1957), p. 61.
87. Ibid., p. 61.
88. Ibid., p. 16.
89. Ibid., p. 17.

90. Hopkins, p. 116.

91. *A Handbook on Anti-Mau Mau Operations.* (Nairobi: Government Printer, November 1954), p. 11.

92. Keen, p. 25.

93. *Time* (3 November 1952), p. 36.

94. CO822/461 (PRO, London).

95. Ibid., p. 21.

96. Ibid., p. 21.

97. Leonard W. Doob, *Propaganda* (New York: Henry Holt, 1935), p. 75.

98. Oliver Lyttelton, *The Memoirs of Lord Chandos* (New York: New American Library, 1963), p. 379.

99. Ibid., p. 384.

100. Ibid., p. 380.

101. Ibid., p. 380.

102. Philip M. Taylor, *The Projection of Britain* (Cambridge: Cambridge University Press, 1981), p. 1.

103. Keen, p. 43.

104. Keen, p. 43.

6. Mau Mau Military and Political Strategy

1. Jeremy Murray-Brown, *Kenyatta* (London: George Allen and Unwin, 1972), p. 274.

2. George Bennett and Alison Smith, "Kenya from Whiteman's Country to Kenyatta's State; 1945–1963," *Oxford History of East Africa,* ed. D. A. Low and Alison Smith (Oxford: Clarendon Press, 1976), p. 130.

3. Basil Davidson, *The People's Cause* (Essex: Longman, 1981), pp. 91–92.

4. Donald Barnett and Karari Njama, *Mau Mau from Within* (New York: Monthly Review Press, 1966), p. 149.

5. Ibid., p. 150. See also Robert Buijtenhuijs, *Essays on Mau Mau* (Leiden/The Netherlands: African Studies Center, 1982), p. 49.

6. Ibid., p. 150.

7. Waruhiu Itote, *Mau Mau General* (Nairobi: East African Publishing House, 1967), p. 139.

8. Buijtenhuijs, *Essays on Mau Mau,* p. 52.

9. Robert Whittier, "Introduction," *The Swords of Kirinyaga* by H. K. Wachanga (Nairobi: Kenya Literature Bureau, 1975), p. xv.

10. Mao Tse-Tung, *Selected Works, Volume Two* (New York: International Publishers, 1954), p. 136. See also Charles W. Thayer, *Guerilla* (New York: Harper & Row, 1963), p. 90.

11. Buijtenhuijs, *Essays,* p. 50.

12. Barnett and Njama, p. 151.

13. Ibid., p. 151.

14. Ibid., p. 154.

15. Ibid., p. 156.

16. Ibid., p. 158.

17. Ibid., p. 226.

18. Ibid., p. 228.

19. Ibid., p. 329.

20. Basil Davidson, *People's Cause,* p. 95.

21. Wachanga, *The Swords of Kirinyaga* p. 40.

22. Barnett and Njama, p. 329.

23. Ibid., p. 376.

24. Carl G. Rosberg and John Nottingham, *The Myth of Mau Mau* (New York: Hoover/Praeger, 1966), p. 300.

25. Gerard Chaliand, "Introduction," *Guerilla Strategies,* ed. Gerard Chaliand (Berkeley/Los Angeles: University of California Press, 1982), p. 1.

26. Carleton Beals, "Guerilla Warfare," *Encyclopedia of the Social Sciences,* Editor-in-Chief, Edwin R. A. Seligman (New York: Macmillan, 1957), p. 197.

27. Thayer, p. xv.

28. Lapping, *End of Empire*, Granada Film/Television, 1985. Videotape.

29. Thayer, p. 39.

30. *The Kenya Police Annual Report, 1954* (Nairobi: Government Printer, 1955), p. 1.

31. *East African Standard* (Nairobi), 15 August 1953, p. 4.

32. Wachanga, p. 36.

33. Ibid. For other general details, see Gucu Gikoyo, *We Fought for Freedom* (Nairobi: East African Publishing House, 1979) and Kiboi Muriithi, *War in the Forest* (Nairobi: East African Publishing House, 1971).

34. Wachanga. Also see Waruhiu Itote, *Mau Mau General* (Nairobi: East African Publishing House, 1967).

35. Wachanga, p. 44.

36. Barnett and Njama, p. 154.

37. Wachanga, p. 44.

38. Ibid., p. 28. Wachanga talks of bribes given to police for the release of Mathenge. On the whole, however, the sale of weapons to Mau Mau guerrillas by Home Guards or African troops remained one of the government's main worries throughout the emergency. In his book *Roots of Freedom*, Kaggia mentions the purchase of weapons from government employees.

39. Amilcar Cabral, *Unity and Struggle* (New York: Monthly Review Press, 1979), p. 99.

40. Mao Tse-Tung, *Selected Works, Volume One* (New York: International Publishers, 1954), p. 106.

41. Frantz Fanon, *The Wretched of the Earth* (New York: Grove Press, 1968), p. 94.

42. Ibid., p. 135.

43. Ibid., p. 136.

44. Buijtenhuijs, *Essays*, p. 55.

45. Barnett and Njama, p. 155.

46. *Kiambu District Annual Report, 1954* (DC/KBU/1/45, KNA), p. 3.

47. Buijtenhuijs, *Essays*, p. 55.

48. *Kiambu District Annual Report, 1954.* (DC/KBU/1/44, KNA), p. 1.

49. Buijtenhuijs, *Essays*, p. 56.

50. Robert Foran, *The Kenya Police, 1887–1960* (London: Robert Hale, 1962), p. 210.

51. Wachanga, p. 63.

52. Barnett and Njama, p. 56.

53. Buijtenhuijs, *Essays*, p. 52.

54. Wachanga, p. 82.

55. Itote, p. 139. For a discussion on other forms of *Komerera* see Muthoni Likimani, *Passbook Number 47927, Women and Mau Mau in Kenya* (London: Macmillan, 1985), p. 92.

56. Itote, p. 140.

57. Wachanga, p. 94.

58. Barnett and Njama, p. 171.

59. Remarks by Wanjugu Mbutu in *End of Empire* (Kenya) by Brian Lapping, Granada Film/Television, London, 1985. Videotape.

60. Wachanga, p. 59.

61. See, for example, the Papers of Sir William R. N. Hinde (RHL, Oxford University), file 9. For further details see chapter 5, "Propaganda and the Oaths."

62. Mao Tse-Tung, *Selected Works, Volume One*, p. 234.

63. Ibid., p. 234.

64. Barnett and Njama, p. 171.

65. L. S. B. Leakey, *The Southern Kikuyu Before 1903, Volume III* (London: Academic Press, 1977), p. 1037.

66. Ibid., p. 1040.

67. Terence Ranger, *Peasant Consciousness and Guerilla War in Zimbabwe* (London: James Currey and Berkeley/Los Angeles: University of California Press, 1985), p. 188.

68. Ibid., p. 189.

69. Ibid., p. 189.

70. Ibid., p. 204.

71. Ibid., p. 214.

72. Johnson Papers (MSS. Afr. S. 1484, RHL, Oxford University), p. 40.

73. Muriithi, p. 40.

74. Barnett and Njama, p. 205.

75. Elizabeth Hopkins, "Racial Minorities in British East Africa," *The Transformation of East Africa*, ed. Stanley Diamond and Fred G. Burke (New York: Basic Books, 1966), p. 114.

76. Ernesto Che Guevara, *Guerilla Warfare* (Lincoln: University of Nebraska Press, 1985), p. 63.

77. Johnson Papers, (RHL), p. 38. The government had certainly expected some amount of sabotage on the railway lines during the war.

78. Ibid., p. 38.

79. MSS. Afr. S. 235, *Mau Mau* (RHL, Oxford University).

80. Ibid.

81. Wachanga, p. 62.

82. Ibid., p. 27.

83. *East African Standard* (Nairobi), 28 August 1953, p. 1. Letter originally published in Swahili in *Habari za Dunia* (Nairobi), 27 August 1953.

84. Ibid.

85. Maina wa Kinyatti, ed., *Kenya's Freedom Struggle: The Dedan Kimathi Papers* (London: Zed Books, 1987).

86. Ibid., p. xviii.

87. Ibid., p. 16.

88. Barnett and Njama, p. 199.

89. Ibid., pp. 349–52.

90. Ibid., p. 351.

91. Ibid., p. 351.

92. Wachanga, p. x.

93. Muriithi, pp. 20–21.

94. Remarks by Joseph Murumbi in *Mau Mau* (CAL/3, KNA), Film.

95. For details on the activities of the KAU, especially in the turbulent period before its proscription in 1953, see John Spencer, *The Kenya African Union* (London: KPI, 1985).

96. Barnett and Njama, p. 377.

97. Ibid., p. 397.

98. Wachanga, p. 42.

99. Maina wa Kinyatti, ed., *Thunder from the Mountains: Mau Mau Patriotic Songs* (London: Zed Press, 1980).

100. Ibid., p. 62.

101. Barnett and Njama, p. 352.

102. Wachanga, p. 111.

103. Chaliand, p. 16.

104. Ian Henderson, *Man Hunt in Kenya* (New York: Doubleday, 1958), p. 15.

105. All accounts and books by former guerrillas never fail to mention this important point.

106. Rosberg and Nottingham, p. 301.

107. *East African Standard* (Nairobi), 15 August 1953, p. 4.

108. Basil Davidson, *Africa in Modern History* (Middlesex, England: Penguin Books, 1978), p. 263.

109. Lord Michael Carver, *War Since 1945* (New York: G. P. Putnam's, 1981), p. 43.

110. Rosberg and Nottingham, p. 310.

111. David Goldsworthy, *Tom Mboya; The Man Kenya Wanted to Forget* (London: Heinemann Educational Books, 1982), p. 29.

112. Ibid., p. 29.

113. R. J. M. Swynnerton, *A Plan to Intensify Development of African Agriculture in Kenya* (Nairobi: Government Printer, 1954).

114. Wachanga, p. 123.

115. Barnett and Njama, p. 455.

7. Rehabilitation

1. *East African Standard* (Nairobi, 11 September 1953), p. 68.

2. Ibid. For details about rehabilitation of Greek communists, see *The War of the Flea* by Robert Taber (New York: Lyle Stuart, 1965), p. 138.

3. Ibid.

4. Defence, Deposit 14, Piece 66 (KNA), p. 2.

5. Dr. Mary Shannon, "Rehabilitating the Kikuyu," *African Affairs* 54, no. 215 (London: April 1955), p. 131.

6. *East African Standard* (Nairobi, 31 August 1953), p. 67.

7. Shannon, p. 130.

8. Papers of Rev. Canon Peter Bostock (PGB/134/80, 28 May 1954, KNA).

9. Ibid.

10. Ibid.

11. Defence Deposit 14, Piece 66 (KNA).

12. Ibid., p. 2.

13. Ibid., p. 3.

14. Ibid., p. 3.

15. Ibid., p. 158/3.

16. Ibid., p. 24.

17. Ibid., p. 24/2.

18. CO822/441 (PRO, London), appendix C, p. 1.

19. *Report on the Treatment of Offenders, 1954* (Nairobi: Government Printer, 1955), p. 16.

20. War Council Papers, (WC/OM/1/96–1/110, reel no. 10, KNA), p. 1.

21. Ibid., p. 2.

22. Ibid., appendix A.

23. Ibid.

24. Ibid., p. 2.

25. Defence Deposit 14, Piece 9 (KNA), p. 73.

26. Defence Deposit 14, Piece 66, (KNA), p. 145.

27. Report on the Treatment of Offenders, 1954, op. cit., p. 14.

28. Defence Deposit 14, Piece 9, vol. 1, (KNA), p. 17/1.

29. Defence Deposit 14, Piece 66, (KNA), p. 24.

30. Defence Deposit 14, Piece 1 (KNA), p. 61/1.

31. Defence Deposit 14, Piece 66, (KNA), p. 145.

32. *Nyeri District Annual Report, 1956* (DC/NY1/1/1, KNA), p. 12.

33. DC/NYK/3/1/40 (KNA), p. 1.

34. Brian Lapping, *End of Empire* (Kenya), Granada Film/Television, London, 1985. Videotape.

35. Ibid.

36. Ibid. Remarks by Barbara Castle.

37. *Report on the Treatment of Offenders, 1953* (Nairobi: Government Printer, 1954), p. 1.

38. Defence Deposit 14, Piece 66, (KNA), p. 17/6.

39. Cmnd. 795 (HMSO, July 1959), p. 35.

40. Charles Douglas-Home, *Evelyn Baring* (London: Collins, 1978), p. 288.

41. Press Office, Department of Information, 4 March 1959, cited in Cmnd. 795 (HMSO), p. 211.

42. Cmnd. 795 (HMSO). Report by Maurice Gerald, police pathologist.

43. Cmnd. 816 (HMSO, July 1959), p. 7.

44. Lapping, *End of Empire* (Kenya), Granada Film/Television. Videotape. Macmillan was especially worried when key conservative politicians like Enoch Powell criticized the government of Kenya for negligence of duty and maladministration in detention camps.

45. War Council Papers (WC/OM/1/43–1/52, reel no. 6, KNA).

46. *Kiambu District Annual Report, 1956* (DC/KBU/1/45, KNA), p. 2. In Kikuyu Division by the end of the year, the administration estimated that all adults had confessed.

47. *Swynnerton Plan (A Plan to Intensify the Development of African Agriculture in Kenya)* (Nairobi: Government Printer, 1954). This scheme represented the government's determination to increase agricultural production in African reserves. Like previous efforts, this scheme envisaged that, on the whole, all African agrarian problems would be solved within the reserves. Provision of land for Africans in the White Highlands was not seriously thought about. The Swynnerton Plan aimed to increase the carrying capacity and productivity of land in the reserves while also raising rural income.

48. *Kenya: An Economic Survey, 1958* (London: Barclays Bank, DCO), p. 21.

49. M. P. K. Sorrenson, *Land Reform in the Kikuyu Country* (Nairobi: Oxford University Press, 1967), p. 118.

50. Ibid., p. 118.

51. "Reconstruction in Kenya," *The Round Table:* A Quarterly Journal of British Commonwealth Affairs, no. 175 (June 1954), p. 255.

52. Ibid.

53. CO822/498 (PRO, London).

54. R. G. Wilson, "Land Consolidation in the Fort Hall District of Kenya," *Journal of African Administration* (HMSO, July 1956), p. 147.

55. DC/KBU/2/1 (KNA), p. 5. For a further illustration of the power of chiefs and loyalists over the release of detainees, see H. K. Wachanga, *The Swords of Kirinyaga* (Nairobi: Kenya Literature Bureau, 1975), chapter 8.

56. Defence Deposit 14, Piece 66, (KNA), p. 158/5.

57. Shannon, p. 135.

58. Defence Deposit 14, Piece 66, (KNA), p. 158/5.

59. CD/5/272 (KNA), p. 1.

60. Ibid., p. 4. (21 February 1953).

61. CD/5/270 (KNA), p. 204.

62. DC/KBU/1/45 (1956) (KNA), p. 2.

63. DC/KBU/1/46 (KNA), p. 2.

64. DC/NY1/1/1 (1956) (KNA), p. 3.

65. DC/NY1/1/1 (1957) (KNA), p. 1.

66. DC/NY1/1/1 (1958) (KNA), p. 1.

67. DC/KBU/1/46 (1958) (KNA), p. 1.

68. Ngugi wa Thiong'o, *A Grain of Wheat* (London: Heinemann Books, 1967), pp. 130, 133.

69. DC/KBU/1/45 (1957) (KNA), p. 2.

70. DC/KBU/1/46 (1959) (KNA), p. 1.

71. Wilson, p. 150.

72. *Swynnerton Plan*, p. 10.

73. Sorrenson, *Land Reform*, p. 119.

74. Tabitha Kanogo, *Squatters and the Roots of Mau Mau* (London: James Currey; Nairobi: Heinemann Kenya; and Athens: Ohio University Press, 1987), p. 164.

75. War Council Papers (WC/OM/1/96–1/110, reel no. 10), KNA.

76. Ibid.

77. DC/NKU/1/7 (1957) (KNA), p. 1.

78. Ibid., p. 1.

79. DC/NY1/1/1 (1956) (KNA), p. 9.

80. DC/NY1/1/1 (1958) (KNA), p. 1.

81. DC/NY1/1/1 (1956) (KNA), p. 9.

82. Defence Deposit 14, Piece 20 (KNA), p. 219. The district commissioner conveyed the views of a local Red Cross worker. Also see DC/KBU/2/1, (KNA), p. 3.

83. DC/KBU/1/45 (KNA), p. 5.

84. PC/COAST/2/1/101 (KNA), p. 2.

85. *Report on Colony and Protectorate of Kenya, 1953* (HMSO, 1954), p. 76.

86. Bishop Walter Carey, *Crisis in Kenya* (London: A. R. Mowbray, 1953), p. 21.

87. *Report of the Committee on African Wages (The Carpenter Report)* (Nairobi: Government Printer, 1954), p. 16.

88. Ibid., p. 142.

89. *Sessional Paper no. 21 of 1954* (Nairobi: Government Printer, 1954), p. 4.

90. Ibid., p. 4.

91. Sorrenson, *Land Reform*, p. 250.

92. PC/COAST/2/1/101 (KNA), p. 2.

93 Cmnd. 9475 (HMSO, June 1955), p. 430.

94. *Sessional Paper No. 10 of 1958/1959* (Nairobi: Government Printer, 1959), p. 9.

95. PC/COAST/2/1/101 (KNA), pp. 1–2. Also see DC/NY1/1/1 (1960), p. 1. The district commissioner for Nyeri thought there was a clear distinction, based on wealth and property, between the opponents and supporters of the government. The"haves" supported the government while the "have-nots" stood in opposition.

96. CO822/498, (PRO).

97. Ibid.

98. Ibid. (Draft on CSB139/349/101).

99. H. K. Wachanga, *The Swords of Kirinyaga* (Nairobi: Kenya Literature Bureau, 1975), p. 154.

100. These were the Lyttelton Constitution of 1954 and the Lennox-Boyd Constitution of 1958.

8. Toward Independence

1. For details see David Goldsworthy, *Tom Mboya: The Man Kenya Wanted to Forget* (Nairobi/London: Heinemann Educational Books, 1982).

2. For details see Tom Mboya, *Freedom and After* (London: Andre Deutsch, 1963).

3. Ibid., p. 73.

4. Ibid., p. 117.

5. George Bennett and Carl G. Rosberg, *The Kenyatta Election: Kenya, 1960–61* (London: Oxford University Press, 1961), p. 34.

6. Oginga Odinga, *Not Yet Uhuru* (London: Heinemann, 1967), p. 143.

7. Mboya, *Freedom*, p. 119.

8. Ibid., p. 51.

9. Bennett and Rosberg, p. 35.

10. See Odinga, *Not Yet Uhuru*, for details.

11. Colin Legum, "Mboya the Professional," *East Africa Journal* (Nairobi: September, 1969), p. 30.

12. Odinga, *Not Yet Uhuru*, p. 171.

13. Goldsworthy, p. 135. The number of African ministers was increased to four out of a cabinet of twelve still to be chosen by the governor.

14. This is now a fairly established fact. For details see Tony Smith, ed. *End of European Empire* (Lexington, Mass.: Heath, 1975).

15. *East African Standard* (Nairobi), 13 October 1956, p. 1.

16. Arthur Skeffington, M. P., "The British Labour Party's Colonial Policy" *Socialist International Information* 4, no. 42 (16 October 1954), p. 748. Colonial achievements by the Labour party enumerated by the M. P. include creation of the Colonial Development Corporation with "a capital of over 100 million to pioneer productive projects in the colonies," long-term buying contracts, establishment of university colleges in the West Indies, Malaya, Gold Coast, Nigeria and Uganda, and an increased number of "colonial students" studying in Britain.

17. James Griffiths, M. P., "From Colonies to Commonwealth," *Socialist International Information* 4, no. 43, (23 October 1954), p. 773.

18. Fenner Brockway, *Toward Tomorrow* (London: Hart-Davis, MacGibbon, 1977), p. 223.

19. Nigel Fisher, *Iain Macleod* (London: Andre Deutsch, 1973), p. 141.

20. Ibid., p. 143.

21. Goldsworthy, p. 131.

22. Dan Horowitz, "Attitudes of British Conservatives Towards Decolonization in Africa," *African Affairs* 69, no. 274 (January 1970). Also see Fisher.

23. Fisher, p. 143.

24. Mboya, *Freedom*, p. 126.

25. Fisher, p. 144.

26. E. A. Vasey, "Kenya: Constitutional Development Today and Tomorrow" (Unpublished paper, RIIA, July 1954), p. 7.

27. Fisher, p. 144.

28. Harold Macmillan, *Pointing the Way, (1959–1961)* (London: Macmillan, 1972), p. 156.

29. Harold Macmillan, cited in Dan Horowitz, p. 16.

30. Mss. Afr. S. 1621 (RHL, Oxford University), p. 42.

31. Brian Lapping, *End of Empire* (New York: St. Martin's Press, 1985), p. 432.

32. Ibid., p. 432.

33. Ibid., p. 433. See also Odinga, *Not Yet Uhuru*, pp. 156–60.

34. Brian Lapping/Granada TV, *End of Empire* (Kenya) (1985). Videotape.

35. Lapping, p. 438.

36. EA07/81 (12) (KNA), p. 1.

37. Ibid., p. 2.

38. *Guardian* (London), cited in *Daily Nation* (Nairobi), 23 November 1960, p. 6.

39. Jomo Kenyatta, *Suffering without Bitterness* (Nairobi: East African Publishing House, 1968), p. 122.

40. Ibid., p. 122.

41. Ibid., p. 123.

42. Jeremy Murray-Brown, *Kenyatta* (London: George Allen and Unwin, 1972), p. 305.

43. 83 MA/7 (Tape) (KNA).

44. Cmd. 960, 1960 (HMSO), cited in Dennis Austin, "The British Point of No Return?," *The Transfer of Power in Africa*, ed. Prosser Gifford and Wm. Roger Louis (New Haven, Conn.: Yale University Press, 1982), p. 236.

45. Odinga, *Not Yet Uhuru*, p. 193.

46. Bethwell Ogot, *Historical Dictionary of Kenya* (London: The Scarecrow Press, 1981), p. 89.

47. C. J. Gertzel, "The Political Legacy," *Government and Politics in Kenya,* ed. C. J. Gertzel, Maure Goldschmidt, and Don Rothchild (Nairobi: East African Publishing House, 1969), p. 6.

48. James Gichuru, "Kenya," (unpublished paper, RIIA, 27 September 1960), p. 1.

49. C. H. Gertzel, "Political Legacy," p. 5.

50. Ronald Ngala, "Kenya's New Constitution," (RIIA, 2 March 1962), pp. 2-3. Ngala also stated that "the apparent national unity today in Kenya is maintained by British rule and the system can only be worked by the British. But once the British quit, the system would collapse, chaos would follow." p. 6.

51. Bennett and Rosberg, p. 43.

52. Ibid., p. 43.

53. Ibid., p. 43.

54. William R. Ochieng, "Kenyatta in Ngugi's Fiction" (unpublished paper, n.d., Kenyatta University), p. 54.

55. Kenya Constitutional Conference, 1962, 16 February 1962 (serial 40, Migrated Archives Project, KNA), p. 26.

56. Ibid. 21 February 1962, p. 81.

57. Ibid. 19 February 1972, p. 34.

58. Ibid. 19 February 1962, p. 45.

59. Ibid. 19 February 1962, p. 41.

60. Tabitha Kanogo, *Squatters and the Roots of Mau Mau* (London: James Currey; Nairobi: Heinemann; and Athens, Ohio: Ohio University Press, 1987), p. 173.

61. Ibid., p. 167.

62. Ibid., p. 168.

63. *The Kanu Manifesto for Independence Social Democracy and Stability* (Nairobi, 1960/61), p. 7. In his address in London, Gichuru thought that Mau Mau was not "a particularly good advertisement" for the country. Gichuru, (RIIA), p. 5.

64. *Kanu Manifesto,* p. 15.

65. Tom Mboya, *Kenya Faces the Future* (New York: American Committee on Africa, 1959), p. 18.

66. Ibid., p. 18.

67. Christopher Leo, *Land and Class in Kenya* (Toronto: University of Toronto Press, 1984), p. 128.

68. Ngugi wa Thiong'o, *A Grain of Wheat* (London: Heinemann, 1967), p. 192. Gikonyo, an ex-detainee, became involved in the affairs of the party at the local level.

69. MAC/KEN/36/7, *KADU's Plan* (KNA), p. 1.

70. Ibid., p. 1.

71. Ibid., p. 1.

72. Ibid., p. 2.

73. Ibid., p. 1.

74. *Kenya Constitutional Conference, 1962,* 21 February 1962 (KNA), p. 77.

75. Gichuru, (RIIA), p. 4.

76. Sir Patrick Renison, "Kenya's Problems at the Start of 1963" (unpublished paper, RIIA, 7 February 1963), p. 4.

77. Odinga, *Not Yet Uhuru,* p. 230.

78. Papers of Dermott Kydd (Landmarks) (KNA), chapter 6, pp. 3-4.

79. Leo, p. 74.

80. Ibid., p. 76.

81. Ibid., p. 120.

82. Papers of Dermott Kydd (Landmarks), p. 2.

83. "It was hoped that the farmers would sell off relatively underdeveloped parts of their land and themselves remain to farm the balance of their holding." Ibid., p. 3.

84. Office of the President, Deposit 3, Serial 199 (KNA), p. 2.

85. Ibid., p. 2.

86. Colin Leys, *Underdevelopment in Kenya* (Berkeley/Los Angeles: University of California Press, 1974), p. 78.

87. Leo, p. 119.

88. Ibid., p. 132.

89. Kanogo, *Squatters*, p. 172.

90. Anthony Clayton and Donald Savage, *Government and Labour in Kenya, 1895–1963* (London: Frank Cass, 1974), p. 461.

91. William R. Ochieng, "The Mau Mau, The Petit Bourgeoisie and Decolonization in Kenya," (Unpublished paper, Kenyatta University, 1984), p. 13.

92. Odinga, *Not Yet Uhuru*, p. 254.

93. Murray-Brown, p. 312.

94. Ngugi wa Thiong'o, *Detained* (London: Heinemann, 1981), p. 162.

95. John Connel Robertson, "The Situation of the European Settler in Kenya" (RIIA, 23 March 1961), p. 5.

96. Sir Michael Blundell, *So Rough a Wind* (London: Weidenfeld & Nicholson, 1964), p. 296.

97. Murray-Brown, p. 309.

98. K. R. Minogue, *Nationalism* (New York: Basic Books, 1967), p. 125.

99. Ibid., p. 125.

100. *Wananchi Declaration;* The Programme of the *Kenya People's Union* (Nairobi: KPU, n.d.) (KNA). The KPU stipulated that "a ceiling will be placed on all individual land holdings in former European settled areas" (p. 7). This remained a vague position avoiding figures. As for land outside the former White Highlands the KPU did not propose to interfere with individual tenure, nor even with the size of individual landholdings.

101. Ibid. "Our goal is a democratic, socialist state, without exploitation by a privileged few" (p. 3).

102. Odinga, *Not Yet Uhuru*.

103. Ibid., chapter 14. Odinga is quite forthright in his condemnation of government policies and how the KANU had turned its back on the masses. Predictably he takes great issue with KANU's agrarian policy, especially its lack of land provision for ex-detainees and former guerrillas. His new party's platform, however, remained general and somewhat evasive on this issue.

104. See Goldsworthy for illuminating details.

105. William R. Ochieng, "Autobiography in Kenyan History" (Unpublished paper, n.d., Kenyatta University), p. 22. Ochieng's position in this well-argued paper is that it would be inaccurate to look at Odinga as a socialist before the formation of the KPU. According to Ochieng, Odinga's ideas appear to be vague, imprecise, and at best populist.

106. Odinga, *Not Yet Uhuru*, pp. 189–92.

107. Gertzel, *The Politics of Independent Kenya, 1963–1968* (Evanston: Northwestern University Press, 1970), p. 37.

108. This issue has been dealt with in great detail in many publications. See, for example, Leys.

109. There can be no doubt that government harassment of the KPU and its activists, as pointed out by Gertzel, *Politics*, chapter 3, affected the opposition party's performance. Still, it is worth noting that "the Opposition was equally limited in the support its headquarters could offer the candidates, not least because they had barely set up their organisation before the campaign began" (p. 81).

110. Murray-Brown, p. 317.

9. The Legacy of Mau Mau

1. This trend has been particularly prominent in the Soviet Union under Gorbachev and his era of *glasnost*. Lenin, who had always remained above criticism, was recently faulted

for some of the errors in the Soviet system. See *New York Times,* 8 June 1988. For a discussion of the supreme place of Lenin in Soviet society, see Nina Tumarkin, *Lenin Lives!* (Cambridge, Mass.: Harvard University Press, 1983). The Communist party of the USSR was suspended and its activities temporarily halted by the Supreme Soviet in an extraordinary session on 29 August 1991. The question of the legacy of the Russian revolution and Marxism as an operative ideology in the USSR is still unfinished business, and it would therefore be irresponsible to predict future developments and realignments.

2. Oginga Odinga, *Not Yet Uhuru* (London: Heinemann, 1967), p. 253.

3. William R. Ochieng, "The Mau Mau, The Petit Bourgeoisie, and Decolonization in Kenya" (unpublished paper, Kenyatta University, 1984), p. 10.

4. This seems to be the view of Dr. Mwangi wa Githumo. See *The Weekly Review* (Nairobi, 28 February 1986), p. 5.

5. It is known, for example, that *FRELIMO* launched its guerrilla wars against the Portuguese in the northern parts of Mozambique bordering Tanzania, its principal external base area. For details see Richard Gibson, *African Liberation Movements* (London: Oxford University Press, 1972), p. 280.

6. A few of these people, like Mr. Argwings-Kodhek (Luo), Mr. Gama Pinto (Asian), and Mr. Achieng Oneko (Luo), were mentioned at the Mau Mau meeting of February 1986. *Daily Nation* (Nairobi) 24 February 1986.

7. Robert Buijtenhuijs, *Mau Mau: Twenty Years After the Myth and the Survivors* (The Hague: Mouton, 1973), p. 84.

8. Remarks by Solomon Memia, in *Mau Mau* (CAL/3; 1973, KNA). Film.

9. Buijtenhuijs, *Mau Mau,* p. 146.

10. Ibid., p. 116.

11. Ibid., p. 117.

12. Tabitha Kanogo, Review Article, *Kenya Historical Review* 5, no. 2 (1977), p. 400. Some of these benefits include "encouragement to form cooperative societies with aid being given either in cash or influence in the purchasing of the farms and general political backing in the transactions for these farms."

13. *Hansard* (Kenya Parliament; First and Second Sittings, 23 July to 29 November 1963), p. 1629.

14. Ibid., p. 1645.

15. Office of the President, Deposit 3, Serial 349 (KNA), 11 March 1964.

16. Ibid. According to the minister, the government was tackling the problem of the needy by "provision of further employment, National Youth Service, exemption from Personal Tax and assistance with hospital and school fees where necessary."

17. Paulo Freire, *Pedagogy of the Oppressed* (New York: Herder & Herder, 1970), p. 31. Freire states that "many of the oppressed who directly or indirectly participate in the revolution intend—conditioned by the myths of the old order—to make it their private revolution."

18. *The Weekly Review* (Nairobi) 1 April 1988, p. 6.

19. Buijtenhuijs, *Mau Mau,* p. 63, notes the changes in Kenyatta's attitude toward Mau Mau from hostility to strategic association with the memory of the revolt for political expedience.

20. *The Weekly Review* (1 April 1988), p. 6.

21. Ilene V. O'Malley, *The Myth of the Revolution; Hero Cults and the Institutionalization of the Mexican State, 1920–40* (New York: Greenwood Press, 1986), p. 3.

22. Ibid., p. 4.

23. *San Francisco Examiner,* 19 April 1987, p. A-13. Sebastian de la Torre, a peasant, was quoted as saying, "Nothing has changed since the revolution. We are still asking for the same things Zapata fought for, namely distributing land to the compesinos who work it. . . . The land is still in the hands of the rich, the politicians, the state governors. What Zapata fought for was never accomplished.

24. Ngugi wa Thiong'o, *Detained* (London: Heinemann, 1981), p. 65. Also see *Barrel of a Pen* (Trenton, N.J.: Africa World Press, 1983).

25. W. Maloba, "Ngugi wa Thiong'o and History," *Joint Centre for African Studies* (Stanford University/U.C. Berkeley, April 1984), p. 5.

26. E. S. Atieno-Odhiambo, Review Article, *Kenya Historical Review* 5, no. 2 (1977), p. 385. For Atieno-Odhiambo's recent views on this issue and on Mau Mau in general; see "Kenyatta and Mau Mau," *Transition*, no. 53 (1991), pp. 147–52. Atieno-Odhiambo strongly urges us to debunk the view that "Kenyatta was not privy to the secrets of Muhimu." He however fails to provide any credible evidence that Kenyatta knew about Mau Mau or managed it. He also fails to make a distinction between Kenyatta's opportunistic embrace of Mau Mau in post-colonial times and actual support for it. It is vital to remember that any views about Mau Mau by former activists and generals have been affected by recent reevaluation of one's individual contribution to Mau Mau and also by the political and social events and forces in postcolonial times.

27. Ngugi wa Thiong'o and Micere Mugo, *The Trial of Dedan Kimathi* (London: Heinemann, 1976), preface.

28. For a detailed discussion of Ngugi wa Thiongo's writings and Mau Mau, see David Maughan-Brown, *Land, Freedom and Fiction* (London: Zed Brooks, 1985). Maughan-Brown in essence accuses Ngugi of being hostile to Mau Mau in his initial writings prior to the publication of *Petals of Blood* (1977). *Petals of Blood*, other than being sympathetic to Mau Mau, establishes "a contrast between the ideals for which the fighters fought, the immense sacrifices they, and the Kikuyu peasantry as a whole, accepted, and the betrayal of those ideals and sacrifices by the rulers of post-independence Kenya" (p. 245).

29. Al-Amin Mazrui, "Ideology, Theory and Revolution: Lessons from the Mau Mau," *Race and Class* 28, no. 4 (1987), p. 60.

30. Maina wa Kinyatti, "Mau Mau: The Peak of African Political Organization in Colonial Kenya," *Kenya Historical Review* 5, no. 2 (1971), p. 294.

31. Maina wa Kinyatti, ed., *Kenya's Freedom Struggle: The Dedan Kimathi Papers* (London: Zed Books, 1987), p. 12.

32. Ngugi wa Thiong'o in Kinyatti, *Kenya's Freedom Struggle*, p. xv.

33. See, for example, Ngugi wa Thiong'o, *Barrel of a Pen* (London: New Beacon Books, 1983).

34. Buijtenhuijs, *Mau Mau*, p. 131.

35. Ibid., p. 141.

36. C. J. Gertzel, *The Politics of Independent Kenya, 1963–1968* (Evanston: Northwestern University Press, 1970), p. 90.

37. Ibid., p. 91.

38. *Daily Nation* (Nairobi), 24 February 1986, p. 1.

39. Ibid.

40. *The Weekly Review* (Nairobi, 28 February 1986), p. 3.

41. Ibid., p. 4. Absent was Kariuki Chotara and Mbaria Kaniu, who were alleged to have "formed their own splinter group to rewrite Mau Mau history and make films on the movement."

42. *Daily Nation* (Nairobi), 28 February 1986, p. 13.

43. Buijtenhuijs, *Mau Mau*, p. 77.

44. *Daily Nation* (Nairobi), 13 March 1986, p. 24.

45. Cora Ann Presley, "The Mau Mau Rebellion: Kikuyu Women and Social Change," *Canadian Journal of African Studies* 22, no. 3 (1988), p. 522. Also see Cora Ann Presley, "Kikuyu Women in the Mau Mau Rebellion," *In Resistance*, ed. Gary Okihiro (Amherst: The University of Massachusetts Press, 1986).

46. Jean O'Barr, "Introductory Essay" in Muthoni Likimani, *Pass Book Number F. 47927: Women and Mau Mau in Kenya* (London: Macmillan Publishers, 1985), p. 9.

47. Presley, "Kikuyu Women," p. 507.

48. O'Barr, p. 10.

49. Margaret Wangui Gachihi, "The Role of Kikuyu Women in the Mau Mau" (M.A. thesis, University of Nairobi, 1986).

50. Ibid., p. iv.

51. Ibid., p. v.

52. Ibid., p. vi.

53. Ibid., p. vi.

54. Presley, "Kikuyu Women," p. 507.

55. Gachihi, p. 111.

56. Ibid., p. 117.

57. Ibid., p. 218.

58. O'Barr, p. 23.

59. Stephanie Urdang, *Fighting Two Colonialisms* (New York: Monthly Review Press, 1979), p. 15.

60. Organization of Angolan Women, *Angolan Women Building the Future* (London: Zed Books, 1984), p. 30.

61. Maria Rosa Cutrufelli, *Women in Africa: Roots of Oppression* (London: Zed Books, 1983), p. 173.

62. Organization of Angolan Women, p. 30.

63. Stephanie Urdang, *Fighting*, p. 307. Also see Stephanie Urdang, *And Still They Dance* (New York: Monthly Review Press, 1989).

64. O'Barr, p. 35. For details about some of the strides and problems of women trade unionists in Kenya see Paul Tiyambe Zeleza's crucial study, *Labour, Unionization and Women's Participation in Kenya, 1963–1987* (Nairobi: The Friedrich Ebert Foundation, 1988).

65. *The Weekly Review* (Nairobi: 9 August 1991), p. 5.

66. *The Weekly Review* (Nairobi: 19 July 1991), Editorial.

67. *Daily Nation* (Nairobi), 17 March 1986.

68. Ibid.

69. Ibid.

70. Ibid. (3 March 1986).

71. Ibid. (30 March 1986). Mr. Paul Ngei, a cabinet minister, stated that "the Mau Mau led struggle for Kenya's independence 'belongs to the past' and should not be the subject of 'futile' public debates." (*Daily Nation*, 7 March 1986).

72. Ibid. (20 March 1986). A letter by Miheso wa Amagalu.

BIBLIOGRAPHY

A. Archives

1. London: Her Majesty's Stationery Office (HMSO)

Cmd. 1922 (1923)
Cmd. 9081 (July 1954)
Cmd. 9475 (June 1955)
Cmd. 795 (July 1959)
Cmd. 778 (June 1959)
Cmd. 816 (1959)
Cmd. 960 (1960)
Cmd. 1030 (1960)

2. London: Public Record Office (PRO)

CO822/435
CO822/436
CO822/437
CO822/438
CO822/439
CO822/440
CO822/441
CO822/442
CO822/443
CO822/444
CO822/450
CO822/461
CO822/474
CO822/495
CO822/496
CO822/497
CO822/498
CO967/168
WO216/857
WO216/879
WO216/883

3. London: Imperial War Museum (IWM)

The Papers of Major-General T. H. Birbeck (83/21/1)
Transcribed tape recordings of Col. I. A. Ferguson
Transcribed tape recordings of Lt. Simon McLachlan
Transcribed tape recordings of Sir Anthony Swann

4. London: Royal Institute of International Affairs (RIIA) (Unpublished Papers)

Francis, Carey E., "The Emergency in Kenya As Seen by a School Master in the Kikuyu Area" (3 March 1955).

Gichuru, James, "Kenya" (27 September 1960).
Ngala, Ronald, "Kenya's New Constitution" (2 March 1962).
Renison, Sir Patrick, "Kenya's Problems at the Start of 1963" (7 February 1963).
Robertson, John Connel, "The Situation of the European Settler in Kenya" (23 March 1961).
Vasey, E. A., "Kenya: Constitutional Development Today and Tomorrow" (1 July 1954).

5. Nairobi: Kenya National Archives (KNA)

Hughes Papers, WM/A 3265, KN. MSS. 16
WC/OM/1/75–1/95
DC/KBU/1/45
WC/CM/1/1/6
ARC/MAA/2/5/183
PGB/134/80
B278 and 279 Church of Scotland Mission
MAC/KEN/34/9
WC/OM/1/96–1/110
MAC/KEN/36/7
DC/KBU/36/7
DC/KBU/1/44
DC/KBU/1/46
DC/KBU/1/43
DC/NY1/1/1
DC/NYK/3/1/40
DC/KBU/1/41
PC/COAST/2/1/101
PC/RVP/64/1/17
CD/5/272
CD/5/270
EAO 7/81 (12)
Defence Deposit 4, Piece no. 66
Defence Deposit 6, Serial no. 19
Defence Deposit 6, Piece no. 16
Defence Deposit 4, Piece no. 9
Defence Deposit 4, Piece no. 1
Police Deposit 5, Serial no. 46
Defence Deposit 14, Piece no. 20
Defence Deposit 13, Piece no. 10
Office of the President, Deposit 3, Serial 119
Office of the President, Deposit 3, Serial 349
City Council of Nairobi, Annual Report, 1953
City Council of Nairobi, Annual Report, 1954
Papers of Dermott Kydd (Landmarks)
Kenya Constitutional Conference, 1962
Hansard (Kenya Parliament)

6. Oxford: Rhodes House Library, Oxford University (RHL)

MSS. Afr. S. 235; *Mau Mau*
MSS. Afr. S. 424
MSS. Afr. S. 1352
MSS. Afr. S. 1484; The Johnson Papers
MSS. Afr. S. 1494

MS. Afr. S. 1534
MS. Afr. S. 1574
MSS. Afr. S. 1580; The Papers of Sir William R. N. Hinde
MS. Afr. S. 1621
MSS. Brit. Emp. S. 486; The Papers of Sir Arthur Young
The Papers of Sir Frank Loyd & Co.

B. Articles, Books, and Pamphlets

Abuor, C. Ojwando. *White Highlands No More* (Nairobi: Pan African Researchers, 1970).
Arnold, Guy. *Kenyatta and the Politics of Kenya* (London: J. M. Dent, 1974).
Asprey, Robert B. *War in the Shadows; The Guerilla in History* (New York: Double-day, 1975).
Atieno-Odhiambo, E. S. "The Colonial Government, The Settlers, and the Trust Principle in Kenya, 1939," *Trans-African Journal of History* 2, no. 2 (1972).
———. Review Article, *Kenya Historical Review* 5, no. 2 (1977).
———. Review Article, "Kenyatta and Mau Mau," *Transition,* no. 53 (1991).
Avrich, Paul. *Russian Rebels (1600–1800)* (New York: Schocken Books, 1972).
Bagdikian, Ben H. *The Shame of the Prisons* (New York: Pocket Books, 1972).
Baldwin, William W. *Mau Mau Man Hunt* (New York: E. P. Dutton, 1957).
Barnett, Donald, and Karari Njama. *Mau Mau from Within* (New York: Monthly Review Press, 1966).
Beals, Carleton. "Guerilla Warfare," *Encyclopedia of the Social Sciences,* Editor-in-Chief, R. A. Seligman (New York: Macmillan, 1957).
Bennett, George, and Alison Smith. "Kenya from Whiteman's Country to Kenyatta's State; 1954–1963," *Oxford History of East Africa,* ed. D. A. Low and Alison Smith (Oxford: Clarendon Press, 1976).
Bennett, George, and Carl G. Rosberg. *The Kenyatta Election: Kenya, 1960–61* (London: Oxford University Press, 1961).
Benston, Margaret. "The Political Economy of Women's Liberation," *Monthly Review* (September 1969). Reissued December 1989.
Berman, Bruce. *Control and Crisis in Colonial Kenya* (London: James Currey; Nairobi: Heinemann; Athens: Ohio University Press, 1990).
Blundell, Sir Michael. *So Rough a Wind* (London: Weidenfeld & Nicolson, 1964).
Brett, E. A. *Colonialism and Underdevelopment in East Africa* (New York: NOK Publishers, 1973).
Brockway, Fenner. *African Journeys* (London: Victor Gollanz, 1955).
———. *Towards Tomorrow* (London: Hart-Davis, MacGibbon, 1977).
Buijtenhuijs, Robert. *Mau Mau: Twenty Years after the Myth and the Survivors* (The Hague: Mouton, 1973).
———. *Essays on Mau Mau* (Leiden/The Netherlands: African Studies Centre, 1982).
Cabral, Amilcar. *Unity and Struggle* (New York: Monthly Review Press, 1979).
———. *Revolution in Guinea* (London: Stage One Publishers, 1969).
Carey, Bishop Walter. *Crisis in Kenya* (London: A. R. Mowbray, 1953).
Carlson, G. "Ape Like Bestial Brutes?" *Socialist Review* 3, no. 7.
Carver, Lord Michael. *War since 1945* (New York: G. P. Putnam's, 1981).
Chaliand, Gerard, ed. *Guerilla Strategies* (Berkeley/Los Angeles: University of California Press, 1982).
———. *The Peasants of North Vietnam* (Baltimore, Maryland: Penguin Books, 1969).
Che Guevara, Ernesto. *Guerilla Warfare* (Lincoln: University of Nebraska Press, 1985).
Chesneaux, Jean. *Popular Movements and Secret Societies in China, 1840–1950* (Stanford: Stanford University Press, 1972).
Clayton, Anthony. *Counter-Insurgency in Kenya* (Nairobi: Transafrica Publishers, 1976).

Clayton, Anthony, and Donald Savage. *Government and Labour in Kenya, 1895–1963* (London: Frank Cass, 1974).

Cooper, Frederick. Review Article, "Mau Mau and the Discourses of Decolonization," *Journal of African History* 29, no. 2 (1988).

Cutrufelli, Maria Rosa. *Women of Africa: Roots of Oppression* (London: Zed Books, 1983).

Davidson, Basil. *Africa in Modern History* (Middlesex, England: Penguin Books, 1978).

———. "African Peasants and Revolution," *Journal of Peasant Studies* 1, no. 3 (1974).

———. *The People's Cause* (Essex: Longman, 1981).

Davis, Fei-Ling. *Primitive Revolutionaries of China* (Honolulu: The University Press of Hawaii, 1977).

Dilley, M. R. *British Policy in Kenya* (New York: Barnes and Noble, 1966).

Doob, Leonard W. *Propaganda* (New York: Henry Holt, 1935).

Douglas-Home, Charles. *Evelyn Baring: The Last Pro-Consul* (London: Collins, 1978).

Eliot, Sir Charles. *The East Africa Protectorate* (New York: Barnes and Noble, 1966).

Erskine, Sir George. "Kenya - Mau Mau," *Royal United Service Institution,* vol. C1, no. 601 (Feb. 1956).

Evans, M. *Fighting against Chimurenga, 1972–1979* (Harare: The Historical Association of Zimbabwe, 1981).

Evans, Peter. *Law and Disorder* (London: Secker and Warburg, 1956).

Fabian Colonial Bureau. *Kenya: Whiteman's Country?* (London: Fabian Publications, 1944).

Fanon, Frantz. *The Wretched of the Earth* (New York: Grove Press, 1968).

Fisher, Nigel. *Ian MacLeod* (London: Andre Deutsch, 1973).

Foran, Robert. *The Kenya Police, 1887–1960* (London: Robert Hale, 1962).

Fourquin, Guy. *The Anatomy of Popular Rebellion in the Middle Ages* (Amsterdam: North Holland, 1978).

Freire, Paulo. *Pedagogy of the Oppressed* (New York: Herder & Herder, 1970).

Frost, Richard. *Race against Time* (London: Rex Hollings, 1978).

Furedi, Frank. "The Social Composition of the Mau Mau Movement in the White Highlands," *Journal of Peasant Studies* 1, no. 4 (1974).

———. "The African Crowd in Nairobi: Popular Movements and Elite Politics," *Journal of African History* 14, no. 2 (1973).

Galula, David. *Counter-Insurgency Warfare* (New York: Frederick A. Praeger, 1964).

Gertzel, C. J. "The Political Legacy," *Government and Politics in Kenya,* edited by C. J. Gertzel, Maure Goldschmidt, and Don Rothchild (Nairobi: East African Publishing House, 1969).

———. *The Politics of Independent Kenya 1963–1968* (Evanston: Northwestern University Press, 1970).

Gikoyo, Gucu G. *We Fought for Freedom* (Nairobi: East African Publishing House, 1979).

Giap, Vo Nguyen. *The Military Art of a People's War* (New York: Monthly Review Press, 1970).

Goldsworthy, David. *Tom Mboya: The Man Kenya Wanted to Forget* (Nairobi/London: Heinemann Educational Books, 1982).

Gordon, David F. *Decolonization and the State in Kenya* (Boulder: Westview Press, 1986).

Gordon, Major J. "Against Mau Mau," *The Journal of Royal Scots Fusiliers* 21, no. 2 (July 1954).

Grandin, Thomas. "The Political Use of the Radio," *Geneva Studies* 10, no. 3 (August 1939).

Griffiths, James. "From Colonies to Commonwealth," *Socialist International Information* 4, no. 43 (23 October 1954).

Grundy, Kenneth W. *Guerilla Struggle in Africa* (New York: Grossman Publishers, 1971).

Heggoy, Andrew Alf. *Insurgency and Counter Insurgency in Algeria* (Bloomington: Indiana University Press, 1972).

Henderson, Ian. *Man Hunt in Kenya* (New York: Doubleday, 1958).

Hilton, R. H., and T. H. Aston, eds. *The English Rising of 1381* (Cambridge: Cambridge University Press, 1984).

Hobsbawm, Eric. *Primitive Rebels* (New York: W. W. Norton, 1959).

———. *Bandits* (New York: Delacorte Press, 1969).

Hoffman, Bruce. *The Failure of British Military Strategy within Palestine, 1939–1947* (Bar-Ilan University Press, 1983).

Hopkins, Elizabeth. "Racial Minorities in British East Africa," *The Transformation of East Africa*, ed. Stanley Diamond and Fred G. Burke (New York: Basic Books, 1966).

Horowitz, Dan. "Attitudes of British Conservatives towards Decolonization in Africa," *African Affairs* 69, no. 274 (January 1970).

Isaacman, Allen. "Peasants and Rural Social Protest in Africa," *African Studies Review* 33, no. 2 (September 1990).

Itote, Waruhiu. *Mau Mau General* (Nairobi: East African Publishing House, 1967).

Jackson, Kennell, and Marshall Clough. *A Bibliography on Mau Mau* (Stanford: Stanford University Press, 1975).

Jones, Steven H. "Jomo Kenyatta: Anthropologist and Cultural Nationalist—And Political Chameleon." (Unpublished Paper, Department of History, Kenyatta University, June, 1986).

Kabiro, Ngugi. *The Man in the Middle* (Richmond, B.C.: LSM Information Center, 1973).

Kaggia, Bildad. *Roots of Freedom* (Nairobi: East African Publishing House, 1975).

Kanogo, Tabitha. Review Article, *Kenya Historical Review* 5, no. 2 (1977).

———. *Squatters and the Roots of Mau Mau* (London: James Currey; Nairobi: Heinemann; and Athens: Ohio University Press, 1987).

Kariuki, J. M. *Mau Mau Detainee* (London: Oxford University Press, 1963).

Keen, Sam. *Faces of the Enemy* (San Francisco: Harper & Row, 1986).

Kenyatta, Jomo. *Harambee* (Nairobi: Oxford University Press, 1964).

———. *Suffering without Bitterness* (Nairobi: East African Publishing House, 1968).

wa Kinyatti, Maina. "Mau Mau: The Peak of African Political Organization in Colonial Kenya," *Kenya Historical Review* 5, no. 2 (1977).

———, ed. *Kenya's Freedom Struggle: The Dedan Kimathi Papers* (London: Zed Books, 1987).

———, ed. *Thunder from the Mountains: Mau Mau Patriotic Sons* (London: Zed Press, 1980).

Kitson, Frank. *Gangs and Counter Gangs* (London: Barrie and Rockliff, 1960).

———. "Counter Insurrection in Kenya," *Guerilla Strategies*, ed. Gerard Chaliand (Berkeley/Los Angeles: University of California Press, 1982).

———. *Low Intensity Operations* (Harrisburg: Stackpole Books, 1971).

Knight, Stephen. *The Brotherhood: The Secret World of the Freemasons* (London: Dorset Press, 1986).

Lapping, Brian. *End of Empire* (New York: St. Martin's Press, 1985).

Larner, Christiana. *Witchcraft and Religion* (New York: Basil Blackwell, 1984).

Lathbury, Sir Gerald. "The Security Forces in the Kenya Emergency," *Oxfordshire and Buckinghamshire Light Infantry Chronicle* 59 (1957).

Lauer, Robert H. *Social Movements and Change* (Carbondale: Southern Illinois University Press, 1976).

Lavers, Anthony. *The Kikuyu Who Fight Mau Mau* (Nairobi: The Eagle Press, 1955).

Leakey, L. S. B. *Defeating Mau Mau* (London: Methuen, 1954).

———. *Mau Mau and the Kikuyu* (London: Methuen, 1952).

———. *The Southern Kikuyu before 1903*, vol. I (London: Academic Press, 1977).

———. *The Southern Kikuyu before 1903*, vol. II (London: Academic Press, 1977).

Legum, Colin. "Mboya the Professional," *East Africa Journal* (September 1969).

Leigh, Ione. *In the Shadow of Mau Mau* (London: W. H. Allen, 1955).

Leo, Christopher. *Land and Class in Kenya* (Toronto: University of Toronto Press, 1984).

Leys, Colin. *Underdevelopment in Kenya* (Berkeley/Los Angeles: University of California Press, 1974).

Likimani, Muthoni G. *Passbook no. F47927: Women and Mau Mau in Kenya* (London: Macmillan, 1985).

Lindsay, Jack. *Nine Days Hero: Wat Tyler* (London: Dennis Dobson, 1964).

Lipscomb, J. F. *We Build a Country* (London: Faber & Faber, 1955).

Lonsdale, John. "Mau Maus of the Mind: Making Mau Mau and Remaking Kenya," *Journal of African History* 31 (1990).

Lugard, Lord. *The Dual Mandate for British Tropical Africa* (Hamden, Connecticut: Archon Books, 1965).

Lyttelton, Oliver. *The Memoirs of Lord Chandos* (New York: New American Library, 1963).

Machel, Samora. *Samora Machel: An African Revolutionary* (London: Zed Books, 1985).

Macmillan, Harold. *Pointing the Way, 1959–1961* (London: Macmillan, 1972).

Maina, Paul. *Six Mau Mau Generals* (Nairobi: Gazelle Books, 1977).

Majdalany, Fred. *State of Emergency* (Boston: Houghton Mifflin, 1963).

Maloba, W. "Ngugi wa Thiong'o and History" (Unpublished Paper delivered at Joint Centre for African Studies, Stanford University/U.C. Berkeley, April 1984).

Mathu, Mohammed. *The Urban Guerilla* (Richmond, B.C.: LSM Information Center, 1974).

Maughan-Brown, David. *Land, Freedom and Fiction: History and Ideology in Kenya* (London: Zed Books, 1985).

Mazrui, Ali. *On Heroes and Uhuru Worship* (London: Longmans, 1967).

Mazrui, Al-Amin. "Ideology, Theory and Revolution: Lessons from the Mau Mau," *Race and Class* 28, no. 4 (1987).

Mboya, Tom. *Kenya Faces the Future* (New York: America Committee on Africa, 1959).

———. *Freedom and After* (London: Andre Deutsch, 1963).

Memmi, Albert. *The Colonizer and the Colonized* (Boston: Beacon Press, 1965).

Minogue, K. R. *Nationalism* (New York: Basic Books, 1967).

Mitchell, Sir Philip. *African Afterthoughts* (London: Hutchinson, 1954).

Mousnier, Roland. *Peasant Uprisings in 17th Century France, Russia and China* (New York: Harper & Row, 1970).

Muchai, Karigo. *The Hard Core* (Richmond, B.C.: LSM Information Center, 1973).

Mungeam, G. H. *Kenya: Select Historical Documents 1884–1923* (Nairobi: East African Publishing House, 1978).

Muriithi, Kiboi (with Peter Ndoria). *War in the Forest* (Nairobi: East African Publishing House, 1971).

Muriuki, G. *A History of the Kikuyu, 1500–1900* (Nairobi: Oxford University Press, 1967).

———. "Background to Politics and Nationalism in Central Kenya," *Politics and Nationalism in Colonial Kenya*, ed. B. A. Ogot (Nairobi: East African Publishing House, 1972).

Murray-Brown, Jeremy. *Kenyatta* (London: George Allen & Unwin, 1972).

Njama, Karari, and Donald Barnett. *Mau Mau from Within* (New York: Monthly Review Press, 1966).

Nottingham, John, and Carl G. Rosberg. *The Myth of Mau Mau: Nationalism in Kenya* (New York: Hoover/Praeger, 1966).

O'Barr, Jean. "Introductory Essay," *Passbook Number F.47927: Women and Mau Mau in Kenya* by Muthoni Likimani (London: Macmillan, 1985).

O'Malley, Ilenev. *The Myth of the Revolution: Hero Cults and the Institutionalization of the Mexican State, 1920–1940* (New York: Greenwood Press, 1986).

Ochieng, William R. "The Mau Mau, The Petit Bourgeoisie and Decolonization in Kenya" (Unpublished Paper, Kenyatta University, 1984).

———. "Autobiography in Kenyan History" (Unpublished Paper, n.d. Kenyatta University).

Odinga, Oginga. *Not Yet Uhuru* (London: Heinemann, 1967).

————. *Wananchi Declaration: The Program of the Kenya People's Union* (Nairobi: KPU, n.d.).

Ogot, Bethwell A. "Revolt of the Elders," *Politics and Nationalism in Colonial Kenya*, ed. B. A. Ogot (Nairobi: East African Publishing House, 1972).

————, ed. *Historical Dictionary of Kenya* (London: Scarecrow Press, 1981).

————. "Introduction," *Kenya Historical Review* 5, no. 2 (1977).

————. "Kenya under the British, 1895–1963," *Zamani*, ed. B. A. Ogot and K. A. Kieran (Nairobi: East African Publishing House, 1968).

Organization of Angolan Women. *Angolan Women Building the Future* (London: Zed Books, 1984).

Orland, Leonard. *Prisons: Houses of Darkness* (New York: The Free Press, 1975).

Paget, Julian. *Counter-Insurgency Operations* (New York: Walker, 1967).

Paine, Lauran. *Sex in Witchcraft* (New York: Tapplinger, 1972).

Parrinder, George. *Witchcraft: European and African* (London: Faber & Faber, 1963).

Perham, Margery. "Struggle Against Mau Mau," *The Times* (London: 22 April 1953).

Pimlott, John. "The British Army," *Armed Forces and Modern Counter Insurgency*, ed. Ian Beckett and John Pimlott (New York: St. Martin's Press, 1985).

Popkin, Samuel. *The Rational Peasant* (Berkeley/Los Angeles: University of California Press, 1979).

Presley, Cora Ann. "Kikuyu Women in the Mau Mau Rebellion," *In Resistance*, ed. Gary Y. Okihiro (Amherst: The University of Massachusetts Press, 1986).

————. "The Mau Mau Rebellion, Kikuyu Women and Social Change," *Canadian Journal of African Studies* 22, no. 3 (1988).

Qualter, Terence H. *Opinion Control in the Democracies* (London: Macmillan, 1985).

Ranger, Terence. *Peasant Consciousness and Guerilla War in Zimbabwe* (London: James Currey; Berkeley/Los Angeles: University of California Press, 1985).

Rimbault, Col. G. A. "Kenya and the Mau Mau," *The Lancashire Land*, vol. 5, new series, no. 3 (1954).

Robertson, John Connel. "The Situation of the European Settler in Kenya" (Unpublished Paper, Royal Institute of International Affairs, 23 March 1961).

Rosberg, Carl G., and John Nottingham. *The Myth of Mau Mau: Nationalism in Kenya* (New York: Hoover/Praeger, 1966).

Savage, Donald, and Anthony Clayton. *Government and Labour in Kenya, 1895–1963* (London: Frank Cass, 1974).

Shannon, Dr. Mary. "Rehabilitating the Kikuyu," *African Affairs* 54, no. 215 (April 1955).

Singh, Makhan. "The East Africa Association, 1921–1925," *Hadith, 3*, ed. B. A. Ogot (Nairobi: East African Publishing House, 1971).

Skeffington, Arthur M. P. "The British Labour Party's Colonial Policy," *Socialist International Information* 4, no. 42 (16 October 1954).

Slater, Montagu. *The Trial of Jomo Kenyatta* (London: Mercury Books, 1965).

Smith, Tony, ed. *End of European Empire* (Lexington, Mass.: Heath, 1975).

Sorrenson, M. P. K. *Land Reform in the Kikuyu Country* (Nairobi: Oxford University Press, 1967).

————. *Origins of European Settlement in Kenya* (Nairobi: Oxford University Press, 1968).

Spencer, John. "The Kikuyu Central Association and the Genesis of Kenya African Union," *Kenya Historical Review* 2, no. 1 (1974).

————. "KAU and Mau Mau: Some Connections," *Kenya Historical Review* 5, no. 2 (1977).

————. *The Kenya Africa Union* (London: KPI, 1985).

Tamarkin, M. "Mau Mau in Nakuru," *Journal of African History* 17, 1 (1976).

Taylor, Philip M. *The Projection of Britain* (Cambridge: Cambridge University Press, 1981).

Thayer, Charles W. *Guerilla* (New York: Harper & Row, 1963).

wa Thiong'o, Ngugi. *A Grain of Wheat* (London: Heinemann, 1967).

————. *Detained* (London: Heinemann, 1981).

———— . *Barrel of a Pen* (Trenton, New Jersey: Africa World Press, 1983).

wa Thiong'o with Micere Mugo. *The Trial of Dedan Kimathi* (London: Heinemann, 1976).

Throup, D. W. "Olenguruone, 1940–1960" (Unpublished Paper, Historical Association of Kenya, Annual Conference Papers, 1981).

———— . *Economic and Social Origins of Mau Mau* (London: James Currey; Nairobi: Heinemann Kenya; Athens: Ohio University Press, 1988).

Thuku, Harry. *An Autobiography* (Nairobi: Oxford University Press, 1970).

Tignor, Robert L. *The Colonial Transformation of Kenya* (Princeton, Princeton University Press, 1976).

Tse-tung, Mao. *Selected Works, Volume One* (New York: International Publishers, 1954).

———— . *Selected Works, Volume Two* (New York: International Publishers, 1954).

———— . *On Guerilla Warfare* (New York: Frederick A. Praeger, 1961).

Urdang, Stephanie. *Fighting Two Colonialisms: Women in Guinea-Bissau* (New York: Monthly Review Press, 1979).

———— . *And Still They Dance* (New York: Monthly Review Press, 1989).

Wachanga, H. K. *The Swords of Kirinyaga* (Nairobi: Kenya Literature Bureau, 1975).

Watene, Kenneth. *My Son for My Freedom* (Nairobi: East African Publishing House, 1973).

———— . *Dedan Kimathi* (Nairobi: Transafrica Publishers, 1974).

Webber, Ronald. *The Peasants' Revolt* (Lavenham: Terrence Dalton, 1980).

White, Luise. "Separating the Men from the Boys: Constructions of Gender, Sexuality and Terrorism in Central Kenya, 1939–1959," *International Journal of African Historical Studies* 23, no. 1 (1990).

———— . *The Comforts of Home: Prostitution in Colonial Nairobi* (Chicago: University of Chicago Press, 1990).

Whittier, Robert. "Introduction," *The Swords of Kirinyaga* by H. K. Wachanga (Nairobi: Kenya Literature Bureau, 1975).

Wilson, R. G. "Land Consolidation in the Fort Hall District of Kenya," *Journal of African Administration* (London: HMSO, July 1956).

Winick, Charles. *Dictionary of Anthropology* (New York: Philosophical Library, 1956).

Wolf, Eric. *Peasant Wars of the Twentieth Century* (New York: Harper & Row, 1969).

Womack, John, Jr. *Zapata and the Mexican Revolution* (New York: Vintage Books, 1968).

Zeleza, Paul Tiyambe. *Labour, Unionization and Women's Participation in Kenya* (Nairobi: The Friedrich Ebert Foundation, 1988).

Zwanenberg, R. M. A. Van. *Colonial Capitalism and Labour in Kenya* (Nairobi: East Africa Literature Bureau, 1978).

C. Dissertations

Barnett, Donald C. "Mau Mau: The Structural Integration and Disintegration of the Aberdare Guerilla Forces" (Ph.D. thesis, University of California, Los Angeles, 1963).

Berman, Bruce J. "Administration and Politics in Colonial Kenya" (Ph.D. thesis, Yale University, 1974).

Gachihi, Margaret Wangui. "The Role of Kikuyu Women in the Mau Mau" (M.A. thesis, University of Nairobi, 1986).

wa Githumo, M. "Land and Nationalism in East Africa: The Impact of Land Expropriation and Land Grievances Upon the Rise and Development of Nationalist Movements in Kenya, 1884–1939. A History" (Ph.D. thesis, New York University, 1974).

Ngunjiri Ngari wa Ndirangu. "The Role of the Gikuyu Land Grievance in the Outbreak of Mau Mau" (Ph.D. thesis, St. John's University, New York, 1984).

Njonjo, A. L. "The Africanisation of the 'White Highlands': A study in Agricultural Class Struggles in Kenya, 1950–1974" (Ph.D. thesis, Princeton University, 1977).

Shiroya, O. J. E. "The Impact of World War II on Kenya: The Role of Ex-Servicemen in Kenya Nationalism" (Ph.D. thesis, Michigan State University, 1968).

Throup, D. W. "The Governorship of Sir Philip Mitchell, 1944–1952" (Ph.D. thesis, University of Cambridge, England, 1983).

D. Newspapers and Magazines

Daily Nation (Nairobi, Kenya)
East Africa Journal (Nairobi, Kenya)
East African Standard (Nairobi, Kenya)
The Economist (London, England)
Guardian (London, England)
Life (USA)
New York Times (USA)
San Francisco Examiner (USA)
Socialist International Information (London, England)
The Socialist Standard (London, England)
Time (USA)
The Times (London, England)
The Weekly Review (Nairobi, Kenya)

E. Government Publications

Government Printer, Nairobi
African Affairs Annual Report, 1948
African Affairs Annual Report, 1949
African Affairs Annual Report, 1950
African Affairs Annual Report, 1951
Report on the Treatment of Offenders, 1953
Report on the Treatment of Offenders, 1954
History of Loyalists, 1961
The Kenya Police Annual Report, 1954
Report of the Committee on African Wages (The Carpenter Report) 1954
Sessional Paper, no 21 of 1954
Sessional Paper, no 10 of 1958/1959
Swynnerton, R. J. M., *A Plan to Intensify Development of African Agriculture In Kenya* (1954)

F. Film

Kenyatta (CAL/2) (KNA): Film by Bellweather Group
Mau Mau (CAL/3) (KNA): Film by Bellweather Group
End of Empire (KENYA) by Brian Lapping and Granada Film/TV

G. Tapes (KNA)

83MA/6	44/11
83MA/7	44/45
15/1	44/62
15/2	44/64
16/4	44/74
44/4	

INDEX

WUNYABARI O. MALOBA is an Associate Professor of History and Coordinator
of the African Studies Program at the University of Delaware. He is also the author
of a number of articles on nationalism and colonialism.